THE ONLY PREGNANCY BOOK YOU'LL EVER NEED

ADVICE ON:
Doctor Visits,
Morning Sickness,
Making the
Announcement,
Choosing a Name,
Eating Right,
Staying Fit,
Maternity Leave,
and More!

Includes expert advice from PAULA FORD-MARTIN, BRITT BRANDON, CFNS, CPT, and others

Avon, Massachusetts

Published by

Adams Media, a division of F+W Media, Inc.

57 Littlefield Street, Avon, MA 02322. U.S.A.

www.adamsmedia.com

Contains material adapted and abridged from *The Everything® Guide to Pregnancy Nutrition and Health* by Britt Brandon, CNFS, CPT with Dr. Heather Rupe, copyright © 2013 by F+W Media, Inc., ISBN 10: 1-4405-6011-0, ISBN 13: 978-1-4405-6011-8; *The Everything® Vegan Pregnancy Book* by Reed Mangels, PhD, RD, LD, FADA, copyright © 2011 by F+W Media, Inc., ISBN 10: 1-4405-2551-X , ISBN 13: 978-1-4405-2551-3; *The Everything® Pregnancy Organizer, 3rd Edition* by Paula Ford-Martin, copyright © 2012, 2007, 2000 by F+W Media, Inc., ISBN 10: 1-4405-2676-1, ISBN 13: 978-1-4405-2676-3; *The Everything® Pregnancy Nutrition Book* by Kimberly A. Tessmer, RD, LD, copyright © 2005 by F+W Media, Inc., ISBN-10: 1-59337-151-9, ISBN-13: 978-1-59337-151-7; *The Everything® Pregnancy Book, 4th Edition* by Paula Ford-Martin, copyright © 2012, 2007, 2003, 1999 by F+W Media, Inc., ISBN 10: 1-4405-2851-9, ISBN 13: 978-1-4405-2851-9.

ISBN 10: 1-4405-7408-1

ISBN 13: 978-1-4405-7408-5

eISBN 10: 1-4405-7409-X

eISBN 13: 978-1-4405-7409-2

Printed in the United States of America.

10 9 8 7 6 5 4 3 2 1

This book is available at quantity discounts for bulk purchases.

For information, please call 1-800-289-0963.

CONTENTS

CHAPTER 3

Clean Up Your Diet **56**

CHAPTER 4

Get Active **86**

CHAPTER 5

The Vegetarian or Vegan Mom-to-Be 108

PART 2: FIRST TRIMESTER 121

CHAPTER 6

Changes in Your Body 122

PART 4: THIRD TRIMESTER 225

What to Expect in Your Third Trimester 226

Your Birthing Plan 246

INTRODUCTION

Congratulations! You're pregnant! This is one of the most special and memorable times in your life. You probably have a lot of questions about the whole process, but *The Only Pregnancy Book You'll Ever Need* has everything you'll need to know while preparing for your little one's arrival, with expert advice that will guide and comfort you each step of this exciting journey.

Right now, you may be feeling a little overwhelmed—after all, you're bringing a new life into the world, and it seems like there are a thousand things you need to do before the big day. There's prenatal care, finding a pediatrician, baby furniture, choosing a name . . . preparing for those sleepless nights. No problem! This in-depth guide will take you through each stage of your pregnancy, from your first trimester to labor and beyond, giving you candid information on what you should anticipate as the weeks go by. No doubt your friends and family are giving you conflicting advice about what you should and shouldn't do, eat, and buy, but *The Only Pregnancy Book You'll Ever Need* is the one-stop resource for what's best for you and your baby.

You'll learn how to cope with morning sickness, fatigue, and food cravings; emotional stress; and your body changing as the baby inside you begins to grow and flourish, among many other things. Need help choosing a birth plan? Find out how to decide which path is best for you and your baby. No idea what to buy to make your home baby-friendly? You'll find information on how to baby proof your house and what kind of car seat and stroller is best for you. Worried about what labor will be like? Ease your fears by being prepared with information on every possible birth scenario.

Use the checklists and worksheets provided to help keep organized throughout every milestone, from the first neonatal doctor's appointment to your first hospital walk through. Keep track of your eating habits and what to eat so you and your baby are in tiptop shape. Also learn what exercises are the most beneficial for a mom-to-be. And this book isn't just for moms, dad-to-be will learn everything he needs to know to be ready for the baby's arrival.

No detail is too small when preparing for your little miracle. There are so many beautiful moments awaiting you, and *The Only Pregnancy Book You'll Ever Need* will help make your pregnancy a happy and healthy one.

PART 1

YOU'RE PREGNANT ... NOW WHAT?

Chapter 1

SO YOU'RE PREGNANT

Congratulations! After you've confirmed the good news that you're pregnant, you can begin to prepare for your pregnancy and beyond. You may be on cloud nine and picking out nursery patterns, or you may be in a state of shock wondering how you're going to handle it all.

Relax. You're normal. Everyone reacts differently for pregnancy. Preparing yourself for the road ahead is the best way to overcome your fears and get a realistic picture of what pregnancy, and motherhood, entails. You'll need to research health-care provider options (from traditional to alternative practitioners), choose a health-care provider, and begin taking prenatal vitamins to provide your baby with a healthy start.

CHOOSING A HEALTH-CARE PROVIDER

Even if you have a picture-perfect pregnancy, you will be seeing a lot of your health-care provider over the next nine months. The American College of Obstetricians and Gynecologists (ACOG) recommends that women see their providers:

- Every four weeks through the first twenty-eight weeks of pregnancy (about seven months)

- Once every two to three weeks between twenty-nine and thirty-six weeks
- Every week after thirty-six weeks

If you have any conditions that put you in a high-risk category, such as diabetes or a history of preterm labor, your provider may want to see you more frequently to monitor your progress.

Who should guide you on this odyssey? If you currently see a gynecologist or family practice doctor who also has an obstetric practice, he or she may be a good choice. If you don't have that choice, or would like to explore your options, consider the following health-care professionals.

- **OB-GYN:** An obstetrician and gynecologist is a medical doctor (MD) who has received specialized training in women's health and reproductive medicine.
- **Perinatologist:** If you have a chronic health condition, you may see a perinatologist—an ob-gyn who specializes in overseeing high-risk pregnancies.
- **Midwife:** There are certified nurse-midwives licensed to practice in all fifty states. They provide patient-focused care throughout pregnancy, labor, and delivery.
- **Nurse practitioner:** A nurse practitioner (NP) is a registered nurse (RN) with advanced medical education and training (at minimum, a master's degree).
- **Combined practice:** Some obstetric practices blend midwives, NPs, and MDs, with the choice (or sometimes the requirement) of seeing one or more throughout your pregnancy.

A doula is a pregnancy and birth support person who cannot replace any of the above professionals, but who can provide emotional assistance to both the mom-to-be and her family. Doulas can assist you at any point in pregnancy, from preconception to postpartum. Because doulas tend to work with a variety of physicians and midwives in many different settings, they may also be helpful in providing information on places and providers as you plan your birth experience.

Whether it's your first or your fifth, this pregnancy is a one-time-only performance. You deserve the best support in seeing it through. Talk to the experts and get referrals. Ask for referrals from the following:

- Friends
- Family members
- State or county medical board
- Patient services department of nearby hospitals and/or birthing centers
- Labor and delivery programs of nearby hospitals and/or birthing centers
- Medical centers
- American Congress of Obstetricians and Gynecologists: *www.acog.org*
- The American College of Nurse-Midwives: *www.midwife.org*

Pregnancy Pointer

While online medical sites are a wonderful source of information, they are also very easy ways to misdiagnose yourself and cause needless worry. Use these sites for information and as a way of learning basic information, but leave diagnosis and treatment up to your health-care provider, who knows your specific situation.

ASK THE RIGHT QUESTIONS

Once you've collected names and phone numbers, narrowed down your list of potential providers, and verified that they accept (and are accepted by) your health insurance plan, it's time to do some legwork. Sit down with your partner and talk about your biggest questions, concerns, and expectations. Then compile a list of provider "interview questions." Some issues to consider:

☐ **What are the costs and payment options?** If your health plan doesn't provide full coverage, find out how much the remaining fees will run and whether installment plans are available.

☐ **Who will deliver my baby?** Will the doctor or midwife you select deliver your child, or might it be another provider in the practice, depending on when the baby arrives? If your provider works alone, find out who covers his patients during vacations and emergencies.

☐ **Whom will I see during office visits?** Since group practices typically share delivery responsibilities, you might want to ask about rotating your prenatal appointments among all the providers in the group so that you'll see a familiar face in the delivery room when the big day arrives.

☐ **What is the provider's philosophy on routine IVs, episiotomies, labor induction, pain relief, and other interventions in the birth process?** If you have certain expectations regarding medical interventions during labor and delivery, you should lay them out now.

☐ **What hospital or birthing center will I go to?** Find out where the provider has hospital privileges, and obtain more information on that facility's programs and policies. Is a neonatal unit available if problems arise after the baby's birth? Many hospitals offer expectant parents the opportunity to tour their labor and delivery rooms.

☐ **What is the provider's policy on birth plans?** Will the provider work with you to create and, more important, to follow a birth plan? Will the plan be signed and become part of your permanent chart in case he or she is off duty during the birth?

☐ **How are phone calls handled if I have a health concern or question?** Most obstetric practices have some sort of triage (prioritizing) system in place for patients' phone calls. Ask how quickly calls are returned and what system the practice has in place for handling night and weekend patient calls.

Belly Basics

According to the U.S. Centers for Disease Control (CDC), 99 percent of U.S. births occur in hospitals, with the majority attended by doctors. Of the 1 percent that do not occur in hospitals, 65 percent are homebirths and 27 percent occur at birth centers.

Some providers have the staff to answer these sorts of inquiries over the phone, while others might schedule a face-to-face appointment with your prospective doctor or midwife. Either way, make sure that all your questions are answered to your satisfaction so that you can make a fully informed choice.

ON YOUR MIND

Although physical wellness and mental health are often perceived as two separate things, the truth is that the mind and body are inextricably linked and what impacts one usually affects the other as well. This connection is particularly strong in pregnancy as the rapid physical changes taking place alter the biochemical balance of the body and brain. Pregnancy is also a precursor to one of the biggest life-changing events there is—the arrival of a baby—and that alone is enough to stir up new and unexpected feelings.

The hormonal changes that occur in pregnancy can have you feeling weepy one minute and irritable the next. And the emotions you experience, especially the negative ones, can be detrimental to your growing child. Depression, stress, and anxiety may alter your eating and sleeping patterns, robbing you and baby of the nutrients and rest you need. Clinical studies have found that depression and stress also have a direct impact on fetal growth and infant development.

If you are feeling blue, you aren't alone; one in ten women experiences depressive symptoms at some point in her pregnancy. Yet women frequently feel guilty that they are feeling so bad during a period of their lives that is supposed to be joyful, and for that reason many do not seek professional help.

Pregnancy Pointer

If you're feeling hopeless, sad, or tired; having trouble sleeping; or losing interest in things that once gave you pleasure, you may be experiencing antepartum depression. Research has linked depression during pregnancy to preterm delivery, lower birth weight, developmental problems in infancy, and a 50 percent chance of developing postpartum depression. Don't wait; talk to your provider about treatment options today.

Pregnancy is a stressful time. A lot of it is positive, exciting stress as you plan for the baby. But you may also be feeling the pressures of impending financial and family responsibilities, fears of labor and delivery, and new career challenges. Trying to keep up with a hectic prepregnancy schedule as your body grows to a very large and unwieldy size is also a sure-fire way to stress out. In high enough amounts, the stress hormone cortisol can cross the placental barrier and impact neuromuscular and brain development in the fetus. That's why it's essential to take time out for yourself to decompress throughout your pregnancy.

Pregnancy Pointer

Many women expect pregnancy to be a time of sheer joy. In reality, it is often a time of ups and downs. This is due in part to the physical changes you are going through and in part to the major changes in your entire life.

Staying focused on the end result of your pregnancy will help you weather the emotions and physical discomforts. Remind yourself that before you know it, your baby will have arrived. It's perfectly okay not to adore being pregnant. While there are women who love it, there are just as many who don't enjoy it at all. The good thing about pregnancy is that above all else, it is only temporary.

During pregnancy, your body may seem to have a mind of its own. You aren't and will never be the same, so expecting yourself to feel and act the same as always is not realistic. Instead, let pregnancy take you on its journey, and try to enjoy what it gives you. You will probably experience very intense emotions that are different from anything you've felt before. This isn't necessarily a bad thing and instead opens you up to the intensity of motherhood.

There are simply going to be days when you feel tired, scared, joyful, frustrated, or cranky during pregnancy. And sometimes there will be nothing you can do to change that, so the easiest thing is to give yourself a break and just ride it through.

COMMON TESTS

Over the course of your pregnancy, you'll be visiting your health-care provider quite a bit. Your provider will administer a number of tests to make sure that you and your baby remain healthy throughout your pregnancy, and that neither you nor your baby are at risk for complications.

Diagnostic Tests and Screenings

As you likely suspect by now, you'll be poked, prodded, swabbed, scraped, and scanned throughout your pregnancy. All these tests have a purpose, of course—a healthy mom and baby. Prenatal tests elicit the full spectrum of maternal emotions, from calm reassurance (the staccato lub-dub of your baby's heart) to amusement (a fast fetal wave from the ultrasound screen) to anxiety and fear of the unknown. Knowing what to expect can make these exams more comfortable.

Pregnancy Pointer

Your urine test is a good excuse to get some of those extra fluids your body and the baby need right now. Down a bottle of drinking water on the way to your checkup so that you can easily provide a sample, but don't overdo it or you may not make it without a pit stop.

At each visit to your provider, you'll have your blood pressure and weight checked and any swelling assessed. Overall, blood pressure tends to go down in pregnancy because of the increase in the size of the circulatory system, a more elastic cardiovascular system, and other factors. A normal blood pressure range in pregnancy is around 120 (systolic) over 70 (diastolic). Anything higher than 140 over 90 (written $^{140}/_{90}$) is considered high. Your doctor will monitor any sudden elevations in blood pressure carefully, as they can be an early sign of pregnancy-induced hypertension or preeclampsia.

Your belly will be examined; just how depends on where you are in your pregnancy, but you might expect a regular measurement of your fundal height (the top of your uterus) starting sometime in the second trimester, and an external check of the baby's position in the third trimester.

At your initial visit and again in month 9 when labor approaches, you will have an internal (pelvic) exam. You're probably familiar with these from your annual gynecological exams, but if you aren't, it's fairly straightforward. If the physician needs to visualize your cervix to perform a Pap smear, check for STDs, or check for amniotic fluid, a speculum (a duck-billed instrument) is inserted into your vagina and opened to form a tube through which your provider can view your vagina and cervix. It isn't painful, but you will probably experience some pressure that you may consider uncomfortable. He will also scrape off some cervical cells for a Pap smear and take a swab of vaginal fluid to test for sexually transmitted diseases. These also should not hurt.

Toward the very end of pregnancy, your doctor or midwife will again do an internal exam, this time to check the cervix for ripening—a sign of approaching labor.

You'll be giving a urine sample for urinalysis at each prenatal visit. Your provider's office or lab will test your urine for ketones, protein, and glucose at each visit, and may also check for the presence of any bacteria. Depending on the protocol followed in your provider's office, you will be asked either to bring a fresh urine specimen to your appointment or provide one upon your arrival.

Ketones

Ketone bodies are substances produced when the body is getting insufficient fuel from food intake and has to metabolize fat for energy. The resulting ketosis process causes ketones to spill into the urine. Ketones may appear in pregnancy if you're suffering from severe nausea and vomiting, and they are signs that you may require intravenous nutrition. They can also be a byproduct of gestational diabetes when blood sugars are consistently high, and can lead to a rare but potentially life-threatening complication called diabetic ketoacidosis (DKA).

The ketone test is generally performed with a reagent test strip, a strip of chemically treated paper that is dipped in your urine sample and then matched against a color chart for the presence of ketones. Test strips allow your provider or her staff to get almost instantaneous results.

Protein

Excessive protein (albumin) in the urine can be a sign of preeclampsia (also known as toxemia). It is also a possible indication of urinary tract infection (UTI) or of renal (kidney) impairment from chronic hypertension and/or diabetes. The presence of white blood cells in urine can be an indication of infection as well.

Your provider will again use a test strip to check for protein. If the strip is positive, it indicates that protein levels above 30 milligrams per deciliter (mg/dL) are detected; this is considered more than the trace amount normally present in urine. A positive protein strip is an indication for further testing with the more specific 24-hour urine test.

Glucose

Glucose (sugar) in the urine (called glycosuria) can be a sign of gestational diabetes mellitus (GDM). It's normal to spill a small amount of sugar into the urine in pregnancy, but consistently high levels along with other risk factors raise a red flag that GDM may be present. Again, test reagent strips (Diastix, Clinistix) are used for screening. If your doctor suspects gestational diabetes, he will order a 1-hour glucose challenge test.

Urine Culture

Your urine will be analyzed and cultured for the presence of bacteria at your first prenatal visit and again in the course of pregnancy if symptoms of a urinary tract infection appear (for example, burning during urination, strong-smelling urine). If you have certain conditions such as sickle cell anemia, a urine culture may be repeated throughout your pregnancy.

BLOOD WORK

Along with common urine tests, you'll be given a handful of blood tests to make sure everything is going smoothly for you and your baby.

Hemoglobin Count

Levels of hemoglobin, the red blood cells that carry oxygen throughout your body, will be assessed at your initial prenatal visit and may be tested again in the second and third trimesters. Low hemoglobin levels (called anemia) occur frequently in pregnancy due to the vast boost of your total blood volume. Levels that are too low can be a risk factor for low-birth-weight babies. If your total hemoglobin levels are below 12 mg/dL, your provider may prescribe iron supplements to build your hemoglobin reserves and may order regular hemoglobin screenings at each prenatal visit to monitor your progress.

Glucose Tests

Your doctor may give you a blood glucose test at your first prenatal visit to check for pre-existing type 2 diabetes, especially if you have risk factors for the condition. Risk factors include being overweight, being a member of a racial or ethnic group with a high prevalence of diabetes, having a history of previous gestational diabetes, a history of delivering a large baby, advanced maternal age, or a first-degree relative with diabetes. There are several variations of blood testing for diabetes, including a fasting plasma glucose test, a random plasma glucose test, and an A1C (hemoglobin A1C) test. If your results indicate diabetes, your provider will test you a second time to confirm.

Pregnancy Pointer

High blood pressure (hypertension) results from an increase in the volume of fluid retained in the bloodstream, and the kidneys must work double time to clean and filter the blood. Eventually, skyrocketing blood pressure damages the nephrons (filtering units of the kidneys) and blood pressure rises further because the kidneys can't keep up.

Once you reach weeks 24 to 28 of pregnancy, your doctor will screen for gestational diabetes mellitus. ACOG endorses use of the glucose challenge test, which requires you to drink 50 grams of a glucose solution, a sugary flavored drink (usually Glucola). One hour later, blood will be drawn and your blood serum glucose levels will be measured. A level of 130 mg/dL or more is considered high. Some medical providers use a cutoff point of 140 mg/dL (ACOG endorses either). If your results exceed the cutoff levels, further testing with the oral glucose tolerance test (OGTT) will be necessary.

Oral Glucose Tolerance Test

Women with high serum glucose levels after the glucose challenge test must take an oral glucose tolerance test to establish a definitive diagnosis of gestational diabetes. The American Diabetes Association recommends use of the OGTT for all pregnant women in weeks 24 to 28 of pregnancy instead of the glucose challenge test.

The OGTT is a fasting test. You will be instructed not to eat for at least 8 hours prior to taking the test (usually midnight the evening before). This test is typically administered first thing in the morning.

When you arrive at the lab, your blood will be drawn for a fasting reading. You will then be given 75 grams of Glucola to drink, and your blood will be taken again at the 1-hour and 2-hour marks. The glucose levels in the blood samples you provide will be analyzed and checked against the diagnostic criteria for GDM.

Other Blood Tests

Your blood type and Rhesus factor will be determined at your first prenatal visit. An Rh factor is either positive or negative. If your Rh is positive, no treatment is necessary. If you are Rh negative and your partner is Rh positive, you are at risk for Rh incompatibility with the blood type of your baby; this can occur when your unborn baby is Rh positive. If some of the baby's blood enters your bloodstream, your body may produce antibodies against the baby's blood, causing her to have severe anemia. When this happens, your immune system may try to fight off the baby as an intruder, causing serious complications. If caught early, however, the disorder can be treated effectively later in pregnancy.

··

Pregnancy Pointer

According to the March of Dimes, one in 2,000 women will develop chickenpox during pregnancy. This virus, known clinically as varicella, has the potential to cause birth defects if it is contracted during pregnancy. Fortunately, there are tests available to determine immunity to varicella; these may be given at the first prenatal appointment if you are unsure whether you have ever had the illness or the chicken pox vaccine.

··

Blood tests also determine whether you are immune to German measles (rubella). German measles can cause birth defects, especially if you contract the infection during the first trimester, and can cause cataracts, heart defects, and deafness in offspring. A majority of women have been exposed to the rubella virus or have been vaccinated against it before becoming pregnant. If you are not immune, you may be vaccinated following the delivery of the baby. Some women will not have immunity despite prior vaccination.

An HIV, hepatitis B, and syphilis test may also be done on your blood. Medications for HIV (human immunodeficiency virus) taken during pregnancy can decrease viral loads and practically eliminate transmission to the fetus in many cases. Treatment for syphilis can also prevent transmission to the fetus. If you test positive for hepatitis B, your baby will be vaccinated shortly after birth to protect him from the effects of hepatitis. He will receive the first three doses of the hepatitis B vaccine and hepatitis B immunoglobulin within 12 hours of birth to protect him from getting hepatitus B.

Blood tests are also offered to screen for inherited sickle cell anemia in at-risk populations, including couples of African, Caribbean, Eastern Mediterranean, Middle Eastern, and Asian descent. Families of Greek, Italian, Turkish, African, West Indian, Arabian, or Asian descent may be screened for the thalassemia trait; if both father and mother are carriers, there is a chance that the fetus could develop the blood disease called thalassemia major.

SWABS AND SMEARS

More bodily fluid tests will be taken throughout pregnancy, particularly at the initial prenatal workup.

Pap Smear

Unless you've had one in the 12 months leading up to conception, your provider will take a Pap smear at your initial prenatal visit. During your pelvic exam, she will scrape a small sample of cells from your cervix using a spatula-like instrument. The cells are collected and sent to a lab for microscopic analysis.

An abnormal Pap smear result tells your doctor that something is going on with your cervix that requires further examination. Most abnormal Pap smears are caused by infection with a common, sexually transmitted virus known as the human papilloma virus (HPV). HPV may remain silent in women infected with the virus, causing no apparent symptoms. However, the virus can cause cellular changes on your cervix. While most of these changes will resolve on their own, some strains of HPV can cause cervical cancer if left untreated. Because of this, most women are regularly screened with Pap smears to detect any early changes that can be treated.

If your Pap smear is abnormal, you may be offered a colposcopy, a way of looking at your cervix with a microscope. Pregnancy should not prevent your colposcopy. However, an endocervical curettage (ECC), a scraping of the cervical canal routinely done as part of the colposcopy, should not be performed while you are pregnant.

Group B Strep

Group B streptococcus (GBS) is a bacterium that can cause serious infections in a newborn, including pneumonia and meningitis. If a pregnant woman tests positive for it, she is usually prescribed intravenous antibiotics during labor and delivery to prevent transmission to her baby.

Swabs of both the rectum and vagina are taken and cultured (put in a medium that will allow the bacteria to grow, if it is present). The Centers for Disease Control and Prevention (CDC) advise that all pregnant women be screened for GBS in weeks 35 to 37 of gestation.

Sexually Transmitted Infections (STIs)

The CDC also recommends that all pregnant women be screened for six sexually transmitted diseases—chlamydia, gonorrhea, hepatitis B, hepatitis C, HIV, and syphilis—because of their potentially devastating effects on a fetus. HIV, hepatitis B and C, and syphilis testing require a blood draw, while chlamydia and gonorrhea are tested by means of a vaginal swab sample followed by laboratory analysis. If you have a history of preterm delivery, your provider may also take a swab sample for bacterial vaginosis.

Chlamydia, gonorrhea, and syphilis are caused by bacteria and can be treated with antibiotics. Viral infections like hepatitis B and HIV cannot be cured, but treatment and precautionary measures can greatly decrease the risk to your baby. HIV medications taken during pregnancy can lower viral loads and dramatically diminish the risk of transmission to the fetus, as can appropriate treatment for syphilis. If you test positive for hepatitis B, your baby will be vaccinated shortly after birth to protect him from the effects of hepatitis.

ULTRASOUNDS

The test that most women look forward to—the ultrasound (sonogram)—gives you your first glimpse at your little one and lets your practitioner assess the baby's growth and development. It may also be used to diagnose placental abnormalities, an ectopic pregnancy, certain birth defects, or other suspected problems.

Baby Basic

If your fetus isn't feeling coy on ultrasound day, a sonogram taken after 16 weeks may reveal its sex. A sighting of a little girl's labia (visible as three parallel lines) or a boy's penis can provide a fairly positive ID, but keep in mind that ultrasound is not foolproof and parents have been surprised in the delivery room.

There are two types of ultrasound scans: the transabdominal, which scans through your abdomen, and the transvaginal, which scans through your vagina. In very early pregnancy, the technician may opt for the vaginal approach, which means that the transducer (handheld wand) will be inserted into your vagina. However, abdominal ultrasounds are the most common in that most ultrasounds take place in the second or third trimesters.

What to Expect

An ultrasound typically takes no longer than a half hour to perform. If you are in the first half of your pregnancy, you will probably be instructed to drink plenty of water prior to the exam and refrain from emptying your bladder. This is probably the most difficult part of the test. The extra fluids help the technician to visualize your baby.

Once in the examining room, you will recline on a table or bed with your upper body elevated and your abdomen exposed. Ask for extra pillows if you tend to get woozy when not lying on your side. The lights may be dimmed to allow the operator to see the sonogram picture more clearly. A thin application of transducer paste, jelly, or oil will be spread on your abdomen, and then the fun begins.

The ultrasound picture (sonogram) is obtained when high-frequency sound waves are passed over your abdomen with a transducer. These waves bounce off the solid structures of your baby, sending back a moving image of the tiny being inside. The resulting picture is transmitted to a computer or television screen.

The ultrasound technician may take a series of measurements during the procedure using the computer attached to the ultrasound unit. These measurements help your provider assess the growth and organ development of the fetus. Depending on the timing of the test and the cooperation of your unborn child, the provider may also be able to get an idea of the gender. Typically, this information won't be given unless you ask for it, in case you prefer to be surprised at birth.

Once the test is over, the technician will help you clean the transducer gel off your belly and you'll be able to empty your bladder if need be. The ultrasound operator can print out pictures for you to take home, so if she doesn't offer, make sure you ask.

A level-two ultrasound uses the same technology as a regular sonogram but involves a more detailed analysis of the results. It is frequently performed by a perinatologist who is specially trained in its use. The doctor will check fetal growth, organ system development, position of the placenta, and amniotic fluid volume. There are a number of reasons for a level-two to be ordered, from the routine to the potentially more serious. Your doctor should keep you informed, so if he hasn't given you a reason, ask.

ADDITIONAL TESTS

Just when you think you're done with testing and diagnostics, there are more screenings to go through. It's all for the safety of the little one growing inside you!

Alpha-fetoprotein (AFP)/Triple or Quad Screen Test

Alpha-fetoprotein is a protein produced by your unborn baby and passed into your circulatory system. The maternal serum AFP test, usually administered between weeks 15 and 18, is a blood test used to screen for chromosomal irregularities such as trisomy 18 and trisomy 21 (Down syndrome), and also for neural tube defects. It can also indicate the presence of twins, triplets, or more. Results of this test are usually available in about a week.

A more precise version of the AFP called the triple screen test (AFP-3) measures levels of hCG and estriol, a type of estrogen, as well as AFP. The quad test, an even more sensitive marker of chromosomal problems, assesses all three of these substances plus inhibin-A.

Most of the time, a high level of AFP is an indication of a multiples' gestation (twins, triplets, or more). However, it could also mean that your fetus has a neural tube defect. If AFP levels are low, it may be an indication of Down syndrome, trisomy 18, or other chromosomal disorders. A level-one or level-two ultrasound or an amniocentesis may be ordered for further evaluation. You may also be referred to a genetic counselor.

Keep in mind that a misdated pregnancy can also affect the results of your AFP or triple or quad screen and give a false positive. Ultrasound can help to confirm or adjust the gestational age.

Amniocentesis

The thought of an amniocentesis makes many women nervous, probably because it involves two critical undertakings: a needle being inserted through the abdomen and breaching your baby's watery environment. It does carry some risk of complications, including a slight chance of miscarriage. However, the amnio (as it is commonly referred to) is one of the best tools available for diagnosing genetic disorders and chromosomal abnormalities. An amniocentesis is typically performed in the second trimester, sometime between weeks 15 and 20 of pregnancy. At this time, there are enough fetal cells present in the amniotic fluid for withdrawal and analysis. A later amnio may be done for various indications or reasons.

An amniocentesis is a relatively short outpatient procedure. First, an abdominal ultrasound is performed to look for an easily accessible pocket of amniotic fluid. Your abdomen is swabbed with an antiseptic solution, and the doctor will then insert a needle into the amniotic sac and draw an amniotic fluid sample into a syringe. The fluid contains sloughed-off fetal cells, which will be analyzed in the lab.

Here are reasons why an amniocentesis may be planned:

- **Age:** Women over age 35 have an increased risk of carrying a baby with a chromosomal disorder like Down syndrome. When the father is over 50, amniocentesis could also be advised because there may be a connection between paternal age and an increased risk of Down syndrome.
- **Family History:** If you've already had a baby with a hereditary or chromosomal abnormality or neural tube defects, or you or your partner have a family history of any of these conditions, an amniocentesis may be recommended.
- **Rh status:** Rh-negative women may have an amnio to determine the Rh status of their fetus. If your baby is Rh isoimmunized, trained professionals can administer an exchange blood transfusion through the fetal cord during an amniocentesis.
- **AFP, triple screen, or quad test results:** If your screen is abnormal, you may be offered an amnio.
- **Ultrasound abnormalities:** If your ultrasound turned up indications of the possibility of a chromosomal disorder, an amnio may be recommended for further evaluation.

- **Lung maturity:** If you're experiencing symptoms of preterm labor or other medical complications (placenta previa, prior classical C-section) that point to an early birth, your provider may perform an amnio to check for markers of fetal lung maturity.
- **Suspected intra-amniotic infection:** If you are experiencing preterm labor, you may be offered an amnio to rule out an intra-amniotic infection (a bacterial infection of the amniotic sac and the surrounding fluid).

After the amnio procedure, the baby will be monitored by ultrasound and will have his heart rate checked for a few minutes to ensure that everything is okay. Minimal cramping may follow the procedure. You will be advised to restrict strenuous exercise for a day (no step aerobics and no sex), although other normal activity should be fine. If in the days following amnio you experience fluid or blood discharge from the vagina, let your provider know as soon as possible.

Baby Basics

The CDC estimates the chance of miscarriage following an amnio at somewhere between one in 400 and one in 200, and the risk of uterine infection at less than one in 1,000. There is also a slight risk of trauma to the unborn baby from a misplaced needle or inadvertent rupture of the sac.

Chorionic Villus Sampling (CVS)

CVS stands for chorionic villus sampling, a test performed in the first trimester (usually in weeks 10 to 12) to assess chromosomal abnormalities and hereditary conditions in the unborn baby. Your provider will use ultrasound guidance to insert a catheter into the placenta, either through the cervix (transcervical) or through a needle injected into the abdomen (transabdominal). The catheter is used to extract a biopsy (sample) of the tiny chorionic villi, the fingers of tissue surrounding the embryo that are the beginnings of the placenta. The villi are a genetic match for the baby's own tissue.

Slight cramping and spotting are normal after the procedure, and you will probably be advised to indulge in some rest and relaxation for the remainder of the day. If bleeding continues, is excessive, or is accompanied by pain or fever, call your practitioner immediately.

CVS has several benefits over amnio. It can be performed earlier (first trimester as opposed to second), and the results are available much faster (5 to 7 days for preliminary CVS results versus 10 to 14 days for amnio). However, the risk of miscarriage is higher with CVS—between one in 200 and one in 100 will experience miscarriage after the procedure. The risk is higher for women with a retroverted (tipped or tilted) uterus who are given a transcervical CVS (about five in 100). For this reason, a transabdominal CVS (through the abdominal wall) is usually advised for these women. A consultation with a genetic counselor can help you analyze the positives and negatives and decide whether a CVS is right for you.

Fetal Monitoring

A fetal heart monitor measures—you guessed it—the fetal heart rate (FHR). A baseline (average) fetal heart rate of 120 to 160 beats per minute (bpm) is considered normal. During your routine prenatal exams, a handheld monitor is used to quickly listen to the fetal heart rate. If you need to be monitored for a longer period of time, belts are used to keep the monitors in place for a period of about 20 minutes. Your health-care provider will look for fetal heart rate accelerations, which correspond to your baby's movement and are a sign of fetal well-being. Reasons to have the prolonged monitoring include going past your due date, intrauterine growth restriction (IUGR), gestational diabetes, and other medical conditions.

Stress and Nonstress Tests (NST)

If there is any concern about fetal well-being or if you are still waiting for baby's belated arrival at week 41 or 42, you'll probably be given a nonstress test (NST) to measure fetal heart rate. It is performed any time after week 26.

The NST is administered while you are lying on a bed or examining table and are attached to a fetal monitor. The monitor belts are strapped around your abdomen. For about 20 minutes, every time you feel your baby move, you'll push a button. The button will record the baby's heartbeat on the paper strip or computer record. Depending on how the monitor is hooked up, the monitor may also detect and note the baby's movement. Rises in the FHR should correspond to fetal movement.

If there is no movement, it's quite possible that baby is sleeping; you'll be given a drink of juice or a small snack in an attempt to rouse her. Sometimes a buzzer or vibrations called vibroacoustic stimulation (VAS) are used to wake up a sleeping fetus. If these methods are unsuccessful, further tests including an ultrasound may be ordered.

In a stress test (also called a contraction stress test or oxytocin challenge test), mild contractions are induced with the synthetic hormone Pitocin to see how your baby responds. You will be hooked up to a fetal monitor, and you will receive an injection of Pitocin (synthetic form of the oxytocin hormone). If the baby cannot maintain his heartbeat during a contraction, immediate delivery may be indicated (possibly by C-section).

Biophysical Profile (BPP)

A biophysical profile (BPP) is simply an ultrasound combined with a nonstress test. A BPP assesses fetal heart rate, muscle tone, body and breathing movement, and the amount of amniotic fluid. The test takes about a half hour. A low BPP score may indicate that the fetus is getting insufficient oxygen. If the fetal lungs are mature, immediate delivery may be recommended.

Women in high-risk pregnancies may undergo regular weekly or biweekly BPP testing in the third trimester. BPP is also a standard test for a post-term pregnancy—one that has gone beyond 42 weeks. Your physician may also order a modified biophysical profile, which is a BPP that consists of the NST and an ultrasound assessment of amniotic fluid only (the amniotic fluid index, AFI).

GENETIC COUNSELING

If you have a history of genetic disease or birth defects in your family or are considered at risk for passing along a hereditary disorder based on your ethnic or racial background, your provider may refer you for genetic counseling, another tool in the prenatal diagnostic arsenal. Genetic counselors certified by the American Board of Genetic Counseling have a "CGC" designation after their names, which indicates that they have passed a certification exam, have a graduate degree in genetic counseling, and have logged significant clinical training experience.

A genetic counselor takes a detailed family and social history and creates a statistical analysis of your child's risk for acquiring genetic or birth defects. She will also provide you with information on the conditions in question and the risks and benefits of further testing and will answer any questions you may have. Some of these tests may involve checking you or your partner for carrier genes, while others test the fetus.

Some women refuse genetic counseling on the grounds that they would never elect to terminate their pregnancy. However, genetic counseling isn't designed to be a survival-of-the-fittest venture but rather a way to help you and your partner reach an informed decision. A genetic counselor is trained to remain objective and not to attempt to influence your choices.

Pregnancy Pointer

If you have a chronic health problem such as diabetes, asthma, or heart disease, you will face some special challenges over the next 9 months as your body adjusts to the major remodeling going on internally. Remember that your baby's health depends on your well-being, so staying on top of your treatment is essential. It's important to bring your primary health-care provider into the pregnancy picture as soon as possible (ideally, when you start planning your pregnancy).

USING MEDICATIONS

Medication use in pregnancy is a thorny issue. There is simply not enough long-term clinical data available on most drugs to provide a 100 percent guarantee of their safety. Ideally, you should avoid all prescription and over-the-counter drugs, except for your prenatal supplements, throughout pregnancy. However, that's an unrealistic expectation given that up to 64 percent of all pregnant women take one or more prescription drugs at some point in their pregnancy. And if you have a chronic disease, such as diabetes, schizophrenia, or HIV, you have little choice but to continue your treatment.

The FDA has a classification system for drugs based on the degree of known risk a medication presents to a fetus. The following chart outlines the five categories currently used for establishing drug safety in pregnancy:

- **Category A**—Controlled studies have shown no risk. Adequate, well-controlled studies in pregnant women have failed to demonstrate a risk to the fetus in any trimester of pregnancy. Unfortunately, very few drugs fall into this category. Prenatal vitamins have a category A rating.
- **Category B**—Animal studies revealed no evidence of harm to the fetus; however, there are no adequate and well-controlled studies in pregnant women. Also in category B are drugs that have been shown to have an adverse effect in animal studies, but adequate and well-controlled studies in pregnant women have failed to demonstrate risk to the fetus.
- **Category C**—Risks cannot be ruled out. Adequate, well-controlled human studies are lacking, and animal studies have shown a risk to the fetus or are lacking as well. A category C implies that the drug may or may not be safe to take.
- **Category D**—Positive evidence of risk exists. Studies in humans, both controlled or observational (noncontrolled) studies, resulted in harm to the fetus. Nevertheless, potential benefits from the use of the drug may outweigh the potential risk. For example, the drug may be acceptable if

needed in a life-threatening situation or serious disease for which safer drugs cannot be used or are ineffective (such as cancer treatment).

- **Category X**—The drug is contraindicated in pregnancy. Studies prove that the drug should never be used in any stage of pregnancy. Tests demonstrate positive evidence of fetal abnormalities or risks, which clearly outweigh any possible benefit to the patient.

The consequences of not taking a medication must also be taken into consideration when evaluating the use of a drug. Do the benefits of the drug outweigh the risks to the mother and/or fetus? Can a safer medication be substituted temporarily? Or can the drug be temporarily stopped during the period of time it is known to potentially harm the fetus? With close observation, well-researched prescribing, and careful dosing, the use of medication can proceed safely in many cases.

Dangerous Drugs

There are a number of drugs that are teratogens—meaning that they have been shown to cause birth defects or other developmental problems in pregnancy. Following is a partial list of some well-known offenders. This list is not all-inclusive, and you should discuss all medication use with your practitioner.

- Angiotensin converting enzyme inhibitors (ACE inhibitors; prescribed for high blood pressure)
- Accutane (isotretinoin; prescribed for cystic acne)
- Androgens (testosterone, danazol; prescribed for endometriosis)
- Anticonvulsants (prescribed for seizure disorders or irregular heartbeats)
- Atypical antipsychotics (prescribed for schizophrenia and bipolar disorder; linked to risk of neural tube defects)
- Certain antibiotics (including streptomycin and tetracycline)
- Certain anticoagulants (warfarin; to prevent blood clotting)

- Tapazole (methimazole; an antithyroid drug prescribed for hyperthyroidism)
- Aspirin and nonsteroidal anti-inflammatory drugs (NSAIDs; for pain relief) during the last trimester
- Chemotherapeutic drugs (used to treat cancer and skin diseases)
- Diethylstilbestrol (DES; not prescribed for pregnant women after the Food and Drug Administration issued a warning in 1971)
- Lithium (used for treatment of depression and bipolar disorder)
- Thalidomide (prescribed for leprosy and inflammatory conditions; in limited use due to its high potential for causing birth defects)

Sometimes women decide to self-treat colds and other illnesses with dietary supplements and herbal and botanical remedies before and during pregnancy, mistakenly assuming that medicine from a botanical source is inherently safe for their fetus. Remember: Natural doesn't necessarily mean harmless; herbs can be potent medicinal substances. Even seemingly benign substances like herbal tea have the potential to interact with other foods and medications and cause harm to your developing child.

AVOIDING ALCOHOL

So what about alcohol? You may have heard that moderate consumption of a drink or two a week is safe in pregnancy. The truth is that there is absolutely no known safe level of alcohol intake in pregnancy, and even a single beer or glass of wine may have an impact on the development of your unborn child. Bottom line—complete abstinence is the safest route for baby. Even if you're not pregnant, if you're thinking about having a baby, now is the time to get a handle on even occasional drinking, not to mention binge or frequent drinking. If you're concerned about your drinking habits, talk to your health-care provider about treatment options or turn to your place of worship or local social service agency for support.

Belly Basics

Suppose that, as you read this, you are pregnant already and realize that you have had a cocktail since conception, perhaps before you even discovered you were pregnant. There is no point in obsessing over that drink. Letting the incident consume you with guilt or allowing it to become a source of undue stress is bad for you and baby. Instead, focus your energies on following a healthy lifestyle now.

The consequences of continuing alcohol use during pregnancy range from risking miscarriage to causing an array of physical, mental, behavioral, and developmental problems known as fetal alcohol spectrum disorders (FASD). One of the most severe is fetal alcohol syndrome (FAS). Babies born with FAS experience growth retardation, central nervous system problems, as well as develop characteristic facial features including small eye openings; a small head; a short, upturned nose; absence of the groove between the upper lip and the nose; and an undeveloped outer ear. FAS is permanent and irreversible.

Since the first eight weeks of pregnancy are a time of rapid development for the limbs, heart, central nervous system, and other organ systems of the embryo, it's important to avoid alcohol to reduce the risk of problems for your baby. Talk to your partner also. Some studies have found that if your partner drinks, smokes, or uses drugs, it can lower his fertility and possibly damage his sperm.

Chapter 2
PLANNING FOR A HEALTHY BABY

Ideally, your prenatal care should begin before you even become pregnant. According to the U.S. Centers for Disease Control and Prevention, almost 4 million American women give birth each year. Nearly one-third of them will experience some type of pregnancy-related complication. Women who do not seek adequate prenatal care increase their risk for complications that may go undetected or are not dealt with soon enough. This can lead to serious consequences for the mother and/or baby. It's never too early to start prenatal care.

IS THAT SAFE?

Now that you are pregnant, you want to make sure that everything you put in your mouth is safe for you and your baby. There are many different products that fall into this group, including everything from food additives to medications. Let this chapter guide you through some of the questions you may have.

Exploring Food Additives

Many of the foods we eat are chock-full of food additives such as preservatives, flavor enhancers, food colorings, and even hormones. These additives are used to add color and flavor, enhance flavor, sweeten, and preserve food freshness. New additives must pass very rigid government safety tests before they are considered safe for consumers. The U.S. Food and Drug Administration (FDA) is the entity responsible for approving additives used in foods. The FDA sets safety standards, determines whether a substance is safe for its intended use, decides what type of foods the additive can be used in, what amounts it can be used in, and how it must be indicated on food labels.

Regulating Additives

Some additives are labeled as "Generally recognized as safe" (GRAS) because they have an extensive history of safe use or because existing scientific evidence indicates their safe use in foods. There is an extensive list of GRAS additives, which the FDA and USDA re-evaluate from time to time.

Additives fall into three categories: prior-approved substances, regulated additives, and color additives. Prior-approved substances are additives that were approved prior to the 1958 Food Additives Amendment, which made the FDA responsible for approving additives. Regulated additives are not considered as GRAS or prior-approved until they are fully approved and go through rigorous testing. Before color additives can be used in food, they need to be tested the same as regulated food additives.

Most food additives are safe during pregnancy unless you have a known reaction or specific allergy to certain food additives. As a pregnant woman, you should get in the habit of reading labels carefully, especially if you are sensitive to any food additives or colorings. If you are concerned about food additives, the best advice is to eat a wide variety of fresh foods. A diet high in whole grains, fresh fruits, fresh vegetables, and fresh meats can help you avoid excessive amounts of some food additives.

MSG

Monosodium glutamate, known as MSG, is used as a flavor enhancer. MSG does not add a flavor of its own to food; instead, it enhances or intensifies the natural salty taste of many processed foods. Although the additive is best known for its use in Chinese food, it is also incorporated into many other processed foods. MSG is made up of sodium and glutamate, or glutamic acid. Glutamic acid is an amino acid that is found naturally in the body and in high protein foods. The FDA classifies MSG as a "generally recognized as safe" additive. Because some people have an adverse reaction to it, the FDA requires all foods that contain MSG to indicate it as an ingredient on the label. In sensitive people, whether pregnant or not, MSG can trigger headaches, nausea, vomiting, sleep disturbances, and dizziness. More severe symptoms include breathing problems, chest pains, and increased blood pressure. Some studies in mice have shown possible birth defects and behavioral problems when MSG is consumed in large amounts, but no correlation has been established for humans. The FDA believes MSG is safe for the majority of the population to consume.

The bottom line is that if you are worried about ingesting MSG during pregnancy and how it may affect you and your baby, you should become aware of what foods contain it and limit your intake.

Olestra

Olean, also known as Olestra, is a noncaloric fat substitute that is made of a synthetic mixture of sugar and vegetable oil. Olestra was certified as safe by the FDA in 1996 and was approved for use in snack foods including potato chips, tortilla chips, and crackers. Some of these products include the Lay's WOW snacks, Doritos, and Pringles. Olestra basically passes through the body undigested. Because it is not absorbed, there is no danger in pregnant women of its reaching the fetus.

....

Pregnancy Pointer

Remember that just because a food contributes no fat, it doesn't necessarily contain zero calories. Foods that contain Olestra will probably not harm you or your baby if eaten in moderation, but there are much better snack choices you can make.

....

However, there can be some negative effects from eating Olestra. It does interfere with the absorption of the fat-soluble vitamins A, D, E, and K. For that reason, the manufacturer is required to fortify Olestra products with those vitamins. The product also causes mild gastrointestinal discomfort such as diarrhea, gas, abdominal cramping, and greasy stools. The FDA initially required that Olestra products be labeled with a warning of the artificial fat's gastrointestinal affects. Recently, the FDA dropped the requirement because the effects are only mild for most people.

During pregnancy, you probably already deal with plenty of gastrointestinal discomforts. There is no need to compound these problems with foods that contain Olestra. In addition, they provide no real nutritional value. This is a time when you need foods that contain loads of nutrition. There are much better choices when it comes to snacks. Don't get yourself into the habit of snacking on chips, whether they contain fat or not. Instead, get in the habit of snacking on fruits, vegetables, yogurt, and other healthier foods.

ARTIFICIAL SWEETENERS

Artificial, or nonnutritive, sweeteners are added to all types of foods including gum, candy, sweets, soft drinks, and even to some over-the-counter medications. If you are trying to avoid these sweeteners or limit your consumption, read labels closely. Artificial sweeteners that are classified as "generally recognized as safe" are acceptable to use during pregnancy in moderation. However, the main health issue behind the use of artificial sweeteners is that they might encourage you to opt out of more nutritious foods. For example, if you drink gallons of diet soft drinks, you may not be drinking other more nutritious beverages such as water, milk, and juice that can be more beneficial. The other concern is that foods with artificial sweeteners are usually lower in calories, and pregnancy is not the time to be eating very low-calorie foods. Artificial sweeteners can be useful to pregnant women who have diabetes.

Aspartame

Aspartame is an artificial sweetener that is found in popular products such as NutraSweet, Equal, and most diet soft drinks. This sweetener has not been shown to cause birth defects, and the FDA considers moderate use during pregnancy to be safe.

Aspartame is a concern for women with phenylketonuria (PKU), a rare genetic disorder. Aspartame contains phenylalanine, an amino acid that is toxic for people with PKU. Women with PKU cannot break down phenylalanine, which can cause high levels in the mother's blood and may affect the developing fetus. Women who have the PKU gene, but not the disease, can break down aspartame well enough to keep from causing harm to their babies. If you have PKU, you should not consume aspartame. All products that contain aspartame have a phenylalanine warning label.

Saccharin

With all of the artificial sweeteners now on the market today, saccharin is much less commonly used. Saccharin is an artificial sweetener that is found in products such as Sweet 'n Low and some diet soft drinks as well as some over-the-counter medications. Saccharin was recently removed from the government's list of possible carcinogens after years of research. However, saccharin still carries a warning label until the FDA or Congress removes it.

Saccharin can cross the placenta and enter the baby's bloodstream. Research has shown that a baby clears saccharin from the bloodstream more slowly than the mother does. Whether this causes harm to the fetus or not is still a controversial issue. Some doctors may ban saccharin from their patients' diets. Because of the controversial and unknown safety of saccharin for unborn babies, it is suggested that saccharin be ingested in moderation if at all during pregnancy. Although there has been no concrete evidence that this sweetener is harmful to you or your baby, it is important to weigh the facts, speak to your doctor, and make your own personal decision.

Acesulfame-K

Acesulfame-K is one of the newer artificial sweeteners on the market. Acesulfame-K is marketed under the name Sunette. Acesulfame-K has recently been used in the product Pepsi One, which also includes aspartame, as well as candy, baked goods, desserts, and tabletop sweeteners such as Sweet One. The use of acesulfame-K within FDA guidelines appears safe for use during pregnancy.

Sucralose

Sucralose is one of the newest low-calorie sweeteners on the market and is the generic name for the product called Splenda. It was only approved by the FDA in 1998. This sweetener is actually made from sugar, but unlike sugar, it is not recognized as a carbohydrate during food digestion or absorption. The sweetener is not digested, absorbed, or metabolized for energy, so it does not affect blood sugar or insulin. Instead, sucralose basically passes through the body unchanged. Splenda can be found in many different products and is also packaged as a tabletop sweetener. Sucralose, or Splenda, is safe for pregnant women to consume, and as with other sweeteners it is best used in moderation.

The safety of FDA-approved nonnutritive sweeteners is expressed in terms of acceptable daily intake (ADI). This measure reflects the estimated amount per kilogram of body weight that a person can safely consume every day over a lifetime without health risk.

SWEETENER	ACCEPTABLE DAILY INTAKE*
Aspartame	50 mg/kilogram body weight
Saccharin	5 mg/kilogram body weight
Acesulfame K	15 mg/ kilogram body weight
Sucralose	0 to 15 mg/ kilogram body weight

*Weight in pounds divided by 2.2 will equal kilograms of body weight.

SOMETHING FISHY

Fish and seafood can be a valuable source of nutrition. Fish contains protein, omega-3 fatty acids, vitamin D, and other essential nutrients that make it an exceptionally healthy food for pregnant mothers and developing babies. However, some fish can contain harmful levels of methylmercury, a toxic mercury compound. Mercury occurs naturally in the environment and is often released into the air through industrial pollution. From the air, mercury can fall and accumulate in streams, lakes, and oceans where fish is caught for consumption. Bacteria in the water can cause chemical changes that transform mercury into the toxic form of methylmercury. Fish in these bodies of water absorb methylmercury as they feed on organisms within the water.

Pregnancy Pointer

Even if you choose to use the canned light tuna, it is best to eat only one average meal of the tuna and choose another meal from another type of fish since the new advisory also suggests eating a variety of fish every week.

Harmful Effects

If consumed regularly by women who can become pregnant, women who are pregnant or nursing, or by a young child, methylmercury can harm a developing brain and nervous system. Just about all types of fish contain trace amounts of methylmercury, which is not harmful to most humans. However, larger fish that feed on other fish accumulate the highest levels of methylmercury. These types of fish pose the greatest risks to people that consume them on a regular basis. Pregnant women as well as women who are trying to conceive, nursing mothers, and young children are advised to also avoid these types of fish in large amounts. Women can avoid any risks associated with methylmercury and still get some of the important health benefits of fish by following the guidelines described in the following section.

Fish Guidelines

Any risk comes from a buildup of mercury in the body and not from a single meal. The Food and Drug Administration (FDA) and Environmental Protection Agency (EPA) have released specific advice concerning fish bought from stores and restaurants, which includes ocean and coastal fish as well as other types of commercial fish. If you follow the advice presented by the FDA and EPA, you can gain the positive benefits of eating fish while still avoiding any developmental problems to your baby due to the mercury content of fish. The FDA and EPA advise women who are pregnant or could become pregnant, nursing mothers, and young children not eat shark, swordfish, king mackerel, or tilefish because these fish contain higher unsafe levels of methylmercury.

Levels of methylmercury in other fish can vary. As a result, these agencies also advise that women who can become pregnant, women who are pregnant, and nursing mothers eat up to 12 ounces (2 average meals) a week of cooked fish or shellfish that are lower in mercury. Five of the most common fish that are low in mercury include shrimp, canned light tuna, salmon, pollock, and catfish. They also advise eating a variety of fish and shellfish and not eating the same type of fish or shellfish more than once per week.

If the fish is caught by family and friends in local lakes, rivers, and coastal areas, you should check local advisories about the safety of the type of fish caught. If no information or advice is available, you are advised to eat up to 6 ounces (one average meal) per week of the fish that was caught in local waters but don't eat any other fish during that same week. Follow these same guidelines for young children but with smaller portions. These guidelines are important when it comes to keeping the total level of methylmercury, contributed by all fish, to low levels in the body. It is smart to keep abreast of guidelines concerning the consumption of fish during pregnancy. Many organizations are trying to enforce stricter guidelines than are currently being recommended by the FDA and EPA. Check out the EPA website, at *www.epa.gov* and the FDA website at *wwww.fda .gov* for the latest advisories.

SOY

Although soy can be a healthy alternative to animal foods, recent controversy questions its safety during pregnancy. Recent studies done on animals found that certain soy components consumed during pregnancy may adversely affect the sexual development of male offspring. Even though no effects have been observed in Asia, where soy is a major part of the diet, the studies have sparked concern and warrant further studies. Other concerns have been the plant-based hormones in soy that mimic estrogen. Research data is far from conclusive on these issues. In the meantime, it is best to remember the rule of thumb, which is moderation. If you are vegetarian, do not rely solely on soy for your main source of protein but choose other foods for variety. Also, it is best to consume soy in the form of whole soy foods rather than from dietary supplements containing soy in the form of pills and powders.

Although pregnancy is a happy and exciting time, health concerns can surface. It is important to understand what health problems can develop and to know the signs and symptoms to look for. You should always contact your doctor if you have signs and/or symptoms that seem abnormal to you or if you just are not feeling right. Listen to your body, and be aware of potential problems.

Belly Basics

The FDA continually monitors the safety of drugs during pregnancy. Drug manufacturers are required to do their part by collecting feedback from pregnant women who are taking their drugs and to report their findings to the FDA.

HYPEREMESIS GRAVIDARUM

The majority of pregnant women experience some form of mild nausea and/or vomiting early in pregnancy. In fact, almost 50 percent of women experience some form of morning sickness. However, a very small percentage of women experience extremely severe and persistent nausea and/or vomiting. This is a condition known as hyperemesis gravidarum (HG). This condition can make it difficult for a mother to consume the number of calories she needs, get enough fluids, and simply perform daily activities. If this condition is left untreated, it can lead to malnutrition, vitamin and mineral deficiencies, electrolyte imbalances, weight loss, dehydration, and even possible liver or kidney damage. These symptoms can all be damaging to the development of the fetus as well as to the health of the mother. When HG is treated properly, any adverse outcome to the baby—such as low birth weight, developmental problems, or prematurity—can be avoided.

IRON DEFICIENCY ANEMIA

Anemia is defined as a deficiency of red blood cells or red blood cells having a decreased ability to carry oxygen or iron. There are different forms of anemia, such as iron, B12, and folate deficiency. During pregnancy, the most common is iron deficiency anemia.

It is important to be tested for anemia during your first prenatal visit so that measures can be taken for treatment if you are found to be anemic. Even if you test negative for anemia at your first visit, the condition can develop as you progress through your pregnancy. This is especially true in the last three months when the baby is using a lot of your red blood cells for growth and development. Most doctors will test you at different stages throughout your pregnancy, including at your first visit, at twenty-eight weeks, once admitted to labor and delivery, and after delivery.

Iron absorption can be increased with vitamin C-rich foods and/or supplements. It is also helpful to take iron supplements between meals or at bedtime as well as on an empty stomach to help absorption. On the flip side, antacids can decrease the absorption of iron.

GESTATIONAL DIABETES

Gestational diabetes mellitus (GDM) is a type of diabetes, or insulin resistance, that develops around the middle of pregnancy and ends after delivery. Women who are pregnant, have high blood sugar (glucose) levels and have never had diabetes before are said to have GDM. Gestational diabetes occurs when the body isn't able to properly use insulin or to make enough insulin to keep blood sugar levels in normal ranges, causing higher-than-normal levels. Without enough insulin, or with the body not using it properly, glucose cannot leave the blood and be used for energy. GDM usually develops around the sixth month of pregnancy, or between the twenty-fourth and twenty-eighth weeks.

It can be unhealthy for both mother and baby if blood sugar levels are too high. Because GDM does not appear until later in the pregnancy when the baby has been formed, it does not cause birth defects seen in some babies whose mother had diabetes before pregnancy. If GDM is not treated properly or controlled, it can cause problems for the baby that include low blood sugar levels, jaundice, breathing problems, and high insulin levels. In addition, it can cause a baby to weigh more than normal at birth, which can make delivery more difficult and possibly necessitate a cesarean section. Babies born with excess insulin run a higher risk of obesity in childhood and adulthood, thereby putting them at higher risk for Type 2 diabetes later in life. GDM is different from other forms of diabetes in that it only occurs during pregnancy and goes away after delivery. Women who have diabetes before becoming pregnant are not classified as having gestational diabetes.

HYPERTENSION AND PREECLAMPSIA

High blood pressure, or hypertension, occurs when there is a consistently higher-than-normal pressure or force of blood against the walls of your arteries. It is normal for a pregnant woman's blood pressure to drop during her first and second trimesters. By the third trimester, however, blood pressure usually returns to normal levels. However, in about 8 to 10 percent of pregnant women, instead of returning to normal, blood pressure begins to increase to abnormally high levels in the second or third trimester. This condition is known as pregnancy-induced hypertension. Women who enter pregnancy with high blood pressure are said to have chronic high blood pressure.

Preeclampsia, which is also sometimes called toxemia, is a disorder that only occurs during pregnancy and can also occur during the period right after delivery. It can greatly affect both the mother and unborn baby. Preeclampsia occurs in about 5 to 8 percent of all pregnancies, and very severe cases of preeclampsia can be life threatening. Typically, this condition develops after the twentieth week of pregnancy, in the late second trimester and into the third trimester, although for some it can develop earlier. High blood pressure that develops before the twentieth week is usually a sign of chronic high blood pressure or pregnancy-induced hypertension, but it can also be an early sign of preeclampsia.

Untreated, preeclampsia can cause high blood pressure, problems with blood supply to the placenta and fetus, problems with the liver, kidney, and brain function of the mother as well as the risk of stroke, seizures, and fluid on the lungs. Because the condition affects the blood flow to the placenta and fetus, the baby has a harder time getting the oxygen and nourishment it needs. These babies are often smaller in size and tend to be born prematurely. Women who develop severe preeclampsia can develop life-threatening seizures called eclampsia.

Both chronic high blood pressure and preeclampsia can develop gradually or suddenly and can be mild or severe. If you develop high blood pressure during your pregnancy, you will be monitored closely for signs of preeclampsia throughout your pregnancy.

HELLP SYNDROME

About 4 to 12 percent of women who develop severe preeclampsia develop a condition called HELLP syndrome, usually in the last trimester. HELLP stands for the following:

- Hemolysis (the breaking down of red blood cells)
- Elevated liver enzymes
- Low platelet count

Symptoms of HELLP include vomiting, nausea, headache, and pain in the right upper abdominal area due to problems with liver bloating. It is possible to experience this syndrome before the classic symptoms of preeclampsia even begin to manifest. Many symptoms of the HELLP syndrome are easily mistaken for the flu or for possible gallbladder problems. Some women develop HELLP syndrome without ever having preeclampsia, within two to seven days after delivery. Treatment for HELLP includes medication to help control blood pressure and medications to help prevent seizures and, occasionally, platelet transfusions. Basically, the only real cure for HELLP is delivery of the baby. Most women who develop HELLP end up delivering their babies early to prevent any serious complications. It is important to listen to your body, and if you have any of these symptoms, contact your doctor immediately.

OVER 35

The over-35 pregnancy is becoming more and more commonplace. When you are over 35, your pregnancy is managed a little more closely than it would be for younger women. You may be aware that screening for Down syndrome is now offered to women of all ages; however it is highly recommended for older mothers. Your physician will discuss testing for this and other disorders with you and may recommend that you go to see a genetic counselor to help you understand your increased risk. While older mothers are at a higher risk of these kinds of problems, the odds are still overwhelming that you will have a healthy baby.

Because you are also at a higher risk for pregnancy complications, such as miscarriages, birth defects, preeclampsia (high blood pressure), gestational diabetes, placenta previa, and a low birth-weight baby, your health-care provider will be checking for these problems. Your health-care provider is there to catch problems early on and prevent complications. Your health-care provider does not expect to find problems simply because you are over 35 but is on the lookout for them with a careful eye. You should remember that risk in medical terms is relative. For example, though your physician may say that your risk of having a live baby born with Down syndrome is increased, the actual risk is only one in 356. Higher than what a younger woman would face, but the actual risk is not very high.

As an over-35 mother, you will not have more frequent prenatal appointments than other women unless you are experiencing problems. You can expect to be referred to a maternal-fetal medicine specialist for testing for things such as Down syndrome and spina bifida, but as long as you are having a normal pregnancy, you won't need to work with the specialist on a regular basis unless you specifically choose to.

Your health-care provider's job is to watch for any possible risks in your pregnancy and step in to manage them if they do appear. All pregnancies are about managing risk, and yours is no different. Your health-care provider is there to minimize risk and take action if risk does arise.

Chapter 3
CLEAN UP YOUR DIET

Focusing on the quality of your diet is a big step toward living the healthiest life for you and your baby. Instead of drastically changing your diet, feeling overwhelmed or deprived, and falling back into an unhealthy diet cycle, you can use some easy-to-apply tips to clean up your diet gradually and painlessly. While you are pregnant and eating for two, you should maintain a diet that optimizes the nutritional content of every bite and sip, and minimizes the unhealthy aspects of foods that won't benefit you or your baby.

THE "EATING FOR TWO" MYTH

Once you become pregnant, you may hear comments like, "Go ahead and eat, you are eating for two now." It is true that you need nutrients through the foods you choose for both you and the healthy development of your baby. Eating plenty of nutritionally dense foods—as opposed to junk that contains calories but very little nutrition—is the way to supply your baby with all the nutrition he needs. On the other hand, you don't need to eat enough calories for two people. In fact, eating too much can cause unnecessary weight gain. At the same time, eating too little may keep your baby from receiving all of the nutrition he needs. The key is to keep a healthy balance.

Calorie needs increase slightly during pregnancy to help support a woman's maternal body changes and the baby's proper growth and development. It is true that your body requires more calories during pregnancy, but "more" here means only a moderate amount. During the first trimester, most physicians recommend no increase in daily caloric intake for women who are of a healthy weight. After the first trimester, you need about 300 calories per day above your maintenance level. That adds up to about 85,000 calories over the nine months that you are pregnant. Calorie needs will be more if you are carrying more than one baby. Your extra daily calorie needs will jump to 500 calories if you breastfeed following pregnancy. It does not take much to consume an extra 300 calories. The key is to choose nutrient-rich foods that contain plenty of lean protein, complex carbohydrates, fiber, vitamins, and minerals for your extra calories.

Max Out Nutrition

Every macronutrient (carbohydrates, proteins, and fats) and micronutrient (vitamins and minerals) is utilized by the body in different ways. Without even one of these essential elements, one or more of the body's systems can pay a heavy price. Each meal and snack you eat should contain foods that supply ample amounts of complex carbohydrates, clean protein, and healthy fats. Vitamins and minerals are plentiful in natural foods, so eating a variety of natural nutritious options should also be a top priority. By including a variety of foods that contain balanced provisions of macronutrients and micronutrients, you can promote optimal system functioning . . . with the added benefit of delicious meals that have a variety of colors, textures, and flavors.

....

Belly Basics

Skipping meals during pregnancy can have serious effects on the proper development of the baby. Skipping meals will force the baby to go too long without proper nourishment, and it can sabotage your efforts to consume enough healthy calories each day.

....

The vibrant colors of foods signify their high content of great, unique nutrition. From blueberries' blue anthocyanins to broccoli's green chlorophyll and phytochemicals, foods you choose to include in your diet should be appealing to the eyes as well as the palate. By focusing your diet on foods that make your plate (or your glass) as colorful as possible, you can benefit from the variety of nutrients contained within each and every food you enjoy.

EAT EVERY THREE TO FOUR HOURS

The body's metabolism is designed to run similarly to a car engine. With fuel, you can run, but without fuel, you can't. Expecting your body to run on little or no food for long periods of time would be like expecting your car to drive long distances at high speeds on nothing but fumes. Expecting your body to be able to create a baby healthfully with little or no fuel would be just as absurd! Fueling up your body every three to four hours with quality nutrition will not only deliver the essential nutrients your body and baby need but also promote a speedy metabolism and provide your body with the energy it needs to function properly. As an added benefit, eating every couple of hours helps satisfy hunger longer and keeps cravings and the temptation to binge on unhealthy foods at bay.

While some people skip breakfast or go long hours without eating under the misconception that fewer meals will result in consuming fewer calories, the reality is that dangerous consequences can result from this short-term starvation. When you choose to forgo your morning meal, it's not just your health at stake—your baby's development is as well. Eating five or six balanced and somewhat proportionate meals will help ensure your baby is receiving adequate amounts of the vitamins, minerals, and macronutrients he needs around the clock.

When your body is forced to function on little or no food, it turns to a sort of "hibernation mode" and begins to burn its own sources of fuel for energy. Because muscle mass provides more energy pound-per-pound compared to fat, the body burns the meatier muscle mass for fuel *and* starts to store consumed calories in preparation for upcoming "hibernation" periods. Breaking the day's total calories into five or six equal meals and snacks allows your body's metabolism to increase and the bodily systems to run at peak performance.

WATER INTAKE

Water is an essential part of a healthy lifestyle that is just as important as macronutrients and micronutrients. Water acts as your body's transportation system to carry nutrients to your body cells as well as your baby's. Water helps to regulate body temperature through perspiration and by transporting oxygen through the body, carrying waste products away from the body cells, cushioning joints, and protecting body organs. Proper hydration before, during, and after any form of exercise or vigorous activity is a vital component of a healthy pregnancy.

How Much Is Enough?

Pregnant women need extra fluid to support their increased blood volume and for amniotic fluid. Because the body has no provision to store water, the amount of water you lose each day must be continually replaced to maintain proper hydration. During both pregnancy and breastfeeding, women should aim to drink eight to twelve (8-ounce) glasses of water per day. This may increase if you are perspiring in hot weather, when exercising, or if you have any type of fever, diarrhea, or vomiting.

Belly Basics

It is normal to get thirsty once in a while, but if you are excessively thirsty and find yourself drinking large amounts of water, this could be a sign of a medical condition such as diabetes. If you feel you are drinking because of severe thirst, as opposed to a healthy habit, speak to your doctor.

Inadequate water intake can lead to problems like fatigue, muscle weakness, and headaches, just to name a few. For the fetus, dehydration can affect adequate nutrient transport, induce poor waste removal, create too warm an environment, and decrease cushioning. These can all affect fetal growth and development. Being properly hydrated can help to reduce swelling and bothersome constipation.

Staying properly hydrated can help you to feel more energized, give you an improved sense of well-being, provide greater endurance and stamina during physical activity, and improve your digestion and elimination.

The best and easiest way to get your fluids is simply by drinking water. Other fluids that can contribute to your daily intake include fat-free or low-fat milk, club soda, bottled water, vegetable juice, seltzer, and fruit juice. Be careful of drinking too many beverages, such as juice, that are healthy but also pack in a lot of calories. Stay clear of alcohol and most herbal teas, and limit coffee, tea, soft drinks, diet soft drinks, and other caffeinated beverages. If you feel thirsty, your body is telling you that it is already becoming dehydrated, so drink up.

Belly Basics

Water contributes close to 55 to 65 percent of an adult's body weight, and during pregnancy your body's water needs expand substantially. Water is present in every part of your body: 83 percent of blood, 73 percent of muscle, 25 percent of body fat, and even 22 percent of bones are made up of water.

A Good Habit to Have

Like everything else, drinking water should be part of your healthy lifestyle—you should make it a habit. Make a commitment today to start drinking water on a regular basis. You should be in the habit before you even become pregnant. You should start out with a moderate goal and work your way up. It may help to start a water diary on a calendar to keep track of your current intake and your progress. If you need help increasing your water intake, follow some of these helpful tips:

- At work or at home, take water breaks instead of coffee breaks.
- Keep a bottle of water at your desk, on your counter at home, or in your car when traveling so you have it available to sip throughout the day.
- Get in the habit of drinking a glass of water before and with meals and snacks. Besides helping you to stay hydrated, it can help take the edge off of your appetite.
- Use a straw to drink your water. Believe it or not, using a straw can help you drink faster and make a glass of water seem a little more manageable.
- Drink water instead of snacking while watching television or reading a book.
- Keep a two-quart container of water in the refrigerator, and make it your goal to drink it all by the end of the day. This also gives you a constant supply of good, cold water.

Easy on the Salt

While sodium is a very important mineral during pregnancy, be careful not to overdo it. For many people, consuming sodium in moderation means making some dietary and lifestyle changes. A strong preference for salty foods is easily acquired and usually starts at a young age. It is all in what your taste buds get used to.

To help moderate the amount of sodium in your diet, begin to gradually decrease your salt intake, especially if you are accustomed to salty tastes. Eat plenty of fresh or frozen fruits and vegetables as well as fresh foods as opposed to processed, canned, or prepared foods. If you eat frozen convenience foods often, look for products that have less than 800 mg sodium per serving. Choose lower-sodium foods by paying attention to the nutrition facts panel on all packaged foods. Keep in mind that condiments such as ketchup, soy sauce, teriyaki sauce, mustard, pickles, and olives can be high in sodium, so go easy on these.

VITAMINS

Vitamins are known as micronutrients because you need them in much smaller amounts than carbohydrates, proteins, and fats. Even though you need them in smaller amounts, that does not make them any less important. Vitamins are involved in all kinds of functions throughout the body. They don't supply energy directly because they do not provide any calories to the body, but vitamins do regulate many of the processes that produce energy. Although all vitamins are important during pregnancy—and you should concentrate on getting enough of all of them—some deserve special attention. Vitamins fall into two categories: water-soluble and fat-soluble vitamins.

Fat-Soluble Vitamins

The fat-soluble vitamins include vitamins A, D, E, and K. Fat-soluble vitamins dissolve in fat, and they travel throughout the body by attaching to body chemicals made with fat. These vitamins can be stored in the body, so it can be harmful to consume more than you need over a long period of time.

Vitamin A promotes the growth and the health of cells and tissues for both the mother and the baby. In the form of beta-carotene, vitamin A also acts as a powerful antioxidant. Beta-carotene does not pose any danger to expectant mothers. Your body converts beta-carotene to vitamin A only when the body needs it. The recommended daily allowance (RDA) of vitamin A is measured in micrograms (mcg). In supplements and on nutrition facts panels, it is measured in international units (IU). The need for vitamin A increases only slightly during pregnancy, from 700 to 770 mcg (for women nineteen to fifty years of age).

Another important fat-soluble vitamin during pregnancy is vitamin D. This vitamin aids in calcium balance and helps your body absorb sufficient calcium for you and your baby. Vitamin D is known as the "sunshine vitamin" because the body can make vitamin D after sunlight hits the skin. It is important to get enough vitamin D throughout your life as a way of helping to avoid osteoporosis (or brittle bone disease). Since vitamin D is stored in the body, too much can be toxic. Excess amounts usually come from supplements and not food or too much sunlight. During pregnancy, women should get 650 IU per day.

Water-Soluble Vitamins

The water-soluble vitamin group consists of the B-complex vitamins and vitamin C. Water-soluble vitamins dissolve in water and are then carried in your bloodstream. Most are not stored in the body in any significant amounts. What your body does not use is excreted through the urine. Since they are not stored in the body, water-soluble vitamins pose less of a risk for toxicity (though moderation is still the best approach). This also means that you need a regular supply from your diet.

Folic Acid

Folic acid is a B vitamin whose main role is to maintain the cell's genetic code or DNA (the cell's master plan for cell reproduction). It also works with vitamin B_{12} to form hemoglobin in red blood cells. Folic acid has gained much attention for its role in reducing the risk for neural tube birth defects, such as spina bifida, in newborn babies. Other risks of folic acid deficiencies include anemia, impaired growth, and abnormal digestive function. It is vital that pregnant women or women of childbearing years consume enough folic acid through food and supplements, especially during the first trimester.

....

Belly Basics

The B-complex vitamins are a family of vitamins that all work together and have similar functions in health. They include vitamin B_1 (thiamin), vitamin B_2 (riboflavin), niacin, vitamin B_6, folate, vitamin B_{12}, biotin, and pantothenic acid. Most B vitamins help the body to indirectly produce energy within its cells.

....

Before pregnancy a woman's need for folic acid is 400 mcg per day. During pregnancy, that amount jumps to 600 mcg per day. Recent studies show that to decrease the risk of birth defects, women planning a pregnancy should increase their daily intake of folic acid to 800–1,000 mcg. Most prenatal vitamins contain 800–1,000 mcg to ensure that women fully absorb the amount they need during pregnancy to help decrease the risk of birth defects. Taking too much folic acid through supplements can mask a vitamin B_{12} deficiency and could interfere with some medications. However, some women may need more folic acid with certain medications.

Vitamin B_6 is necessary in helping your body make nonessential amino acids (the building blocks of protein). These nonessential amino acids are used to make necessary body cells. Vitamin B_6 also helps to turn the amino acid tryptophan into niacin and serotonin (a messenger in the brain). In addition to those functions, this vitamin helps produce insulin, hemoglobin, and antibodies that help fight infection. Requirements are increased slightly in pregnancy due to the needs of the baby. The recommended level during pregnancy is 1.9 mg.

Requirements are also increased for vitamin B_{12} during pregnancy to help with the formation of red blood cells. The increase is slight, from 2.4 mcg before pregnancy to 2.6 mcg during pregnancy. This vitamin is found mostly in foods of animal origin, so vegetarians need a reliable source of vitamin B_{12}, such as fortified breakfast cereal or supplements.

Vitamin C produces collagen, a connective tissue that holds muscles, bones, and other tissues together. In addition it helps with a variety of other functions, including forming and repairing red blood cells, bones, and other tissue; protecting you from bruising by keeping capillary walls and blood vessels firm; keeping your gums healthy; healing cuts and wounds; and keeping your immune system strong and healthy. Vitamin C also helps your body absorb iron from plant sources, which is not as easily absorbed as iron from animals. Vitamin C is one of the very powerful antioxidants that attacks free radicals (unstable molecules with a missing electron formed when the body's cells burn oxygen) in the body's fluids. These free radicals can damage the body's cells, tissues, and even DNA (your body's master plan for reproducing cells).

With pregnancy, a woman's need for vitamin C increases slightly, from

75 mg to 85 mg (for women nineteen to fifty years). Because vitamin C is so readily available in numerous food sources like papayas, bell peppers, pineapple, broccoli, kiwis, cantaloupe, kale, oranges, and strawberries, it is not difficult to get the extra you need.

MINERALS

Minerals are also micronutrients. As with vitamins, your good health and your healthy pregnancy require an optimal supply. Minerals do not supply energy to the body directly, because they do not contain calories, but they do fulfill many vital functions. Minerals are part of a baby's bones and teeth. Along with protein and certain vitamins, minerals help to produce blood cells and other body tissues. Minerals aid in numerous body functions that support a normal pregnancy.

Minerals are categorized as either major minerals or trace minerals. Though they are all important, trace minerals are needed in smaller amounts than major minerals. Minerals are absorbed into your intestines and then are transported and stored in your body in various ways. Some minerals pass directly into your bloodstream. They are then transported to the cells, and the excess passes out of the body through the urine. Again, the rule of moderation is the best policy. Although all minerals are important during pregnancy and you should concentrate on getting enough of all of them, some deserve special attention.

Calcium

You already know how vital calcium is to strong bones and teeth. You also know that if your growing baby can't get what she needs, the fetal development process will rob your calcium stores. You need enough calcium to protect your stores and for the development of the baby's bones. Consuming enough calcium during pregnancy may also reduce your chances of developing high blood pressure and toxemia. Calcium requirements do not change throughout pregnancy, but many women still don't consume enough. Regardless of whether you are pregnant, you should consume at least 1,000 mg per day (for women aged nineteen to fifty years). If you do not consume enough calcium-containing foods, such as dairy products, speak to your doctor about calcium supplements. Keep in mind that the upper limit for calcium intake during pregnancy is 2,500 mg per day; this limit will keep you safe from "hypercalcemia," a condition resulting from excessive calcium intake that can lead to unnecessary calcium accumulation in cells (other than bone) that can result in soft tissue calcification.

Iron

As your blood volume increases during the time you are pregnant, your iron needs increase as well. Iron is essential for making hemoglobin, the component of blood that carries oxygen throughout the body and to the baby. Foods rich in vitamin C can help iron be absorbed into the blood. Many women start their pregnancies with less than optimal stores of iron, which can increase their risk of becoming anemic. Women who have iron deficiency anemia may be prescribed a higher dose of iron supplements. You should never increase your iron intake, especially through supplements, without first speaking with your doctor. Iron toxemia, otherwise known as "iron poisoning," is the condition that results from excessive iron intake (most commonly associated with the supplement variety) and can cause symptoms like nausea and vomiting, but also more serious conditions like shock, liver failure, and damage to the lining of the intestinal tract. You can easily avoid any of these possible consequences by simply consulting with your physician prior to taking any kind of iron supplements.

....

Pregnancy Pointer

Women who are having multiple babies have slightly higher recommended intakes for some vitamins and minerals. Your doctor can advise you as to your recommended nutritional intake.

....

Zinc

Almost every cell in the body contains zinc, which is also part of over seventy different types of enzymes. Zinc is known as the second most abundant trace mineral in the human body. Your requirement for this mineral increases slightly during pregnancy from 8 to 11 mg (for women nineteen to fifty years). Zinc is needed for cell growth and brain development. Too much iron from supplements can inhibit the absorption of zinc. Rather than supplementation, you can always opt to include high-zinc foods like oats, yogurt, sesame seeds, pumpkin seeds, and turkey in your diet on a regular basis.

Sodium

Although sodium sometimes gets bad press, it is still a mineral that is essential to life and to good health—and that is still true during pregnancy. Sodium has many important functions in the body, such as controlling the flow of fluids in and out of each cell, regulating blood pressure, transmitting nerve impulses, and helping your muscles relax (including the heart, which is a muscle). Sodium, chloride, and potassium are known as electrolytes, compounds that transmit electrical currents through the body. As a result of these currents, nerve impulses can also be transmitted.

....

Belly Basics

Fluid retention, or edema, is very normal during pregnancy and is not always the result of eating too much sodium. Instead, this condition is usually the result of increased estrogen production and a greater blood volume. Do not decrease your sodium intake to relieve edema. Restricting sodium too much can disrupt the body's fluid balance. Extra fluids, especially water, can help relieve some edema. If you are experiencing excessive edema, see your doctor before making any dietary changes.

....

The terms "salt" and "sodium" are often used interchangeably, yet they are two different things. Sodium is an element of table salt, which is technically known as sodium chloride. How much sodium is in table salt? A single teaspoon of salt contains 2,000 mg of sodium. Generally, articles and guidelines that warn of the dangers of eating too much salt are concerned with sodium only.

Although pregnant women should not decrease their sodium intake, excessive intake is not recommended either. During pregnancy, your body's need for sodium increases. Most women get plenty of sodium in their regular diets, and it is almost never necessary to arrange for extra sodium. In fact, the typical American consumes 4,000 to 8,000 mg per day, well above daily recommended levels. The moderate goal for adults, including pregnant and breastfeeding women, is approximately 2,400 mg of sodium per day.

In healthy people, the kidneys help regulate the sodium level in the body. Sodium levels usually don't become too high because most excess sodium is excreted from the body in urine and through perspiration. For example, when you eat foods that are high in salt, you probably urinate more frequently because the body is trying to rid itself of the extra sodium. Even though your sodium intake may vary from day to day, your body is very efficient at maintaining a proper balance.

PROTEIN

Protein is a powerful macronutrient. During pregnancy, protein provides the material needed for the physical growth and cellular development of the growing baby. Protein is also needed to build the mother's placenta, amniotic tissue, and other maternal tissues. A woman's blood volume increases by almost 50 percent during pregnancy, and additional protein is needed to produce those new blood cells.

Belly Basics

A low protein intake during pregnancy can increase the risk of having a low birth-weight baby. These babies are more prone to health problems and learning disabilities later in life.

During your pregnancy, you need slightly more protein than you did before, and during breastfeeding your needs will continue to increase. The body does not store protein, so you must consume a continuous supply. You need about 10 extra grams of protein from your extra daily calories, or 60 grams of protein daily, compared with the 50 grams a nonpregnant woman requires. Women expecting multiple babies may need more. Here are some examples of where you might find an extra 10 grams of protein:

- In a 1.5-ounce serving of lean meat
- In about 10 ounces of fat-free milk
- In 1.5 ounces of canned tuna in water

Most women do not have a problem meeting their protein requirements. Eating plenty of lean meat, fish, eggs, legumes, and dried beans as well as increasing your dairy servings will ensure you meet your protein needs. If you are a vegetarian and consume plenty of legumes, grain products, soy foods, and vegetables and fruits like summer squashes, cauliflower, collard greens, black beans, split peas, kidney beans, pinto beans, garbanzo beans, and crimini mushrooms, you should not have a problem consuming the recommended amount of protein.

CARBOHYDRATES

You can count on carbohydrates to be your body's main source of energy, especially for the brain and nervous system. Carbohydrates quickly and efficiently convert to energy for mom and baby. Carbohydrates are found in fruits, vegetables, dairy products, starches, and foods in the meat group such as beans and soy products. The only foods in which they are not found are meat, poultry, and fish. Fiber is also considered a carbohydrate and is important to health. However, fiber is not considered a nutrient because most of it is not digested or absorbed into the body.

Good Carbs and Not-So-Good Carbs

Carbohydrates are classified into two different categories: simple carbohydrates, or sugars; and complex carbohydrates, or starches. Sugars are carbohydrates in their simplest form. Refined sugars are found in foods such as table sugar, honey, jams, candy, syrup, and soft drinks. Refined sugars provide calories, but they lack nutrients like vitamins and minerals, and fiber. Some simple sugars, such as those that occur naturally, are found in more nutritious foods, such as the fructose found in fruit or the lactose that is part of dairy products. Complex carbohydrates are basically formed of many simple sugars linked together. They are found in foods such as grains, pasta, rice, vegetables, breads, legumes, nuts, and seeds. Complex carbohydrates are much more nutrient-rich than simple sugars.

How Many Carbs?

On average, women should get approximately 45 to 65 percent of their calories from carbohydrates. Since pregnancy increases calorie needs, more calories must be ingested from carbohydrates. The key is to increase your calories by eating more complex carbohydrates and not more sugar. Take in more complex carbohydrates by eating more fruits and vegetables, whole grains, rice, breads, and cereals. Try adding more beans, lentils, and peas to your daily meals.

Belly Basics

Before complex or simple carbohydrates can be used as energy, they must be broken down into glucose, or blood sugar. Glucose is carried through your bloodstream to your body's cells, where it is converted to energy. Since simple carbohydrates or sugars are already in their simplest form, they go straight into the bloodstream. Complex carbohydrates must be broken down into glucose. Some glucose is used as energy, and some is stored. The hormone insulin helps to regulate your blood sugar.

Following the USDA's MyPlate guidelines and eating the suggested number of servings from each food group during pregnancy will give you a safe suggested guideline to follow so that you are consuming the amount of carbohydrates your body needs for a healthy pregnancy and a healthy baby. Even though carbohydrates are extremely important, they need to be balanced with the other two macronutrients: protein and fat.

FAT

Fat is an important nutrient that sometimes gets a bad rap. Its major functions in the body include providing an energy source; aiding in the absorption and transport of the fat-soluble vitamins A, D, E, and K; cushioning organs; and regulating body temperature. All women, pregnant or not, should get 20 to 35 percent of their calories from fat. Fat can be dangerous to health if consumed in excess or if the wrong kinds of fat are eaten. It is important to include fat in your daily diet but in moderation. Fat is a very concentrated source of calories. A gram of fat has 9 calories, twice as many as a gram of carbohydrates or protein (both of which contain 4 calories per gram). A small amount of fat can go a long way!

Good Fat versus Bad Fat

There are different types of triglycerides, or dietary fats. Some of these fats are more harmful than others. The major kinds of fats in the foods you eat are saturated, polyunsaturated, monounsaturated, and trans-fatty acids or hydrogenated fats.

The unsaturated fats (polyunsaturated and monounsaturated) are referred to as the "healthy" fats. These fats can help to lower cholesterol levels, and they also have heart-protective factors. Most of the fat in your diet should be unsaturated. Following is a list of foods that contain healthy fats:

- Almonds
- Avocado oil
- Bee pollen
- Canola oil
- Cashews
- Coconut oil
- Flaxseeds
- Hemp seeds
- Olive oil
- Pistachios
- Walnuts

Sources of monounsaturated fats include certain plant-based oils, such as olive, canola, and peanut. Avocados are also good sources of monounsaturated fats. Sources of polyunsaturated fats include certain other plant-based oils such as corn, cottonseed, safflower, sunflower, sesame, and soybean. Nuts and seeds are also good sources. This group also includes the omega-3 fatty acids found in some fish. There are two polyunsaturated essential fatty acids that your body does not make and you must get from the food you consume. These two fatty acids are linoleic acid (or omega-6) and linolenic acid (or omega-3).

Saturated fats and trans-fatty acids tend to increase blood cholesterol levels, which can lead to health problems such as heart disease and stroke. The major sources of saturated fat are animal foods such as meat, poultry, and whole-milk dairy products. However, some plant sources also provide saturated fat, including palm and palm kernel oils. Food that contains trans-fats includes some margarines, cookies, crackers, and other commercial baked goods made with partially hydrogenated vegetable oils, as well as French fries, donuts, and other commercial fried foods.

....

Belly Basics

Eating a totally fat-free diet is not part of a healthy eating style. Fat is an essential nutrient, and some fats—such as omega-3 fatty acids—are necessary for certain parts of a baby's development. A totally fat-free diet may also fail to provide sufficient calories.

Trimming the Fat

Fat is definitely a needed nutrient in a healthy diet. The problem is that most Americans consume too much and the wrong kinds. Don't cut fat completely out of your diet, but it is important to cut back and to choose the right types. This means lowering your intake of dietary cholesterol and saturated fat. You should also lower your blood cholesterol or maintain it at safe levels as a way of decreasing your risk for heart disease.

Belly Basics

Cholesterol is not the same as fat. Cholesterol is a fat-like substance, but it has a different structure and different functions in the body than fat does. Because cholesterol provides no energy to the body, it has no calories.

You can cut the fat and cholesterol from your meals without losing any flavor. For example, try using egg whites or egg substitute in place of whole eggs. Choose leaner meats, cook with skinless poultry and fish, or occasionally opt for a vegetarian meal with beans or soy products as your main protein source. Read the nutrition facts panel to keep an eye on your daily intake of total fat, saturated fat, and cholesterol.

FIBER

Fiber is exclusively found in plant foods; it is the part of the plant that your body cannot digest. Fiber, also called dietary fiber, is categorized as a complex carbohydrate, but because it cannot be digested or absorbed into your bloodstream, it is not considered a nutrient. There are two types of fiber: soluble and insoluble. Each type has a different beneficial health function in the body. It is important to eat a variety of fiber-rich foods every day that will provide you with the health benefits of both soluble and insoluble fiber.

Soluble Fibers

Soluble fibers naturally found in plants include gums, mucilages, psyllium, and pectins. Foods that contain these fibers include peas, beans, oats, barley, and some fruits (especially apples with skin, oranges, prunes, strawberries, and bananas) and some vegetables (especially carrots, broccoli, and cauliflower). Soluble fiber binds to fatty substances and promotes their excretion, which in turn seems to help lower blood cholesterol levels.

Belly Basics

According to the American Heart Association, soluble fibers, when part of your everyday low-fat and low-cholesterol diet, can aid in slowing the absorption of sugar into the bloodstream, which in turn can help to control your blood sugar levels.

Insoluble Fibers

Insoluble fiber is known as "roughage." The insoluble fibers give plants their structure. Insoluble fibers naturally found in plants include cellulose, hemicellulose, and lignin. Foods that contain these fibers include whole-wheat or whole-grain products, wheat bran, corn bran, some fruits (especially the skin), and many vegetables including cauliflower, green beans, potatoes with skin, and broccoli. Insoluble fibers do not dissolve in water, but they hold on to water as they move waste through your intestinal tract. By holding on to water, they add bulk and softness to the stool and therefore promote regularity and help prevent constipation. Insoluble fibers also help accelerate intestinal transit time, which means they decrease the amount of time that waste stays in the colon. This cuts the time that potentially harmful waste food substances can linger in the intestines.

Fiber Benefits

Basically, fiber comes in and goes out of the body. However, it does some pretty amazing things on its travels. Fiber helps to promote good health in many ways. Studies show that a diet rich in fiber as part of a varied, balanced, and low-fat eating pattern may help to prevent some chronic diseases. No matter how good your present health is you can certainly benefit from adding more fiber to your diet. Fiber not only promotes health but also may help to reduce the risk for digestive problems, heart disease, some types of cancer, and diabetes. A fiber-rich diet can also help to promote weight management.

Belly Basics

There is such a thing as too much of a good thing. Eating more than 50 to 60 grams of fiber per day may cause a decrease in the amount of vitamins and minerals, such as zinc, iron, magnesium, and calcium, that your body absorbs. Large amounts of fiber can also cause gas, diarrhea, and bloating.

How Much Is Enough?

A diet rich in fiber is important at all times, but it can be especially helpful during pregnancy. A fiber-rich diet can help to prevent constipation, which plagues many pregnant women. The average American only eats about 12 to 17 grams of fiber daily, which is well below the recommended levels, so make sure you make the necessary changes to your diet to boost your fiber! Adults under the age of fifty should get 25 grams a day; adults over fifty should get 21 grams. When boosting your fiber intake, it is important to increase your intake gradually and to make sure you are drinking plenty of fluids.

Adding fiber to your diet may be easier than you think. Just looking at the fiber content on the nutrition facts panel on packaged foods can help you be aware of what you need to do to increase your fiber intake. Choose foods that are good sources of fiber and have at least 2.5 grams or more of fiber per serving. Make simple switches by substituting higher-fiber foods, such as whole-grain breads, brown rice, whole-wheat pasta, fruits, and vegetables for lower-fiber foods such as white bread, white rice, candy, and chips. Eat more raw vegetables and fresh fruits, and include the skins when appropriate. Lightly steam these foods, which can preserve a lot of the fiber content. Plan your meals to include high-fiber foods such as fruits, vegetables, legumes, or whole-grain starches. Simply adding extra vegetables to your favorite sandwiches, soups, and casseroles can make a world of difference.

....

Belly Basics

Don't consider juice for daily servings of fruit! Whole fruits contain more fiber than juice because much of the fiber is found in the skin and pulp, which is removed when the juice is made.

....

What better way to start your day than with a high-fiber breakfast cereal such as bran cereal or oatmeal? Look for cereals that contain at least 3 to 5 grams or more of fiber per serving. Add some fresh fruit to the top of your cereal for an extra fiber boost. Since both soluble and insoluble fibers are important for good health, eat a variety of high-fiber foods to ensure you get a mix of both types of fiber. Make good use of your snacks by choosing those that will increase your fiber intake. Nibble on dried fruits, popcorn, fresh fruit, raw vegetables, whole-wheat bagels, or whole-wheat crackers. Try something different and add legumes, or dried beans, to your diet at least two to three times per week. You can add them to salads, soups, casseroles, or spaghetti sauce.

WEIGHING IN

Comparisons between different pregnancies and the weight gained with each may make for great social conversation, but should never be considered a standard by which to gauge your own healthy weight gain while pregnant. Every pregnancy is as different as every mom, and trying to mimic someone else's ideal pregnancy can be a dangerous path to travel. Your goal for weight gain in pregnancy should focus on the needs of *your* body and *your* baby.

BMI

Your Body Mass Index is commonly referred to as your BMI by health and fitness professionals. Rather than looking at your weight as a number that you feel should be higher or lower, or aiming for an arbitrary weight that you assume is where you should be, your BMI takes into account your height and weight in order to determine whether your weight falls into a category that is healthy or unhealthy. With five categories that range from "underweight" to "severely obese," calculating your BMI can be an easy way to determine whether you have risks for weight-related health issues and need to focus more heavily on reaching a more optimal weight range with less associated risks.

To figure out your BMI, use the following formula:

Weight (pounds) ÷ 2.2 = weight in kilograms (kg)
Height (inches) ÷ 39.37 = height in meters (m)
Weight (kg) ÷ height (m) squared = BMI

Check your BMI against the following chart to see where your present weight places you for risk of health problems related to your body weight:

BMI	RISK FOR HEALTH PROBLEMS RELATED TO BODY WEIGHT
20–25	Very low risk
26–30	Low risk
31–35	Moderate risk
36–39	High risk
40–plus	Very high risk

If your BMI is greater than 30, you should consult your personal physician for further evaluation, especially before becoming pregnant.

DETERMINE YOUR CALORIC NEEDS

There are many different methods for estimating caloric needs. It is important to remember that these methods result only in estimates; still, you can get a general idea of the number of calories your body needs. Everyone's caloric needs differ, depending on factors such as age, gender, size, body composition, basal metabolic rate, and physical activity.

Basal metabolic rate (BMR) is the number of calories your body would burn if you were at rest all day. By figuring your basal metabolic rate, you know the minimum number of calories you must consume to maintain your weight. On average, a moderately active woman needs between 1,800 and 2,200 calories per day. A pregnant woman needs about 2,500 calories after the first trimester. However, because you don't spend every day lying in bed, you have additional calorie needs on top of your basal rate. The next section describes how to determine the number of calories you should ingest every day.

You Do the Math

Use this simple equation to figure your basic calorie needs:

1. First, figure your basal metabolic rate to get the minimum number of calories your body needs to maintain a healthy weight. To do this, multiply your healthy weight (in pounds) by 10. For instance, a woman whose

healthy weight is 165 pounds would have a basal metabolic rate of 1,650—in other words, this woman needs to take in a minimum of 1,650 calories to maintain her body weight.

2. Figure how many additional calories you need to sustain your level of physical activity. To do this, choose the activity level from the following list that best describes you and take the appropriate percentage of your basal metabolic rate.

- **Sedentary**—You mainly engage in low-intensity activities throughout your day, such as sitting, driving a car, lying down, sleeping, standing, typing, or reading. Take 20 percent of your basal metabolic rate (multiply by 0.2).

- **Light activity**—Your day includes light exercise, such as walking, but for no more than two hours of your day. Take 30 percent of your basal metabolic rate (multiply by 0.3).

- **Moderate activity**—You engage in moderate exercise throughout the day, such as heavy housework, gardening, dancing, with very little sitting. Take 40 percent of your basal metabolic rate (multiply by 0.4).

- **High activity**—You engage in active physical sports or have a labor-intensive job, such as construction work, on a daily basis. Take 50 percent of your basal metabolic rate (multiply by 0.5).

3. Figure out how many additional calories you need to sustain your body's digestion and absorption of nutrients. To do this, add your results from steps 1 and 2, then take 10 percent of the total (multiply by 0.1).

4. To find your total calorie needs, add your basal metabolic rate from step 1, the calories to sustain your level of physical activity from step 2, and the number of calories needed for digestion from step 3.

Take the example of the 165-pound woman from step 1, with the basal metabolic rate of 1,650. She is moderately active, which means she needs an additional 660 calories to sustain her activity level. She needs

231 calories to fuel her body's digestion and food absorption processes (1,650+660×0.1=231). Adding those values gives us a total of 2,541, which is the total number of calories a moderately active 165-pound woman should ingest to maintain her weight.

5. To account for the additional calories you need to sustain your body weight during pregnancy, add 300 to the total from step 4. This final value represents your estimated basic calorie needs.

A Little Extra Help

Doing the math will only give you an estimate of your calorie needs. Some women have special needs. If you are having problems figuring out your calorie needs, or if you are not sure what to eat to get those extra calories in, don't hesitate to contact a registered dietitian to help you out. Some women may need a little extra nutritional help to ensure they are getting everything that they need. It is recommended that you seek extra help if you are younger than seventeen or older than thirty-five; pregnant with more than one baby; underweight or overweight prior to becoming pregnant; a strict vegetarian; lactose intolerant; gaining too much or too little during pregnancy; having trouble eating due to nausea and/or vomiting; on a special diet due to allergies, diabetes, or gastrointestinal or digestive disorder; or if you have suffered with eating disorders. Don't go it alone if you are not sure what to do. Nutrition and calorie intake is vital to a healthy baby and a healthy pregnancy. Never hesitate to ask for help!

HEALTHY PREGNANCY WEIGHT GAIN

The health and weight of your baby at birth depend greatly on how much weight you gain over the course of your pregnancy. The weight of your baby factors into your weight gain, but your body also gains weight through its increase in blood volume—about 50 percent—as well as muscle, fluid, and tissue. Your body weight increases at a different rate depending on your stage of pregnancy. During the first trimester, weight gain is slow, only about 2 to 4 pounds for the whole time period. During the last six months, weight gain should increase to about 1/2 to 1 pound per week, depending on your total target weight gain. Even though all women differ slightly, it is best to gain weight at a steady pace.

TRIMESTER	WEIGHT GAIN
First trimester (1–3 months)	2 to 4 pounds
Second trimester (4–6 months)	12 to 14 pounds
Third trimester (7–9 months)	8 to 10 pounds

Your body weight before pregnancy will help to determine a healthy weight gain for you during pregnancy. The American College of Obstetricians and Gynecologists recommends the following target weight gains for healthy women. Keep in mind that these are only guidelines and that every woman is unique.

PRE-PREGNANCY WEIGHT	SUGGESTED WEIGHT GAIN
Normal weight (BMI of 19.8 to 26)	25 to 35 pounds
Overweight (BMI 26 to 29)	15 to 25 pounds
Obese (BMI greater than 29)	At least 15 pounds
Underweight (BMI of less than 19.8)	28 to 40 pounds

Because all women are different, suggested weight gains are expressed in ranges. Shoot for your target weight gain, and if you are not sure where your pre-pregnancy weight falls, speak to your doctor or calculate your pre-pregnancy BMI.

Your goal should be to maintain a steady weight gain throughout your pregnancy. Your baby requires a daily supply of essential nutrients during your entire pregnancy, and that comes from what you eat every day. Expect your weight gain to fluctuate a bit from week to week and to gain more or less depending on the stage of your pregnancy. However, if your weight fluctuates too much or changes suddenly, that could be a warning sign. Be aware of some of the following red flags:

- Gaining more than 3 pounds in any one week during your second trimester
- Gaining more than 2 pounds in any one week during your third trimester
- Not gaining any weight for more than two weeks in a row at any time during the fourth through the eighth months
- Gaining more weight than you anticipated (given that you are diligent about sticking to a well-balanced, healthy meal plan daily)

If you experience any of these or other warning signs, you should discuss it with your doctor at your next visit.

Belly Basics

Women who are African-American or in their teenage years (younger than eighteen) are advised to gain toward the upper limit of the weight range to help decrease the risk for delivering a low birth-weight baby. Taller women should shoot for the higher end of the weight gain ranges, and shorter women (62 inches or under) should shoot for the lower end of the range for weight gain.

Don't be obsessive about weighing yourself every day. Your weight can fluctuate too much from day to day to pinpoint possible problems this way. Instead, make regular doctor's visits, and weigh yourself at home every week or two to make sure you are on the right track.

Dieting During Pregnancy

Pregnancy is not the time to worry about losing weight, no matter what your pre-pregnancy weight was. Nor is it the time to worry about spoiling your girlish figure. Once you become pregnant, your focus should be on gaining the recommended amount of weight and on living a healthier lifestyle for a healthy pregnancy. It is the time to eat healthy and stay fit, not skimp on calories. Your baby is constantly growing and needs constant nourishment. You can think about weight loss and reaching a healthier weight once your pregnancy is over and you have finished breastfeeding your baby.

Pregnancy Pointer

Never take any type of diet pill or weight-loss supplement, even those claiming to be "safe and natural," while trying to conceive or once you are pregnant. These can be harmful to the fetus.

Even when you are trying to conceive, it is advisable to stay away from extreme fad diets since you may not know you are pregnant immediately. Fad diets can be too low in the calories and essential nutrients you need from the very start of pregnancy. If you need to reach a healthier weight before pregnancy, do it by sticking to a low-fat, high-fiber, well-balanced diet and exercising regularly.

If you've had gastric bypass surgery, doctors recommend that you stay at a stable weight for six months before trying to conceive. Also, be sure to see a nutritionist to determine your specific nutritional needs during pregnancy.

Dieting either before or during pregnancy can lead to nutritional deficiencies that can affect the proper development of your baby. Dieting by decreasing your caloric intake can lead to too little weight gain during pregnancy, which can lead to problems such as premature labor and delivering a low birth-weight baby. Do not try to lose weight in order to keep from gaining too much during your pregnancy. Bigger women are unlikely to gain as much weight during pregnancy as smaller women might. Keep your weight gain to the advised levels, and do not try to lose weight!

EATING DISORDERS

Maintaining a positive body image can be tough for any woman. During pregnancy, body image concerns seem to become even more prevalent. Eating disorders such as anorexia and bulimia seem to be more prevalent in women and tend to peak around the childbearing years. For women who are already struggling with an eating disorder, pregnancy can be a difficult time that can cause the disorder to worsen. Any type of eating disorder can affect the reproductive process and be dangerous during pregnancy.

Types of Eating Disorders

Anorexia nervosa is an eating disorder in which a person starves herself by eating little to no food. These people have a strong fear of body fat and weight gain. The most dangerous hazard of anorexia is starvation and its extreme health consequences. Obviously, for someone who is pregnant and whose food intake is responsible for supporting a fetus, anorexia could be detrimental. Not eating during pregnancy deprives the baby of essential nutrients she needs for proper growth and development.

Bulimia nervosa is an eating disorder in which a person binges, or consumes a very large amount of food all at once, and then purges by forcing herself to vomit or by taking laxatives or diuretics (water pills). The dangers of bulimia nervosa include electrolyte imbalances from repeated vomiting. Many people with bulimia are able to maintain normal body weight, making the disorder more difficult to detect.

Binge-eating disorder is very common in women. With a binge-eating disorder, a person is unable to control the desire to overeat. These people are not necessarily overweight or obese. The food they binge on is usually not nutritious but instead filled with fat, sugar, and calories.

Effects on Pregnancy

Eating disorders can have a very negative impact on pregnancy. There are numerous complications that can occur and put you and your baby at higher risk. Some of these complications include the following:

- Premature labor
- Low birth-weight baby
- Stillbirth or fetal death
- Higher risk of C-section
- Low Apgar scores (the Apgar score is an evaluation of a newborn's physical condition after delivery)
- Delayed fetal growth respiratory problems
- Gestational diabetes
- Complications during labor
- Low amniotic fluid, miscarriage
- Preeclampsia (toxemia)
- Birth defects

Pregnancy can exacerbate other medical problems that are related to eating disorders, such as liver, kidney, and cardiac damage. Women who struggle with bulimia usually gain excess weight during pregnancy, putting them at higher risk for hypertension or high blood pressure. Women who struggle with eating disorders through pregnancy also tend to have higher rates of postpartum depression, and they can have difficulty with breastfeeding.

If a women abuses laxatives, diuretics, or other medications to help get rid of calories during pregnancy, she can cause harm to her baby in many ways. These types of over-the-counter medications can also rid the body of valuable fluids and nutrients before they can be used to nourish and feed the baby. Over-the-counter medications, even if they are considered safe during pregnancy, can be dangerous when used in this manner or when used excessively.

Chapter 4

GET ACTIVE

Before you start, or continue, your prenatal exercise routine, there are a couple of things you can do to make the transition a little easier. From identifying your current fitness level and your goals, to how to fit exercise into your busy schedule and what to wear, you can set yourself up for exercise success by thinking ahead and creating a plan.

TALK TO YOUR DOCTOR

Talking with your doctor or midwife about exercise might seem way down on your list of things to discuss in the precious few minutes you have during a regular prenatal appointment. But you can't afford *not* to talk about this issue. Looking at the benefits of pregnancy exercise, you now know it is important to exercise, but it is also crucial that you receive guidance from those taking care of you during your pregnancy.

Ask your practitioner his opinion on exercise during pregnancy. Does he seem to agree with the current guidelines for pregnancy fitness released by the American College of Obstetricians and Gynecologists (ACOG)? If he doesn't, ask if there is a specific reason you should not exercise or should not exercise to the extent that you believe you should be able to during this pregnancy.

If he doesn't seem to have an answer that is satisfactory, ask him if he is aware of the latest guidelines from ACOG. If he is not aware, offer to share your copy. This education process can benefit not only you but also other patients who are seeing this practitioner.

Pregnancy Pointer

If you and your practitioner can't see eye to eye about exercise, you may have bigger troubles looming. Remember that you are the consumer and that you can switch to a practitioner who is supportive of your decisions concerning exercise. If you can't decide together on this issue, you may not be able to agree on other important decisions later, such as medication during labor, genetic testing, and so on.

Maybe you're one of the lucky women who has a practitioner who is very up to date on the latest exercise guidelines and is actually encouraging you. Perhaps your provider has a belief in exercise that exceeds the ACOG guidelines. Finding a happy medium—the middle of the road that both you and your practitioner can live with—goes both ways. Talking to your doctor or midwife will help you tailor a fitness program for you and your baby that is safe and effective. This will help ensure a healthy and safe pregnancy fitness course.

WHAT'S YOUR FITNESS LEVEL?

A fitness level is simply defined as what "shape" your body is in, meaning how fit you are on a cardiovascular level as well as your level of muscle tone. To gauge your fitness level, you might look at how often you exercise. Do you walk every day? Perhaps you take one aerobics class per week. Maybe you get in six exercise sessions a week and if you don't, you feel awful. Each of these categories would represent a different fitness level.

The importance of a fitness evaluation cannot be understated. Choosing a place to start your activity will depend largely on this evaluation. How successful and safe your performance is will also be attributed to the proper determination of your pre-pregnancy fitness level.

How Fit Are You?

Finding your fitness level is the first step in any pregnancy or pre-pregnancy exercise program. By using some simple questions about your fitness level, you can then decide on the appropriate place to begin for your current pregnancy. An evaluation should be done with each pregnancy, as your fitness level will change throughout your life.

One of the most important elements of the evaluation, however, will not be which category you are in, but rather your determination and dedication to the exercise program. Remember that intermittent exercise can be more harmful to your body than no exercise at all.

When you exercise irregularly, you're always in the initial phases of exercise. You never really build up to anything, as you can't get past the initial stages of the training. There are also mental reasons why irregular exercise is harmful—because it never gets "any better." You are always doing something that feels difficult to do. This can make you lack the desire to exercise and can also make you more prone to injury.

Let's look at three main fitness levels—sedentary, moderately active, and athletic—and determine where you fit in:

If you are sedentary, you probably have not been participating in any type of formal exercise program. You may not exercise at all, or very little. Just because you fit into these criteria does not mean that you are necessarily overweight or unhealthy. You might simply just not be as fit as you potentially could be.

....

Belly Basics

It used to be said that athletes should quit competing when a pregnancy was confirmed.

Now we see many pregnant athletes enjoying their sports well into their pregnancy. If you had been athletic prior to becoming pregnant, barring health issues with the pregnancy, there are few reasons you would need to change your athletic ways.

....

Moderately Active

Do you consider yourself moderately active? If so, you probably enjoy exercise but do not go out of your way to make it a regular part of your life. You may exercise when it is convenient or fits into your social schedule, like a walk in the neighborhood with a friend, or a random aerobics or yoga class. You are more likely to add small portions of exercise to your life, like walking short distances rather than driving, or parking in the back of the parking lot. This category is more for the social exerciser.

Do you value your exercise highly and would you be very lost without your regular routine? Perhaps you go to a regular exercise class or schedule exercise on a near daily basis. You may be a competitive athlete, or perhaps you may compete in more than one sport. This category is not restricted to only professional athletes; many people enjoy rigorous exercise.

ASSESS YOURSELF

Looking at these three categories of fitness, you might think you fit neatly into one of them. However, you should only use the fitness level category as a starting point. Consulting with a trainer who specializes in pregnant populations or asking your physician, you can get an objective assessment of your fitness that can give you a good idea of where and how you could improve your fitness level. On your own, you can use some simple self-check evaluations to determine your fitness level right in the privacy of your own home.

Professional Evaluation

Some women prefer to have a professional evaluation of their fitness level. This can be done in most major fitness centers, including some hospital gyms. If you are having trouble finding someone to perform this assessment, you might try a professional association that trains fitness instructors or personal trainers. Fitness evaluation is a basic skill of personal trainers and fitness instructors.

Pregnancy Pointer

If you choose to have a professional evaluation, be sure to ask your evaluator about her certification in the area of pre- and postnatal fitness and nutrition. Choosing a certified fitness instructor or personal trainer will make a huge difference in your evaluation. Having an evaluator with previous experience working with pregnant women will also make it easier for you to ask questions and trust her advice.

A few practitioners might require a professional evaluation before giving you the go-ahead to exercise. If your doctor or midwife requests one from you, ask if he has a recommendation for where to have your fitness levels tested. In most cases, you will be able to use self-evaluation to figure out where to begin your exercise routine.

Self-Evaluation

Begin your self-evaluation by asking yourself the following questions about your body, your pregnancy, and exercise:

- What injuries have you experienced in the past (including broken bones, accidents, falls, previous surgeries, or other problems)?
- Do you have old injuries that still require nurturing? If so, can you find ways to alter different exercises to accommodate this injury?

- What medical conditions, if any, did you have before your pregnancy (e.g., chronic conditions including high blood pressure, heart disease, diabetes, arthritis, etc.)? Are they under control now? Do you have any specific concerns about these conditions?
- Are you suffering from current pregnancy discomforts (e.g., swelling, nausea, backache, etc.)?
- Have you developed potential complications during pregnancy, like gestational diabetes, anemia, or pregnancy-induced hypertension (PIH)? If so, how can you still fit in exercise? Will there be restrictions on which exercises you are able to complete?

FITTING IT IN

You know that exercising will be good for you, but between work, carpool, family, to-dos, and the new tired or nauseous challenges of pregnancy, you may find yourself wondering where you could find the time. You're not alone. Not having time to exercise is reported as one of the most common reasons for people to quit exercising. Don't let it be yours. If you find yourself searching for excuses not to exercise, try to remember all of those health benefits to you and your baby that result from regular prenatal exercise . . . and the negative outcomes of not exercising consistently or at all. By implementing just a few quick and easy strategies, you can work exercise into even your busiest of days, and feel great for helping yourself and your baby by doing so.

....

Pregnancy Pointer

Picking a gym can be a big decision. You should shop around for a gym that will fit your needs during pregnancy as well as after. For example, don't pick a gym based solely on the prenatal classes. What about a nursery? Can you bring the baby back with you once he or she is born? Look at location in relation to your home or work. What would keep you from coming to the gym? What would make you go?

....

Making a Schedule

One of the best secrets to finding the time to exercise is to schedule the time. Many women find that if they select a morning time, the exercise gets done. If you wait to do your exercise after work or before bed, things might come up during the day making it easily forgotten. Write the time in your planning calendar—and be faithful to it!

What if you don't quite feel up to it one day? Or what if you have trouble getting out of bed? Simply get up and do a modified program. Perhaps instead of doing an aerobics video, you choose to walk the dog leisurely around the block. You are still committing yourself to exercise.

Scheduling the time to exercise into your day is the best way to ensure that you stick to your plan. Just as you make the time to nourish your body with food, be sure to find time to nourish your body with exercise.

Adding Exercise to Your Daily Life

Perhaps there are times when you simply cannot fit exercise into a hectic life, despite scheduling. As long as this does not become a habit, never fear! Find sneaky ways to add exercise into your schedule, "a little bit here, and a little bit there." You'll probably be surprised at how easy it can be to reach your daily goals with a little creativity and dedication.

- Skip the elevator! You should consider taking the stairs when you can. Even if you can't walk up all sixty flights, walking five of them and then taking the elevator the rest of the way up still gives you quite a workout.

- Walk instead of ride. Rather than spending ten minutes circling the parking lot to find the absolutely best space available, try parking at the back of the parking lot and walking to the store. Not only will this give you exercise, but it often saves you time.
- Take your dog for a much-needed walk. Getting out and enjoying the fresh air can be good for you and Fido, not to mention the added benefits to your body.
- Go the extra step. Are you the type of person who carries things to the stairs or one particular room, and leaves a pile to carry up later? Consider taking your belongings up the stairs or to their rightful spot every time you would normally just pile them up. Six or seven trips up the stairs or to the other end of the house throughout the day is a great way to add to your workout without stressing your time limits or lifestyle. The fringe benefit is that you do not have anything to trip over at the bottom of the stairs and your house could look so clean. Just make sure you are not carrying heavy loads, following the guidelines of your particular caregiver.
- Work out with housework. Doing dishes, folding laundry, sweeping, mopping, and vacuuming can all be transformed from boring chores to exhilarating workouts. You can do calf raises while washing dishes, squats and lunges while doing laundry, or challenge yourself to a certain number of bicep curls or crunches every time you finish sweeping or mopping a room. If you get creative, you can think of tons of new and exciting ways to create workout opportunities from everyday activities you'd have to do anyway.
- Walk it out! If you work at a desk or in an office, you might try taking a walk during a break period or lunch. Not only will it help you fit exercise in, but it will also get you out of the office and give you a chance to

clear your head. Be sure to bring a change of shoes so that you are comfortable and safe when you walk.

THE PHYSIOLOGICAL EFFECTS OF EXERCISE

The physiological benefits of exercise on pregnancy are great. Not only can exercise improve the course of your pregnancy and of your labor, but it can also help you reduce stress. The benefits also go well into the postpartum period and beyond.

....

Belly Basics

Backache in pregnancy is one of the most common complaints women have. Not only does exercise help with alleviating back pain, but it also helps prevent back pain from occurring to begin with. Exercise also makes caring for your baby easier after the birth because your muscles are more used to being held appropriately.

....

Body awareness is a key component to exercise in pregnancy (and pregnancy in general!). As you begin to exercise, your body awareness increases. This attention to your body can help you become more attuned to problems before they become larger issues. This can in turn lead to an increase in attention to proper body mechanics and body posture, both of which are key to a comfortable pregnancy.

THE PHYSICAL BENEFITS OF EXERCISE

The improved body awareness that you gain from exercising will help you manage the physical symptoms of pregnancy with greater ease. This directly corresponds with feeling more comfortable as your body goes through the many changes of the three trimesters. Exercising will also decrease the number of physical complaints commonly associated with pregnancy.

Other physical benefits of exercise in pregnancy include:

- Decrease in headaches
- Decrease in shortness of breath
- Improved digestion
- Improved bowel function
- Increased sense of well-being
- Decreased tendency toward depression
- Maintained or improved cardiovascular strength
- Increased pelvic floor strength
- Improved posture
- Better sense of control over body issues

Belly Basics

The physical complaints of pregnancy are many. Among the most often-heard complaints are fatigue, backache, digestion problems, constipation, and swelling. Exercise can help you prevent many of these complaints for a variety of reasons.

Reducing Fatigue and Strength Building

The physical movements of exercise can help you combat the fatigue that is so common in the first and third trimesters. Additionally, exercise helps alleviate problems with insomnia that can plague pregnant women at all stages of pregnancy and recovery.

When you physically utilize your body during the day, your body responds by requiring a recuperation period. The physical demands of exercise, even when not intense, will also help you clear your mind and rest more easily at night.

Certain exercises also increase the strength and the flexibility of your body, which will be very handy advantages for the physical demands of pregnancy and labor. This added strength and mobility will also make the tasks of caring for a newborn seem less extreme.

Blood Volume Increase

When you are pregnant, you experience an increase in your blood volume—as much as 50 percent of your blood volume with one baby and more if you are carrying multiples. Exercise also helps increase the circulation of your blood, which can prevent a number of circulatory issues common to pregnancy: varicose veins of the legs and rectum (hemorrhoids), blood clots that occur during pregnancy and after, and some forms of swelling associated with pregnancy.

THE PSYCHOLOGICAL EFFECTS

By now, you have read a lot of information about the physical benefits of exercise for you and your baby in different periods during the child-bearing years. But there are many emotional and mental benefits as well to gain from exercise. It has long been shown that, in general, exercising helps to lower your stress levels. This stress reduction is very important during such a tense, albeit happy, time in your life.

There is an increased pride in your pregnancy and your pregnant body when you are physically meeting your body's needs through exercise. This sense of confidence and self-esteem that comes from exercise helps you envision your newly rounding figure with pride and pleasure. No longer do you see yourself as a "beached whale" awaiting the delivery of your calf. You now see the beauty and function of your new pregnant form. This is just another benefit of knowing the body you live in.

Finally, as exercise becomes a part of your way of life, it becomes a habit—a healthy habit that can be shared as a family. Exercising moms rarely just quit exercising after the birth of their babies. They begin exercising *with* their babies. This starts the baby on a lifelong journey to seek out fitness for himself or herself, because it is what he or she has learned by Mom's great example.

LABOR AND BIRTH BENEFITS OF EXERCISE

While people tend to want immediate gratification from everything they do, exercise in pregnancy doesn't always fall into this category. Sometimes it can be difficult to get up and exercise when the benefits aren't seen immediately. However, the exercises you do in pregnancy will certainly affect how you give birth when the time comes.

Having a well-toned and fit body for labor has its advantages. If you have been used to the physical rigors of exercise, you will tend to do better in labor. You will be more prepared for the physical demands placed on your body. The muscles that have been prepared with the strength that you will need for pushing, and perhaps even specifically for the task of labor and birth, are not only stronger as a result of exercise but are also more easily put into action when they are exercised on a regular basis.

Beyond the feelings of having more strength and stamina, there are some specific benefits to you for exercising in pregnancy. Studies have shown that women who exercise during pregnancy often have shorter labors. These women also tend to require cesarean surgery less often, as well as experiencing a decrease in the use of forceps and vacuum extractors. By decreasing the risks of surgery and instrumental deliveries, you will also speed your recovery period.

Some childbirth classes will offer a few prenatal exercises to incorporate into your regular exercise routine. These exercises are usually specially designed to prepare specific muscles in your body for labor and birth. An example might be teaching the class about squatting. It's a great exercise to strengthen your legs and glutes, but is also the perfect position to give birth in as it opens the pelvic outlet by an additional 10 percent.

Postpartum Advantages

Possibly some of the most surprising benefits of exercise in pregnancy are the postpartum benefits. If you've spent time building strength and flexibility during pregnancy, you will tend to have an easier recovery period after the birth of your baby. Coupled with the fact that you will tend to have an easier birth with fewer cesareans and episiotomies, it makes sense.

Not only is exercise beneficial in terms of your weight loss but in your body tone and fitness levels in general. Returning to your pre-pregnancy body is a huge issue for women in the postpartum period. When you stay fit before birth, you have a huge leap ahead of the crowd toward getting your old body back. There also seems to be a protective benefit from postpartum depression when you have exercised during pregnancy.

EXERCISE BENEFITS FOR BABY

In the past, one of the main concerns about exercise during pregnancy was that it would have a negative effect on your baby. Some researchers predicted growth restriction, oxygen reduction, and other scary outcomes for babies born to moms who exercised. To the contrary, researchers have now found that there are many physical and psychological benefits for a baby when Mom exercises during pregnancy.

As you become more aware of your pregnant body and your baby, you focus on taking proper care of that body and baby. By watching how and what you eat, you decrease the risks of preterm labor. The decrease in preterm birth rates alone prevents many neonatal deaths, as preterm birth is one of the leading causes of death in newborns.

Healthier Placenta

The improved blood circulation of the mother through exercise can help grow a healthier placenta, which is the baby's lifeline during pregnancy, as it uses the placenta to get nutrients and oxygen and to expel waste products. The heartier the placenta, the healthier the baby will be.

Improved Labor Tolerance

Babies of mothers who exercise also seem to tolerate labor better. These babies are used to having Mom work hard while exercising, so that when it is time for Mom to have contractions, it is just another workout for them. This tolerance level has also been shown to decrease the incidence of meconium (baby's first stool) in the amniotic fluid at birth. Having too much meconium in the amniotic fluid is potentially life-threatening and something you would prefer to avoid.

Leaner, Healthier Babies

If you exercise during pregnancy, your baby will tend to be of a lower birth weight. While this might seem like a negative outcome, the lower weight is not from fetal growth restriction, but rather the reduction in deposits of unnecessary fat for the baby. These leaner babies at birth are also healthier and leaner later in life. Some studies even report that babies born to mothers who exercised during pregnancy were easier to care for after birth and seemed to adjust to their environments more readily.

Perhaps these babies are reported to be easier because the rocking motions associated with maternal exercise during pregnancy offered stimulation to enhance baby's brain development. One study, "Morphometric and neurodevelopmental outcome at age five years of the offspring of women who continued to exercise regularly throughout pregnancy" (*J. Pediatr.* 1996 Dec; 129[6]:856–63), shows that these babies actually had better language and intelligence scores at five years of life.

WHY EXERCISE IS DIFFERENT DURING PREGNANCY

As with many other aspects of your lifestyle that change with pregnancy, your new body and new responsibilities make exercise very different from when you're not expecting. Simply knowing what physical changes can possibly lead to potentially dangerous situations can help you understand how to avoid them and keep yourself and your baby safe from harm.

Center of Gravity

Your center of gravity is located in the middle of your abdomen, just above your belly button or umbilicus. Usually, you will not notice any changes to this area until you are into your third or fourth month of pregnancy. Once your uterus has begun to grow out of your pelvic region, your center of gravity will shift upward.

This shift itself is not painful, nor is it cause for alarm. In fact, you will probably not even notice the changes taking place, as it is a gradual process. Your body will naturally adapt to most center of gravity changes. What you do need to watch for is the natural loss of balance that may occur that will probably continue throughout pregnancy, steadily growing as your abdomen does.

Many women report that they feel off balance as their abdomen grows. You might experience this as well. The biggest danger is that the shift makes falls more likely. The good news is that even a serious fall is generally not harmful to your baby. He or she is tucked safely away in the amniotic sac, blissfully unaware of your most recent belly flop. A shift in the center of gravity is more likely to cause problems with your posture as well. Posture is key to feeling good and looking good during your pregnancy. While exercising, simply be aware of your abdomen and try to remain conscious of the movements you are making and how you are moving. This awareness can help with any problems you might experience.

Joints and Flexibility

As with everything in pregnancy, your joints are also affected. This includes your elbows, shoulders, hips, knees, wrists, and ankles. The usual culprits, your hormones, namely relaxin, are to blame for the increased risk of injury to these areas.

Joints can be injured very easily during pregnancy. Using warmup sessions and cool-downs, you can greatly reduce the risk of harming the joints during pregnancy. These exercises also have the added benefits of working your range of motion.

TRUST YOUR BODY

We have all heard the "no pain, no gain" mantra that is so common in health centers today. And as a society, we all seem too eager to buy into that theory. While it is true that you have to expend energy to get the benefit of exercise, pain has no place in exercise, particularly during pregnancy.

Pain

Pain is your body's way of saying something is wrong. When you are pregnant, it is even more important that you pay attention to these signals from your body. Remember, your baby is counting on you to listen.

Pain should be something that makes you stop exercising immediately. No matter where the location of the pain or what the feeling is like, stop doing whatever you are doing. Sometimes pain is a signal that you have a hurt muscle or a leg cramp. While these may not have a direct negative effect on your pregnancy, they can harm your body.

This type of cramping pain may be more likely to occur during pregnancy. For example, if you have a leg cramp, it may be a sign that your electrolytes are out of balance and that you need to watch your nutritional intake more closely or stretch more often. An injured muscle could result from your body's release of the hormone relaxin, which helps to facilitate the birth but also has the effect of making injuries more likely.

Falls

Due to the changes in your center of gravity and the hormones coursing through your body, falls may be more likely when pregnant. For this reason, some exercises (e.g., horseback riding) are never recommended during pregnancy.

While you may be at an increased risk for falls, learning to take certain precautions can certainly help reduce this likelihood. During your normal daily life avoid high heels, walk on pathways whenever you can, and avoid uneven surfaces or stones. Whenever you work out, remember to wear the appropriate footwear.

If you do fall, try not to panic. Check yourself out completely before standing back up. In general, your baby is well protected by the amniotic sac in your uterus. However, if you experience any abdominal pain, bleeding, contractions, or changes in the baby's movements, report this immediately to your practitioner.

Pregnancy Pointer

Remember to eat something a few hours before you work out. The meal you have prior to a workout should be snack-sized with lots of quality nutrition like complex carbs and protein. Some yogurt and a piece of fruit is one example. This will help your body sustain your energy through your fitness session.

Feeling Weak or Dizzy

Feeling weak or dizzy is a sign that you probably need to skip your exercise today. These feelings can be a normal part of your pregnancy, or they may indicate a problem. Sometimes you feel weak from the exhaustion of pregnancy, more typically in the first and third trimesters. Other issues for feeling weak or dizzy would be a dramatic fluctuation in your blood sugar levels.

If you begin to feel weak or lightheaded during your workout, stop immediately. Sit down or lie down. Have someone bring you water. You should not try to drive or walk. If you actually pass out, be sure to call your doctor or midwife as soon as you awake. Call your doctor or midwife right away if the symptoms don't go away within a few minutes. Otherwise, report your symptoms to your practitioner during normal office hours. They may suggest you alter your exercise plan going forward.

Sometimes simply not feeling right is a perfect indicator to stop. It could be you're having an off day. Maybe you've not eaten recently enough or perhaps you're tired. Whatever the reason, listen to your body's signals and stop exercising.

The Talk Test

The "talk test" is one of the simpler ways for you to determine whether or not you are exercising at the right intensity for your body and your baby. It is much easier to do than taking your pulse and can be done without any equipment and at any location.

The only thing you have to do is to ask yourself whether you can carry on a conversation with the person next to you without sounding out of breath or winded. It's as simple as that.

So if, for example, you are out walking with your family or friends in your neighborhood and you are discussing weekend plans, can you do this without huffing and puffing? Or do you sound like you are in need of a breathing machine? If you can carry on the conversation without being winded, you are exercising at the appropriate intensity for you.

....

Pregnancy Pointer

While exercising, it is normal to be somewhat out of breath. You should exert yourself enough to work your heart and lungs during your exercise sessions, but not to a dangerous extent. The difference between a good windedness and being too short of breath is going to be your ability to carry on a conversation, either real or imagined. Talk to yourself if you need to, just to be sure you're not pushing yourself too hard.

....

Now, what do you do if you are winded? Very simple—slow it down. This doesn't mean coming to a complete stop (unless it's severe), but rather shorten your strides when walking and drop the pace, even if this means you fall behind the group. If you are doing aerobics, you might consider doing only leg motions and keeping your arms at your sides instead of including them in the workout, too. If that doesn't work, you can also try walking in place until you can talk at a normal conversational pattern.

When conversation has returned to a normal pace, slowly add speed or activity to what you are doing, being careful not to overexert yourself again. Remember, as you exercise more, your tolerance will increase. The walking pace that winded you last week might be perfect this week.

WHEN NOT TO EXERCISE

While there are not many reasons that exercise would be contraindicated during pregnancy, it is important to know what to look for in terms of protecting yourself. In general, here are some problems that you may experience that would signal you to stop exercise during portions or all of your pregnancy.

Bleeding

About 30 to 40 percent of women will experience some form of bleeding during pregnancy. The majority of these women, more than 60 percent, will go on to carry a healthy baby to the end of pregnancy. However, it is wise to find out the source of the bleeding, which will determine whether or not you can exercise.

For example, the cervix region becomes much more vascular during pregnancy. Sometimes something as simple as a vaginal exam or sexual intercourse can cause the cervix to bleed slightly. While this is definitely scary, it does not necessarily mean an impending miscarriage or other problems with the pregnancy. However, bleeding from the uterus, or between the uterus and the placenta, also called a *partial abruption*, would be a reason not to exercise during this pregnancy until the issues were resolved and your doctor or midwife gave you the go-ahead.

Belly Basics

Placenta previa, detected via ultrasound prior to twenty weeks of gestation, may or may not interfere with the birth process. As you enter the second trimester, the body of the uterus begins a major growth spurt, often helping the placenta move from the cervical region in 95 percent of women. If the placenta does not move far enough away by the end of your pregnancy, your baby will be born via a cesarean surgery to ensure the safety of both mom and baby.

Placenta previa is a condition in which part of or the entire placenta covers the opening of the uterus, the cervix. This can lead to bleeding, with or without pain, as well as pregnancy loss and other trauma to the pregnancy. There may not be an opportunity for you to exercise during this type of pregnancy because of the inherent risks. Ask your provider about how this will affect your pregnancy and birth. You might also ask how often and how they intend to monitor the location of the placenta. Many times this condition will spontaneously resolve itself during the second trimester as the body of the uterus grows, helping to move the placenta away from the cervix.

History of Preterm Labor

If you have previously given birth to a baby before thirty-seven weeks, you will want to talk to your practitioner about exercise. In certain cases, your previous birth may have had a non-repeating factor that caused you to have your baby early. This means that this particular pregnancy is not at a higher risk for preterm birth. Some practitioners, however, will advise that exercise for the first portion of pregnancy is best avoided to confirm the fact that it was a non-repeating factor. And then again, they may advise taking it easy during the later portion of pregnancy.

Contractions

The rhythmic tightening of the uterus that leads to cervical changes is not good; if you feel it, you should discontinue exercising immediately. These contractions are an indicator of preterm labor, even if they are not painful or even noticeable. Any regularly occurring contractions you feel prior to thirty-seven weeks of pregnancy should be immediately reported to your doctor or midwife.

Belly Basics

Timing contractions is very simple. Using a watch with a second hand, make a note of when a contraction begins. When the contraction ends, make note of that time as well. The third number to write down will be when the next contraction starts. The period from the beginning of the first contraction to the beginning of the second contraction is how far apart your contractions are. How long they last is from the beginning of one contraction until it ends.

It can be perfectly normal to have slight contractions for about twenty to thirty minutes after exercising. However, the contractions that do not stop after this short period of time or those that become very painful or intense need to be reported to your practitioner. Drinking water and lying on your left side should also help contractions decrease in frequency.

Incompetent Cervix

Incompetent cervix is a condition in which your cervix dilates prior to being full term. This can happen with or without noticeable contractions. You may have been previously diagnosed with an incompetent cervix in this or a previous pregnancy, in which case you will probably be treated with a cervical cerclage, a stitch placed in the cervix to attempt to delay labor. Exercise is usually contraindicated because of the risk of preterm labor.

Membrane Ruptures

If your water breaks, you will likely be confined to bed rest for the remainder of your pregnancy in an attempt to prevent the preterm birth of your baby. While on bed rest, there may be opportunities to do certain types of physical therapy to help prevent muscle loss. Talk to your medical team about utilizing these services. Regular exercise is simply not possible.

Pregnancy-Induced Hypertension (PIH)

When your blood pressure is elevated in pregnancy, one must worry about the effects on mom and baby. Overall, exercise will tend to lower blood pressure, but during the actual exercise it does raise your blood pressure. Some practitioners advise that you avoid all exercise if you experience any episode of high blood pressure. Other practitioners take a wait-and-see approach, often depending on the severity of your symptoms and the timing of the onset of the symptoms.

Multiple Gestation

When you are carrying more than one baby, it is simply not well studied as to whether or not exercise is acceptable or beneficial. The general consensus is that with twins, moderate exercise in the beginning of pregnancy is acceptable. Since you will be more closely monitored during the second half of pregnancy, you can look for signs of impending preterm birth, like a shortening cervix. This will alert you and your provider to what changes you need to make in your physical activity levels.

In the later portion of pregnancy, exercise will have to be considered on a case-by-case basis. For those women carrying more than two babies, higher order multiples (HOM), greater restrictions on exercise during pregnancy will exist. However, physical therapy and some forms of stretching may be perfectly acceptable. Again, working with your practitioner is the best option.

Some of these conditions might not make exercise impossible for you, though you may wish to consider modifying your program. It's very important to discuss your current fitness status with your doctor or midwife.

Chapter 5

THE VEGETARIAN OR VEGAN MOM-TO-BE

Becoming a vegetarian is an important step for many women, usually fueled by a desire to create optimal changes within the self or for the world. Regardless of the type of vegetarian you are, it is completely safe to remain vegetarian throughout pregnancy. Although many decades of speculation have led people to consider vegetarianism inadequate in certain nutrients like protein, B_{12}, iron, and other vitamins and minerals, studies have shown that a well-planned vegetarian diet can include more than enough of the essential nutrients needed. During pregnancy, including a variety of highly nutritious foods providing bountiful protein, omega-3s, and vitamins and minerals will ensure the health of mom and baby from conception to delivery and beyond.

IS A VEGETARIAN DIET SAFE DURING PREGNANCY?

Regardless of the vegetarian category you choose for your lifestyle, you and your baby will not only benefit from the foods you consume, you can thrive! By focusing on including a wide variety of natural foods in your diet, you can keep your diet cleaner and healthier than most with the added benefit of naturally occurring phytochemicals that have been shown to safeguard health and promote healthy development. While a pregnant diet will require a little extra persistence, focus, and planning, a vegetarian mom-to-be can remain vegetarian throughout pregnancy by being aware of the types of foods included in every meal to ensure that no specific foods such as greens or grains are being excluded or consumed on a minimal basis. Each fruit, vegetable, seed, grain, nut, and legume provides a very different combination of macro- and micronutrients, so a deficiency in one food group would likely result in a deficiency in the diet and, eventually, within the body.

A healthy vegetarian pregnancy diet must be balanced. In other words, it must contain all of the nutrients essential to good health and a healthy pregnancy. It may take a little work, but keep in mind that knowledge is power. The more you know about the foods you eat, the more nutritious your diet can become. The nutritional adequacy of a vegetarian diet depends more on the overall food choices made over several days than what you consume at each meal.

The Benefits

Vegetarian diets can be very healthy if designed correctly. A healthy, well-planned vegetarian diet usually contains more fiber. It is also lower in total fat, especially saturated fat and dietary cholesterol, which can help lower the risk for diseases such as heart disease, stroke, and some cancers. In addition, LDL blood cholesterol (the "bad" cholesterol) levels are generally lower in vegetarians, which can decrease the incidence of death from heart disease. Vegetarians tend to have a lower incidence of hypertension, type 2 diabetes, obesity, and some forms of cancers, such as lung and colon, than people who eat meat.

Vegetarian diets that are high in fruits, vegetables, and whole grains also tend to be higher in folic acid, antioxidants such as vitamins C and E, carotenoids, and phytochemicals. All these benefits give this eating style an extra disease-fighting punch. However, the key to being at a lower risk for these health problems is following a properly balanced vegetarian diet.

Keep in mind that not all vegetarian protein sources are low in fat. Popular protein sources, such as nuts and seeds, can be high in fat. These contain unsaturated (or healthy) fats, but small amounts can pack in lots of calories.

THE PITFALLS

It is important to keep in mind that being a vegetarian does not guarantee that you are eating a healthy diet. A poorly planned vegetarian diet can cause some nutritional deficiencies. It can also be high in fat, cholesterol, and calories and low in fiber. Some vegetarians may have a high saturated-fat intake from consuming too many eggs, cream, butter, whole-milk products, and cheese. Vegetarians may get into the rut of eating too many low-fiber starches without including enough of the other food groups, such as plant-based proteins, fruits, vegetables, whole grains, and dairy foods (if included in their eating style).

Belly Basics

Vegetarian women who are breastfeeding need to make sure they are consuming plenty of vitamin B_{12} sources because intake can affect levels in breast milk. While you are on prenatal vitamins, you should get all of the nutrients you need. After delivery, your doctor will most likely take you off your prenatal vitamins. Talk to your doctor or a dietitian about starting a multivitamin/mineral supplement that will ensure optimal nutritional intake.

Despite some of the pitfalls of a vegetarian diet, you can still reap the benefits of a vegetarian lifestyle as long as you plan your meals correctly and you eat higher-fat, higher-sugar foods in moderation.

THE VEGETARIAN FOOD GUIDE PYRAMID

The Vegetarian Food Guide Pyramid is very similar to the regular Food Guide Pyramid. The vegetarian version provides recommended guidelines for the vegetarian population. The lacto-ovo vegetarian diet can be modified to meet the guidelines of the Food Guide Pyramid with only a few modifications. If you consume eggs and/or dairy products, choose lower-fat or nonfat products to limit the amount of saturated fat and cholesterol you consume each day.

The following list describes the minimum number of servings you should consume from each food group during pregnancy:

- **Use fats, oils, and sweets sparingly.** This includes candy, butter, margarine, salad dressing, and cooking oil.
- **Eat three to four servings from the milk, yogurt, and cheese group.** Examples of single servings from this group include 1 cup of milk or yogurt or 1½ ounces of cheese. Those who choose not to eat milk, yogurt, or cheese should select other food sources rich in calcium, such as calcium-fortified juice, cereal, dark-green leafy vegetables, and soy milk.
- **Eat two servings (6–7 ounces each) from the dry beans, nuts, seeds, eggs, and meat substitutes group.** Examples of a single serving from this food group include 1 cup of soy milk, ½ cup of cooked dry beans or peas, one egg or two egg whites, ½ cup of nuts or seeds, or 2 tablespoons peanut butter. Shoot to eat at least three to four servings of cooked dried beans weekly. They are a good choice because they are full of zinc, iron, protein, and fiber.
- **Eat four servings from the vegetable group.** Examples of a single serving from this group include ½ cup of cooked or chopped raw vegetables or 1 cup of raw leafy vegetables. Choose dark-green leafy vegetables often for higher calcium intake.

- **Eat three servings from the fruit group.** Examples of a single serving from this group include ¾ cup of juice, ¼ cup of dried fruit, ½ cup of chopped raw fruit, ½ cup of canned fruit, or a medium-size piece of fruit, such as a banana, apple, or orange.
- **Eat nine servings from the bread, cereal, rice, and pasta group.** Examples of a single serving from this group include one slice of bread, 1 ounce of ready-to-eat cereal; ½ cup of cooked cereal; ½ cup of cooked brown rice, pasta, or other grains; or half a bagel. Those consuming gluten should choose whole-wheat and whole-grain breads and pastas more often, as well as fortified and enriched products, while gluten-free diets should include more rice, rice pastas, and gluten-free breads and cereals.

VEGETARIAN MEAL PLANNING TIPS

The key to a healthy vegetarian diet is making the right choices and eating a variety of foods. It never hurts to take an overall look at your diet to make sure it is well balanced, nutritious, and in line with your new pregnancy needs. There are all kinds of specialty foods out there that you may have never thought of trying. Here are a few suggestions to get you started:

- Explore new foods at your grocery store. Instead of going with the same old foods, try new grains (such as barley, bulgur, kasha, and quinoa), vegetables, and/or legumes each week.
- Try different meat-free or soy products from the selection located in the freezer section or the health section. Soy can boost the protein, calcium, and iron content of almost any meal.
- Add different types of legumes or dried beans to casseroles, stews, soups, salads, and chili for a protein, iron, zinc, and fiber boost to your meal.

- Prepare some of your favorite dishes with a soy substitute, such as using textured vegetable protein in Sloppy Joes or spaghetti sauce or adding cubed tofu to a stir-fry along with your favorite vegetables.
- Next time you grill out, try a marinated portabella mushroom or veggie burger marinated in teriyaki sauce or your favorite marinade.
- Buy a vegetarian cookbook, or search out vegetarian recipes that meet your specific criteria, likes, and dislikes on the Internet for new ideas. The websites *www.vegweb.com*, *www.fatfree.com*, and *www.vegkitchen.com* should get you started.
- When looking for a place to dine out, suggest Chinese, Vietnamese, Thai, or Italian. You can always find plenty of vegetarian entrées on these menus.

Belly Basics

If you are a vegan, you may have a tougher time making sure you consume all of the essential nutrients you need during pregnancy. You need to make modifications to the Food Guide Pyramid to fit your lifestyle, but also ensure your nutrient intake is meeting your requirements. Seek the guidance of a dietitian who can make sure you are planning your diet correctly.

SPECIAL VITAMIN AND MINERAL CONSIDERATIONS

If you are not careful, eliminating animal foods from your diet can cause a shortfall of several nutrients in an otherwise healthy eating plan. Nutrients that should be given special attention include calcium, vitamin D, iron, vitamin B_{12}, and zinc. You should notify your doctor of your vegetarian eating style so that she is aware of your nutrient intake and can prescribe supplements you might need. In addition, careful meal planning and good choices can ensure the intake of all these essential nutrients each day. Keep in mind that you should never take additional supplements without first speaking to your doctor. It is possible to overdo a good thing! If you have questions about how you can combine foods to incorporate essential vitamins and minerals, speak to a registered dietitian.

Calcium

Calcium is vital for strong bones and teeth for both the baby and the mother. Pregnant women need 1,000 mg per day. For vegetarian moms who consume dairy products (at least three servings of dairy foods each day), consuming enough calcium should not be a problem. For vegans, however, calcium intake can be a concern. However, calcium can be found in both plant and animal foods.

Though it may take a bit more planning, as a pregnant vegan you can definitely find foods that fit your eating style and contain enough calcium to help you meet your daily needs. Some of these foods include tofu processed with calcium, calcium-fortified beverages such as orange juice and soy milk, calcium-fortified breakfast cereals, broccoli, seeds such as sunflower and sesame, tahini, nuts such as almonds, soy beans, legumes, some greens such as kale, mustard greens, and collards, bok choy, okra, dried figs, and almond butter.

....

Belly Basics

If you can't get enough calcium from the foods you choose, a supplement can be a good idea. The rule of thumb should always be food before supplements, though. First, include calcium-containing foods in your diet as much as possible, and then supplement on top of that. Never let a supplement take the place of an entire food group or nutrient such as calcium.

....

Vitamin D

Vitamin D is essential to help the body absorb calcium and phosphorus and then deposit them into teeth and bones. Your body can also make vitamin D when your skin is exposed to sunlight. With the exception of milk, very few foods are naturally high in vitamin D. If you are a vegetarian who drinks milk, vitamin D should not be a concern if you consume the recommended number of servings. However, if you are a vegan, you need to be careful that you get enough vitamin D in your diet. The best way for vegans to get vitamin D is from fortified foods. Check the nutrition facts panel on the labels of foods fortified with vitamin D, such as breakfast cereals, soy beverages, and some calcium-fortified juices. Your prenatal vitamin should also ensure that you are receiving the amount of vitamin D you need daily for a healthy pregnancy. The requirement for pregnant women is 5 mcg per day.

Iron

Regardless of whether you are a vegetarian, it is likely that you don't get enough iron. This nutrient is often lacking in women's diets. As a result, during pregnancy, women are often prescribed a prenatal vitamin and mineral supplement that includes iron to meet their increased needs and to prevent iron-deficiency anemia. As a pregnant vegetarian, it can be difficult to get enough absorbable iron to meet your daily needs.

Some plant foods do contain iron. Called nonheme iron, it is not absorbed as well as the iron found in animal foods, or heme iron. The challenge for vegetarians is to improve the absorption of nonheme iron foods. You can start by consuming iron-rich plant sources every day, such as legumes, iron-fortified cereals and breads, whole-wheat and whole-grain products, tofu, some dark-green leafy vegetables, seeds, nuts, tempeh, prune juice, blackstrap molasses, and dried fruit.

If your vegetarian diet allows you to consume eggs, keep in mind that they too contain nonheme iron. You can increase your body's absorption of nonheme iron by including a vitamin C–rich food with these nonheme iron sources at every meal, such as orange juice and other citrus juices, citrus fruits, broccoli, tomatoes, and green or red peppers. If you are a semi-vegetarian, eat a little meat, poultry, or fish with nonheme iron sources to help your body better absorb the iron.

Vitamin B$_{12}$

Vitamin B$_{12}$ is mainly found in animal foods. Because plant foods are not a reliable source of vitamin B$_{12}$, it can be a concern for vegetarians, especially vegans. Vitamin B$_{12}$ is important for helping the body make red blood cells and use fats and amino acids. It is also part of the structure of every cell in the body. The body only needs small amounts of vitamin B$_{12}$. Because it is stored and recycled in the body, a deficiency in the short term is not likely. Over time, however, a deficiency of vitamin B$_{12}$ can result in anemia.

Belly Basics

Some products, such as seaweed, algae, spirulina, tempeh, and miso, are not good sources of vitamin B$_{12}$ even though their packages may make a different claim. The vitamin B$_{12}$ that is contained in these products is inactive and is not in a form that the body can utilize.

Every day, vegans need to consume at least one (preferably more) serving of foods fortified with vitamin B$_{12}$, such as fortified breakfast cereals, soy milk products, rice milk beverages, or meat substitute products such as vegetarian burgers.

If you are a vegetarian who eats dairy and eggs, vitamin B$_{12}$ intake should not be a problem as long as you consume the recommended number of daily food group servings. Vitamin B$_{12}$ is usually a standard vitamin included in most prenatal supplements. Most prenatal vitamin supplements contain cyancobalamin, the form of vitamin B$_{12}$ most easily absorbed by the body.

Zinc

It is tough to get enough zinc when you do not consume meat, poultry, or seafood of any kind. Zinc can be found in eggs and milk, as well as other dairy products. You can also get zinc from plant foods, though it is not absorbed as well as the zinc from animal foods. Zinc-containing plant foods include whole-wheat bread, whole grains, bran, wheat germ, legumes and peas, tofu, seeds, and nuts. Most well-balanced vegetarian diets supply enough zinc, but you should make sure that you consume sufficient amounts. Even mild deficiencies can have an effect on mental performance for both adults and children. Though your prenatal vitamin contains zinc, you should also be sure to get zinc from foods in your diet.

THE POWER OF PROTEIN FOR VEGANS AND VEGETARIANS

When you become pregnant, your protein needs increase by 30 percent. Protein can be found in both animal and plant foods, which makes it easy for both meat-eating and vegetarian women to get all of the protein they need. If you are a vegan, as long as you eat a wide variety of plant foods including whole grains, cereals, legumes, and soy products at each meal, you too should have no problem consuming all of the protein you need for a healthy pregnancy.

Protein is considered a macronutrient because it provides the body with energy, or calories. Protein is part of every cell in the body. Your body requires a constant supply of protein to repair body cells as they wear out. During pregnancy, you need protein to make new cells. Your body's tissues are all unique because of the differing amino acid patterns in their proteins. Amino acids are the building blocks of proteins. Your body uses about twenty different amino acids to make body proteins. Of those, nine are considered essential—your body cannot make them, and you must get them from the foods you eat. The others are considered nonessential amino acids because your body does make them as long as you consume enough essential amino acids and enough calories each day. Animal foods such as meat, poultry, fish, eggs, milk, cheese, and yogurt contain all nine essential amino acids. These foods are said to contain "complete proteins" or "high-quality proteins." Plant foods, on the other hand, contain essential amino acids, but not all nine together. These sources are said to be "incomplete proteins."

Soy is the exception to the incomplete protein rule. Soy is the only plant food that is a complete protein and contains all nine of the essential amino acids.

Gone are the days when vegans were instructed to eat foods in special combinations at each meal to make sure they were getting the right mix of essential amino acids to make proteins. Instead, vegans need only make sure they are eating a balanced diet that includes a wide variety of plant foods and that provides enough calories each and every day. If you are a vegan, this eating plan will ensure you are receiving all of the essential amino acids in needed amounts each day to make the proteins that your body needs. It is more important to think about your total day's intake rather than each individual meal's.

OMEGA-3 ESSENTIAL FATTY ACIDS

Fats are made up of two types: saturated and unsaturated. Unsaturated fats include monounsaturated and polyunsaturated. Two polyunsaturated fatty acids, linoleic acid (omega-6) and alpha-linolenic acid (omega-3), are considered essential because the body cannot make them. Omega-3 fatty acids are essential fats that can be very heart-healthy as well as vital to the development of a baby's brain and nerves. They are also vital to eye development, growth, and vision. In addition, researchers are studying the question of whether omega-3 fatty acids are helpful in preventing preterm labor and possibly protecting against postpartum depression.

Sources of Omega-3 Fatty Acids

Vegetarians are advised to consume omega-3 fatty acids from eggs as well as from plant-based ingredients such as canola oil, soybean oil, walnuts, walnut oil, ground flaxseed (which you can add to baked goods or smoothies), flaxseed oil, soybeans, wheat germ, and other nuts and seeds. For vegetarians who sometimes consume fish, fatty fish such as salmon, mackerel, herring, trout, tuna, and sardines also supply omega-3 fatty acids.

NOTES AND CHECKLISTS

Use the space below to write down questions you have for your doctor during your prenatal visits.

Food Log

Start a diet log! Use the space below to record the food you've eaten for a few days to see what kind of nutrients you may need more of.

_____

_____

_____

_____

_____

_____

_____

_____

_____

_____

_____

_____

_____

PART 2

FIRST TRIMESTER

Chapter 6
CHANGES IN YOUR BODY

During the first trimester of pregnancy, which lasts approximately 14 weeks from the first day of your last menstrual period, your body is hard at work forming one of the most intricate and complex works of nature. By the end of your first official month of pregnancy (6 weeks after your last menstrual period, but 4 weeks since conception), your developing child will have grown an astonishing 10,000 times in size since fertilization.

MORNING SICKNESS

Your stomach flutters, then lurches. As your mouth starts to water, you run for the bathroom for the fifth time today. Sound familiar? Morning sickness (NVP) is arguably the most debilitating and prevalent of pregnancy symptoms. While most women find that NVP symptoms subside or stop as the first trimester ends, for some they continue into the second and even third trimesters. If you're having twins or more, your NVP may be longer and more intense.

The exact cause of NVP has not been pinpointed, but theories abound. Some possible culprits: the human chorionic gonadotropin (hCG) hormone that surges through your system and peaks in early pregnancy; a deficiency of vitamin B_6; hormonal changes that relax your gastrointestinal tract and slow digestion; and immune system changes. Another hypothesis is that morning sickness is actually a defense mechanism that protects both mother and child from toxins and potentially harmful microorganisms in food. No matter what the trigger, it's a miserable time for all.

Pregnancy Pointers

Pregnancy causes a heightened sensitivity to certain odors—coffee, cigarette smoke, and fried foods are frequent offenders—that can contribute to stomach unrest. One theory is that these olfactory aversions are your body's way of keeping you away from substances that could harm your developing baby.

REMEDIES AND SAFETY

The following treatments have met with some success in lessening symptoms of NVP in clinical trials. (Speak with your health-care provider before adding any new supplements to your diet.)

1. Ginger. Gingersnaps and other foods and teas that contain ginger (*Zingiber officinale*) may be helpful in settling your stomach.
2. Acupressure wristbands (Sea-Bands). Sometimes used to ward off motion sickness and seasickness, these wristbands place pressure on what is called the P6, or Nei-Kuan, acupressure point. Available at most drugstores, they are an inexpensive and noninvasive way to treat NVP.
3. Vitamin B_6. This supplement has reduced NVP symptoms in several clinical trials. It has been suggested that NVP is a sign of B_6 vitamin deficiency.

Belly Basics

Kava-kava (*Piper methysticum*), licorice root (*Glycyrrhiza glabra*), rue (*Ruta graveolens*), Chinese cinnamon (*Cinnamomum aromaticum*), and safflower (*Carthamus tinctorius*, false saffron) are just a few of the many botanical remedies that are known to be dangerous in pregnancy. Don't pick up that supplement or cup of herbal tea without asking your health-care provider first.

Other treatments that women report as helpful include:

- Eating smaller, more frequent meals. An empty stomach produces acid that can make you feel worse. Low blood sugar causes nausea as well.
- Choosing proteins and complex carbohydrates. Protein-rich foods (for example, yogurt, beans) and complex carbs (for example, baked potato, whole-grain breads) are good for the two of you and may calm your stomach.
- Eat what you like. Most pregnant women have at least one food aversion. If broccoli turns your tummy, don't force it. The better foods look and taste, the more likely they are to stay down.
- Drink plenty of fluids. Don't get dehydrated. If you're vomiting, you need to replace those lost fluids. Some women report better tolerance of beverages if they are taken between meals rather than with them. Turned off by water and juice right now? Try juicy fruits like watermelon and grapes instead.
- Brush regularly. Keeping your mouth fresh can cut down on the excess saliva that plagues some pregnant women. Breath mints may be helpful, too.

Talk to your provider about switching prenatal supplements. If it makes you sick just to look at your vitamins, perhaps a chewable or other formulation will help. Iron is notoriously tough on the stomach, so your provider might also recommend a supplement with a lower or extended-release dose. And if you can't keep your vitamins down no matter what you try, your doctor may suggest forgoing them until your NVP has passed.

How to Cope

Constant queasiness and vomiting may have you wondering why on earth you got pregnant in the first place. Try to take solace in the fact that for most women, NVP is primarily a first-trimester affair. Stick close to home and take it easy, if at all possible. When staying home isn't an option, talk to your employer about allowing some flexibility with your work schedule. If your stomach is at its worst first thing in the morning, ask about starting later in the day on a temporary basis. Depending on your occupation, working from home on some days may be an option.

When It May Be More Than Morning Sickness

When your body can't get what it needs from food to keep things running, it will start to metabolize stored fat for energy. This condition, called ketosis, generates ketones that circulate in your bloodstream and can be harmful to your fetus. Your provider may test your urine for ketones if you're having severe and persistent nausea and vomiting.

A small percentage of pregnant women (0.3 to 3 percent) experience a severe form of morning sickness called hyperemesis gravidarum (excessive vomiting during pregnancy). If you can't keep any food or fluids down, are losing weight, and are finding it impossible to function normally, you may be in this category.

EATING THROUGH MORNING SICKNESS

If you're dealing with morning sickness, eating healthfully (and keeping it down) is a particular challenge. Your stomach will have definite opinions on what it will and will not tolerate; when you're feeling nauseated, let it guide you. Stick to what works—even if it's the same thing three times daily. Morning sickness won't last forever, and prenatal vitamins will help even out your nutrient intake while you get through this difficult period. Don't worry if you don't gain weight in the first trimester due to morning sickness. It's more important to have weight gain in the following trimester.

Pregnancy Pointer

Put together a morning sickness survival kit for the car. Items to include: wet wipes, tissues, small bottle of water, travel-sized toothbrush and toothpaste, breath mints, graham or soda crackers, and a bundle of large freezer-grade zip-top baggies (for obvious reasons!).

Preparing meals when you're not feeling well can be even more challenging than eating them, so try to get help in the kitchen from your spouse or significant other, if possible. If not, stock up on foods that require minimal prep work, such as frozen entrees and canned soups, so that you can eat with little effort.

As you have likely already discovered, both the taste and the smell of fatty and spicy foods can aggravate an already sensitive stomach, so try to stick to some bland basics. Traditional comfort foods nourish many women suffering through morning sickness; staples like soup, rice, pasta, and potatoes can be a filling way to get needed calories.

Changing your meal patterns to small but more frequent snacks can make eating more tolerable. Remember that low blood sugar is a nausea trigger, so the worst thing you can do for your morning sickness is to skip meals. And you need those calories and nutrients for that growing baby!

Dehydration can also contribute to nausea. If drinking fluids makes your stomach turn, opt for foods with a high fluid content, such as frozen juice bars, grapes, and melon.

MONTH 1: CHANGES TO YOUR BODY

At this point in your pregnancy, you might not notice any significant changes in shape and size. Although you aren't menstruating, you feel slightly bloated, and your waistband may begin to feel a bit snug. Your breasts may also start to increase in size, and the areolae around your nipples may enlarge and darken. No period? Bigger breasts? This baby is doing wonders for you already! Now for the cloud around that silver lining: fuller breasts are often more tender in pregnancy (although a supportive sports bra can help).

Belly Basics

Some women experience minor vaginal blood flow, called spotting, as the embryo implants itself into the uterine wall. Because of the timing—1 week to 10 days after ovulation—it's often mistaken for the beginning of the menstrual period. The spotting, which usually lasts only a day or two, is pink to brown and may be accompanied by minor cramps.

You may also experience another hormonal side effect: increased vaginal secretions similar to those you get premenstrually. These typically last throughout pregnancy and may actually worsen in the third trimester. Normal vaginal secretions in pregnancy are clear to white in color, mucus-like, and both odor- and pain-free. If you experience discharge that is thick, foul-smelling, off-color, or accompanied by itching, blood, or pain, contact your health-care provider immediately to rule out infection or other problems.

MONTH 2: CHANGES TO YOUR BODY

Even though you may not have put on any additional weight yet, your growing uterus is pushing the boundaries of your waistline. On average, most women gain 2 to 4 pounds in the first trimester.

....

Pregnancy Pointer

If you are concerned over a possible risk of using hair dye during your pregnancy, you may opt for a vegetable-based or temporary color treatment until the baby is born. Some experts also recommend holding off on all chemical hair treatments during the first trimester.

....

Changes in skin and hair are common in pregnancy. Hair that was fine and thin may become thick and shiny during pregnancy, and that fabled pregnancy glow may actually be your flawless, blemish-free complexion. On the other end of the spectrum, acne problems and hair breakage and thinning may occur.

Chloasma (also known as melasma) may cause a mask-like darkening or lightening of your facial skin. Freckles and moles are prone to darkening as are other pigmented areas of your skin (for example, areolae). To minimize chloasma and other hyperpigmentation, use a good sunscreen (SPF 30 or higher) to cover exposed skin when you're out in the sun.

Your gums may start to bleed when you brush your teeth, a condition known as pregnancy gingivitis. Be sure to floss and brush regularly to keep your teeth and gums healthy. A warm saltwater rinse may soothe swollen gum tissues. Now is a good time to schedule a thorough cleaning with your dentist; in a few months, leaning back in a dental chair will be uncomfortable, if not impossible. Gum disease has been associated with preterm labor, so keep up with regular dental checkups during pregnancy.

MONTH 3: CHANGES TO YOUR BODY

Your uterus is about the size of a softball and stretches to just about your pubic bone. Four to six pounds of total weight gain is about average for the first trimester; if you've been down and out with nausea and vomiting, you may be below the curve. Weight gain will pick up in the second trimester and peak in the third as your baby starts to fill out your womb.

Don't take the "eating for two" cliché literally: 300 extra calories per day is about all you'll require to meet your baby's nutritional needs. Gaining too much can exacerbate the aches and pains of pregnancy, place an extra strain on your back, increase the risk of having a large baby, and put you at risk for hypertension (high blood pressure) and gestational diabetes. On the other hand, if you find the aversions and nausea of pregnancy have you keeping down only a certain type of not-so-nutritious food (pepperoni pizza, for example), don't feel bad about it. The most important thing right now is keeping some food down and your energy up. Try experimenting with healthier variations if your stomach will take it (skip the pepperoni in exchange for extra cheese or veggies), and hang in there. By the end of the first trimester, most women report that their morning sickness gets better or (fingers crossed) completely disappears.

GASTROINTESTINAL COMPLAINTS DURING YOUR FIRST TRIMESTER

Several gastrointestinal complaints can strike during your pregnancy. Knowing how to deal with them can help to decrease your discomfort. The way you eat and the lifestyle you live can go a long way in relieving some of these problems.

Controlling Constipation

Constipation can be a very common problem during pregnancy. Hormonal changes relax muscles to help accommodate your expanding uterus. In turn, this can slow the action in your intestines and the movement of food through your digestive tract. If you are taking iron from either an iron supplement or a prenatal vitamin, this can also cause constipation. Increased pressure on your intestinal tract as the baby grows can also cause hemorrhoids. Preventing constipation (as much as possible, anyway) can help you to avoid hemorrhoids. Some circumstances, such as hormonal changes and the growing baby, can't be helped, but there are plenty of dietary and lifestyle changes you can make that will make a difference.

Never discontinue your prescribed supplements. If you feel they are causing constipation or other problems, speak with your doctor before you stop taking them. Your doctor can recommend a different brand, maybe with a stool softener, or break up your iron dosages throughout the day.

A high-fiber diet can help to relieve constipation, but you must drink plenty of fluids or this option can make your constipation worse. Women under fifty should shoot for 25 grams of fiber daily. Make sure you are drinking eight to twelve cups of fluid daily. The majority of your beverages should be water, but you should also include fruit juice and milk in your total fluid intake. Include high-fiber foods to help alleviate your symptoms, such as whole-wheat breads and pastas, high-fiber breakfast cereals, bran, vegetables, fruits, and legumes. Some foods are known to act as natural laxatives, such as prunes, prune juice, and figs; other dried fruits may help as well. It is also essential to be physically active each day. Regular activity can help to stimulate normal bowel function. If nothing seems to help, speak to your doctor about possibly taking a fiber supplement such as bran, Metamucil, or a similar product mixed with water or juice once a day.

....

Belly Basics

Do not use over-the-counter laxatives or stool softeners while you are pregnant to help relieve your constipation unless you have talked to your doctor first. Some may not be safe to use during pregnancy. Before relying on medications to relieve your symptoms, first make sure your diet, fluid intake, and activity level is adequate.

....

Taming Gas

The same changes in a pregnant woman's body that cause constipation can also cause excess gassiness. Increase your fiber intake slowly and drink plenty of fluids each day. Increasing fiber too quickly, especially when you are used to a lower-fiber diet, can cause gas and other gastrointestinal problems. Some foods can exacerbate gas problems, such as broccoli, beans, cabbage, onions, cauliflower, and fried foods. Carbonated drinks can also cause problems with gas. All women are different as to what foods they can tolerate, so keep track of what bothers you so that you can cut back on those things.

Oh, the Heartburn

In the beginning stages of pregnancy, heartburn is usually due to hormonal changes. Heartburn has nothing to do with your heart but everything to do with your stomach and esophagus. The irritation you feel and the sour taste in your mouth comes from acidic stomach juices that back up into your esophagus. As your pregnancy progresses, your growing baby puts more and more pressure on your stomach and other digestive organs, which can cause heartburn. Although this problem can happen at any time during your pregnancy, it is more prevalent during the last three months when the baby is rapidly growing.

To help relieve symptoms, take the following steps:

- Eat small, frequent meals throughout the day, every hour or two if possible.
- Avoid known irritants that cause heartburn, such as caffeine, chocolate, highly seasoned foods, high-fat foods, citrus fruits or juices, tomato-based products, and carbonated beverages.
- Keep a food diary to track foods that might be triggering your heartburn. Everyone is different, so what bothers someone else may not bother you.
- Eat slowly and in a relaxed atmosphere.

- Do not lie down right after eating a meal. Instead, remain seated upright for an hour or two after eating. Even better is to walk after you eat to help your gastric juices flow in the right direction.
- Avoid large meals before bedtime.
- Limit fluids with meals, and drink them between meals instead.
- Sleep with your head elevated to help prevent acid backup.
- Wear comfortable, loose-fitting clothing.
- Talk to your doctor before taking any over-the-counter medications, such as antacids. Your doctor can advise you on what is safe to use.

HEADACHE PAIN

Headaches can be very common in pregnancy, especially during the first trimester. The most common are tension headaches, which most people experience whether pregnant or not. If you suffered with chronic headaches before, they may become worse during pregnancy. Though experts are not sure why, the factor behind headaches in pregnancy is probably the crazy hormone levels and the changes in your blood circulation. The good news is that for most women, headaches during pregnancy will probably lessen—and maybe even disappear altogether—by the second trimester. That is when the sudden rise in hormones stabilizes, and your body gets used to its altered chemistry. Other causes can include quitting your caffeine habit too abruptly as well as lack of sleep, fatigue, allergies, eyestrain, stress, depression, hunger, or dehydration.

Though most headaches during pregnancy are harmless, some can be a sign of a more serious problem. In the second or third trimester, a headache can be a sign of preeclampsia, a serious pregnancy-induced condition that includes high blood pressure, protein in the urine, and other indicators.

Relieving the Pain

The concern in pregnancy is over the products that can be used to relieve the pain of headaches. Most commonly used headache medications, such as aspirin and ibuprofen, are not recommended for use during pregnancy. Acetaminophen, or Tylenol, is safe to take but only as directed. Never take more than the bottle directs. In addition to over-the-counter medications, other remedies may help to relieve pain and should be tried first. For tension headaches, try a warm or cold compress applied to the forehead or back of the neck.

Pregnancy Pointer

WHEN SHOULD YOU CALL YOUR DOCTOR ABOUT A HEADACHE?

If you are in your second or third trimester and experience a bad headache, or a headache for the first time during your pregnancy, you should contact your doctor. If you have a severe headache that comes on suddenly, won't go away, and is unlike any you have ever experienced, you should call your doctor. You should contact your doctor if you have a headache that worsens and is accompanied by vision problems, speech problems, drowsiness, and/or numbness. Also call your doctor if your headache is accompanied by a stiff neck and fever.

Pinpointing the trigger of your headache can help you to relieve it. If you are in a hot, stuffy room, get some fresh air. If the trigger is your screaming kids, drop them off with a relative or friend and take a break. Figure out what is triggering the problem, and try to defuse the situation. Take a warm shower or bath; if you have the time and money, get a professional to give you a massage and work out the knots. Since low blood sugar can be a trigger for headaches, make sure you keep your stomach full. Eat small meals every few hours so you don't become hungry. Avoid food that is high in sugar like candy, which can cause blood sugar to rapidly spike and crash. If possible, avoid fatigue and take daily naps if you need them. Regular sleep patterns can be very helpful in reducing the number of headaches you get.

Regular exercise can also help decrease the stress that sometimes causes tension headaches. Try to adopt regular relaxation techniques into your daily routine. Meditation and yoga can be very helpful in reducing stress and headaches. Find a professional to show you safe yoga and other relaxation techniques. Headaches can be caused by something you don't even realize is happening, such as eyestrain. If you find that after reading or sitting at your computer you get headaches, visit your eye doctor.

Even if you are a headache veteran, talk to your doctor about your headaches so that he can decide what type of treatment might be best for you during your pregnancy. Do not treat or diagnose yourself. If you have a headache that worries you, don't hesitate to call your doctor.

MIGRAINES AND PREGNANCY

Migraine headaches are fairly common in women of childbearing age. About two-thirds of women who suffer from migraines before becoming pregnant note an improvement in their symptoms after the first trimester. This is especially true if their migraines were normally caused by hormonal changes during their menstrual cycle. Others, however, notice no change, and some even experience more frequent and intense headaches.

....

Belly Basics

About 15 percent of migraine sufferers experience these terrible headaches for the first time during pregnancy, usually in the first trimester.

....

Migraines are much different than tension headaches. A migraine is a type of vascular headache that occurs when the blood vessels in the brain constrict and then dilate rapidly. Some people experience visual disturbances or an aura before the headache occurs. The pain is usually concentrated on one side of the head and takes the form of severe throbbing. Some people also experience nausea and vomiting as well as sensitivity to light and noise. Little is known about what causes migraines. The best way to treat your migraine headache during pregnancy is to try to avoid one.

If you are a regular migraine sufferer, you won't be able to take the medication that you were taking before pregnancy. You should talk to your doctor right away about what is safe to take so you know ahead of time what to do. When a migraine does hit, try to sleep it off in a quiet, dark room and apply a cold compress to your forehead or neck. A cold shower can help to constrict the dilated blood vessels. If you can't take a shower, at least splash some cool water on your face and the back of your neck.

Some migraines are triggered by certain foods. If you know what these foods are, avoid them. If you don't know, keep a food diary to try to pinpoint the culprits. Common offenders include foods containing MSG, red wine, cured meats, chocolate, aged cheese, and preserved meats such as hot dogs or bologna. As in treating other headaches, it is important to keep your stomach full and your blood sugar level up. Low blood sugar can also trigger migraines.

Try to stay physically active during your pregnancy. Evidence has shown that regular exercise can reduce the frequency and severity of migraines. Start slowly, though, because sudden bursts of activity, especially if you are not used to exercise, could trigger a migraine. Get plenty of rest, and adopt regular sleep patterns by going to bed at the same time every night and waking up at the same time every morning. Irregular sleeping patterns can be a big trigger for migraines. As with tension headaches, it is important to practice stress-relieving techniques.

MOUTH AND GUM DISCOMFORT

Because of the hormonal changes that affect the blood supply to the mouth and gums, pregnancy can be demanding on your teeth and can make you more susceptible to mouth and gum discomfort. Increases in hormones can make your gums sensitive and make you more susceptible to gum disease such as gingivitis.

Gingivitis is especially common during the second to eighth month of pregnancy and can cause red, puffy, or tender gums that tend to bleed when you brush your teeth. Having a sore mouth and gums can make it hard to eat certain foods, which can result in lower calorie intake or not eating from all of the food groups.

Taking Care of Your Teeth

It is important to see your dentist early in your pregnancy and to have regular checkups. Brush your teeth and tongue at least twice per day, and floss regularly. Chew sugarless gum after meals if you are not able to brush. Make sure you are taking your prenatal vitamins and calcium supplements daily, or as directed, to help strengthen your teeth and keep your mouth healthy. If you have any mouth or gum problems, see your dentist to keep them from interfering with your healthy diet.

If you experience problems with taste changes or recurring bad tastes, try using mouthwash. Often, chewing gum, mints, or hard candy can help lessen unpleasant tastes.

....

Pregnancy Pointer

The taste of mint in toothpaste or mouthwash can trigger nausea in some pregnant women. If you experience this, try children's bubblegum-flavored toothpaste so that you can continue good dental care.

....

The Fluoride Connection

Fluoride is a trace mineral found in most tap water. It is known for its dental cavity-fighting properties. It also bonds with calcium and phosphorus to form strong bones. A baby needs fluoride in the second to third month, as her teeth begin to form. During pregnancy, the recommended intake is 3 mg, with a tolerable upper intake level of 10 mg. There is no need for a supplement as long as you drink or cook with fluoridated tap water. Bottled water usually does not contain fluoride. Fluoride is not widely found in food. Significant sources include tea, especially if brewed with fluoridated water, fish with edible bones, kale, spinach, apples, and nonfat milk.

BATTLING LEG CRAMPS

Muscle cramps, especially leg cramps, can be another bothersome discomfort during pregnancy. They usually surface late in the second trimester and in the third trimester of pregnancy. They can occur at any time of day, but they occur most often at night.

The truth is that no one really knows exactly why women experience leg cramps during pregnancy. Fatigue in muscles that are carrying around extra weight, as well as circulation problems later in pregnancy, can cause leg cramps. Some believe they are caused by excess phosphorus and too little calcium, potassium, and/or magnesium in the blood. Though there is no concrete evidence that supplementing with these minerals decreases leg cramps during pregnancy, some doctors may prescribe them anyway. The best idea is to make sure you are getting plenty of these nutrients by eating a healthy, well-balanced diet that includes all of the food groups. Some also believe that cramps can be due to inactivity, decreased circulation, and not enough fluids during pregnancy. Do not take any additional supplements unless you have talked with your doctor first. No matter what the reason, the good news is that there are ways that you can both prevent and alleviate your leg cramps. Here are a few tips:

- Avoid standing or sitting in the same position for long periods of time. That includes sitting with your legs crossed, which can decrease blood circulation in your legs.
- Stretch your calf muscles periodically during the day and especially before going to bed at night and when waking up in the morning.
- With your doctor's permission, take a walk or engage in some other physical activity every day to help the flow of blood in your legs and extremities.

- Stay well hydrated throughout the day by drinking eight to twelve glasses of water daily.
- Make sure you are getting plenty of calcium in your diet through food and prescribed supplements. Aim for three servings of dairy foods per day.
- If you get a cramp, massage the troubled area. You can also try applying a hot water bottle or heating pad to your leg. Straighten your leg and flex your ankle and toes slowly up toward your nose.

Do not go overboard with your calcium intake to relieve leg cramps. Consume no more than three dairy servings per day, and take your calcium supplement only as directed by your doctor. Too much calcium and phosphorus may decrease the absorption of magnesium, which also may be needed to prevent muscle cramps. Too much calcium over an extended period of time can also inhibit the absorption of iron and zinc as well as cause other problems. The upper tolerable limit for calcium is 2,500 mg per day.

SLEEP PROBLEMS

During the day, pregnant women seem to fight fatigue, but at night many end up fighting sleeplessness, especially during the first and third trimesters. During the first trimester, sleepless nights can be the result of endless trips to the bathroom due to increased need to urinate or from symptoms of morning sickness. Excitement, anxiety, and worrying about becoming a new mother can also disrupt normal sleep patterns. During the third trimester, physical discomfort due to the size of the abdomen, heartburn, backaches, leg cramps, and anxiety can all be culprits.

Pregnancy Pointers

If you experience insomnia, it may help to take afternoon naps—but not so many that you find it hard to sleep at night—to drink warm milk, or to take a warm bath before bedtime. Find ways to relax yourself to sleep, such as yoga, meditation, guided imagery, or reading before bedtime. Make sure your bedroom is at a comfortable temperature and that it is dark and quiet. Regular exercise during the day can also help. Above all, don't worry or get yourself all worked up about not being able to get to sleep. That will only exacerbate the problem. Do what you can to relax and fall asleep. Do not take sleeping pills or other herbal remedies without talking to your doctor first. If you feel you have a serious sleep disorder, talk to your doctor.

Chapter 7
YOUR BABY'S DEVELOPMENT

During the first trimester of pregnancy, which lasts approximately 14 weeks from the first day of your last menstrual period, your body is hard at work forming one of the most intricate and complex works of nature. By the end of your first official month of pregnancy (6 weeks after your last menstrual period, but 4 weeks since conception), your developing child will have grown an astonishing 10,000 times in size since fertilization.

YOUR BABY DURING MONTH 1

Making its longest journey until the big move 9 months from now, your developing baby (at this point called a zygote, or fertilized ovum) travels from the fallopian tube into the uterus (womb). After fertilization, the zygote begins a process of rapid cell division, and by day 4 it has formed a small, solid cluster of cells known as a morula (after *moris*, Latin for mulberry). The morula finishes the trip down the fallopian tube, reaching the uterus about 3 or 4 days after fertilization.

The Blastocyst

By the fifth or sixth day, your baby takes on its third name change in less than a week as the morula grows to a blastocyst. The blastocyst contains two distinct cell layers with a cavity at the center. The inner layer will evolve into the embryo, and the outer layer will develop into the placental membranes—the amnion and the chorion. Within days, the blastocyst nestles into the nutrient-rich lining of your uterus (the endometrium) as implantation begins, about 1 week after conception. Wispy fingers of tissue called chorionic villi from the chorion layer will anchor the blastocyst firmly to your uterine wall, where they will begin to build a network of blood vessels. These villi are the start of the placenta, a spongy, oval-shaped structure that will feed the fetus (via the umbilical cord) with maternal nutrients and oxygen throughout pregnancy.

The Embryo

About 15 days after conception, the blastocyst officially becomes an embryo. Next to the embryo floats the yolk sac, a cluster of blood vessels that provide blood for the embryo at this early stage until the placenta takes over. The embryo is surrounded by a watertight sac called the amnion (amniotic sac). The amniotic fluid that fills the sac provides a warm and weightless environment for your developing baby. It also serves as a sort of embryo airbag (in this case, fluid bag), protecting baby from the bumps and bustle of your daily routine. Nature efficiently double-bags your baby, surrounding the embryo and the amnion with a second membrane called the chorion.

During these first 4 weeks of development, your embryo has laid the groundwork for most of its major organ systems. As month 1 draws to a close, baby's heart is beating (although you won't be able to hear it for several weeks yet), lung buds have appeared, and construction of the gastrointestinal system and liver is well under way. The neural tube, the basis of the baby's central nervous system, has developed, and the forebrain, midbrain, and hindbrain are defined. The embryo is starting to look more like a person, too. The first layer of skin has appeared, facial features are surfacing, and arm and leg buds—complete with the beginnings of feet and hands—are visible. It's an amazing list of accomplishments considering your baby is about the size of a raisin (less than ¼ inch long).

AT YOUR DOCTOR'S VISIT FOR MONTH 1

Set up your first prenatal care visit as soon as you know you are pregnant. For now through the seventh month, you'll be seeing your provider on a monthly basis (unless you are considered high-risk, in which case you may have more frequent appointments). If you're seeing a new doctor or midwife, expect your initial visit to be a bit longer than subsequent checkups because you'll be asked to fill out medical history forms and insurance paperwork. Some providers will send you these materials in advance so that you can complete them at home.

Your provider will ask plenty of questions about your health history and the pregnancy symptoms you have been experiencing. Make sure that you take advantage of this initial appointment to ask about issues that are on your mind as well. In addition, you will undergo a thorough physical examination, give a urine sample (the first of many), and have blood drawn for routine lab work. If you haven't had a Pap smear within the last year, your provider may also take a vaginal swab of cells scraped from your cervix for this purpose.

Your provider will probably supply you with educational brochures and pamphlets on prenatal care, nutrition, office policies, and other important issues. There will be a lot of new information to absorb, so don't feel as though you have to study everything on the spot. However, do take everything home to read and refer to later.

Confirming Your Pregnancy

Today's home pregnancy tests are highly sensitive (many claim a 99 percent or higher accuracy rate) and provide many women with a convenient and private way to confirm their pregnancy. However, juggling sticks, strips, and tiny plastic cups while trying to decode the magic-answer window does leave some room for operator error.

If your provider hasn't yet officially confirmed your pregnancy with a lab test, he will do so at this first visit, typically with a urine test, although a blood (serum) test may be used. The pregnancy test measures the amount of hCG in your system. Blood tests may be performed in cases where a urine test is negative but pregnancy is still suspected (usually in the early weeks of pregnancy) or when an abnormal pregnancy may be suspected.

Estimating Your Due Date

Although pregnancy lasts approximately 280 days or about 9 calendar months, your estimated date of delivery (EDD) is based on a 10-lunar-month pregnancy. Each lunar month is four 7-day weeks. Why lunar months instead of following a good old-fashioned calendar? Lunar months are based on a 28-day menstrual cycle, which is considered the average cycle length.

It's important to remember that most providers determine gestational age (how far along you are) from the first day of your last menstrual period (LMP). This means that you are officially 2 weeks pregnant at the moment of conception. How's that for an existential twist? Of course, if your cycle is longer or shorter than 28 days, or if you have an irregular menstrual period, or if you're hazy on the date of your LMP, the EDD could be harder to pinpoint.

To avoid confusion, your provider probably makes good use of the printed EDD charts in her office. However, if you do have a regular 28-day cycle, you can figure out your own EDD by taking the date of your last period, counting 3 months back, and then adding 7 days. For example, if your last period began on September 1, you would go back through August, July, and June, to June 1. Then add 7 days to come up with an estimated due date of June 8 (of the following year). An alternate method is to count 280 days (40 weeks) from the first day of your last period.

YOUR BABY DURING MONTH 2

Your unborn child has now advanced from raisin to raspberry size—about a half inch in length. By the end of the month, she will be about an inch long (like a good-sized grape). The fetus is lengthening and straightening from the shrimplike, curled form it held last month. The tail she was sporting disappears around week 8, and her closed eyes start to move from the sides of the head to their permanent location. The face is further defined by a nose and jaw, and the buds of twenty tiny baby teeth are present in the gums by week 10. The palate and vocal cords also form around this time, although baby isn't ready to make herself heard just yet.

Important organ systems are nearly completed by the end of this second month. The right and left hemispheres of your baby's brain are fully formed, and brain cell mass grows rapidly. Soft bones begin to develop, and the liver starts to manufacture red blood cells until the bone marrow can take over the job in the third trimester.

Your unborn baby is also giving his brand new organs a workout. Heart chambers form, the pancreas begins to produce insulin, and the liver secretes bile. The stomach produces gastric juices, while the intestines, which have developed in the umbilical cord, move up into the abdomen by the end of the month.

Floating in about 1.5 ounces (approximately 10 teaspoons) of amniotic fluid, your baby has plenty of room for flexing the muscles she is now developing. Because of her small size and spacious accommodations, chances are you won't notice these movements now. At about weeks 18 to 20, when the second trimester is in full swing and her quarters become a bit closer, you will feel the first flutterings, known as quickening.

ON YOUR MIND

Now that you're feeling more symptoms of pregnancy, the reality of impending parenthood may suddenly hit home. "So much to do, so little time," you may be thinking. Understanding and recognizing your emotional changes can help you better control your stress levels.

Mood Swings

Find yourself laughing hysterically or sobbing uncontrollably? If you're normally the even-keeled type, these emotional outbursts can be downright alarming. You aren't losing control or losing your mind; you're just experiencing the normal mood swings of pregnancy. Although this emotional roller coaster may continue throughout pregnancy, it is typically strongest in the first trimester as you adjust to hormonal and other changes.

Given the transformation your body is going through and the accompanying aches and pains, you have every right to be cranky. In fact, when you factor in your physical discomforts with the spectrum of emotions you're experiencing as motherhood approaches, you've got a license to be hell on wheels. Of course, no one is happy when that happens (just ask your partner), so take steps now to reduce your stress level and achieve some balance.

Stress and Stress Management

It's easy to get stressed out over what may seem like an overwhelming amount of preparation for your new family member. Your body is already working overtime on the development of your child; try to keep your commitments and activities at a reasonable level to prevent mental and physical overload.

Controlling outer stress is especially important when your pregnant body is under the physical stress of providing for a growing baby. And added psychological stress can make the discomforts of pregnancy last longer and feel more severe.

....

Pregnancy Pointers

Some traditional stress-control methods, such as relaxation techniques involving certain strenuous yoga positions or martial arts, are not appropriate for pregnant women. You should also not try fad diets, herbal preparations, or over-the-counter medications (which are generally not good stress control methods, in any case). When in doubt, check with your health-care provider.

....

Anxiety may also impact your unborn child's health. An increase of corticotropin-releasing hormone (CRH), a stress-related substance produced by the brain and the placenta, has been linked to preterm labor and low birth weight. Research has also suggested a possible connection between first-trimester maternal stress and congenital malformations.

As you rush to get everything just so, remember that your little one is not going to care if the crib matches the dresser, but he will feel the effects of your excess tension. Keeping the ups and downs of pregnancy in perspective is important. So is taking steps to decompress when you feel the pressure building.

Effective stress management involves finding the right technique for you. Relaxation and meditation techniques (for example, progressive muscle relaxation, yoga), adjustments to your work or social schedule, or carving out an hour of "me time" each evening to decompress are all ways you can lighten your load. Exercise is also a great stress-control method, but be sure to get your doctor's approval regarding the level of exercise appropriate for you.

YOUR BABY DURING MONTH 3

By the end of this month, baby will grow to over 2 inches in length and almost 1 ounce, about the size and heft of a roll of Life Savers. If you could look at his face, you'd see that his ears and closed eyelids have now fully developed. His head accounts for one-third of his total length, and his tongue, salivary glands, and taste buds have also formed. Even though he's a long way from his first meal, studies indicate he may already be getting a taste of what you've been snacking on from the amniotic fluid.

He is now getting all of his nutrients through the fully formed placenta (from the Greek *plakuos*, meaning "flat cake," its approximate shape), an organ that you and your fetus share. The umbilical cord tethers the fetus to the placenta, which provides it with nutrients and oxygen and transports waste materials away.

Your baby's heart is pumping about 25 quarts of blood each day, and a lattice of blood vessels can be seen through her translucent skin, which is starting to develop a coat of fine downy hair called lanugo. The gender is apparent because the external sex organs have now fully differentiated, but it will take a combination of luck and technical skill for an ultrasound technician to reveal whether you have a son or daughter.

Belly Basics

As you enter the second trimester, your risk of miscarriage drops dramatically. While an estimated 15 percent of recognized pregnancies result in miscarriage in the first trimester, by the time you hear your baby's heartbeat around week 12, the risk of miscarriage for most women drops to 1 to 5 percent.

AT YOUR DOCTOR'S VISIT FOR MONTH 3

Make sure your husband or partner makes this month's prenatal appointment. You're both in for a treat as you begin to experience the sights and sounds of your growing child.

Tests This Month

Depending on your provider's policy on ultrasound exams and on your personal medical history, you may be seeing your baby this month.

Your provider will also start estimating the size of your baby by taking a tape measure to your belly and counting the centimeters from your pubic bone to the tip of your fundus—the top of your uterus. Taking this measurement at each visit gives your practitioner a way to assess your baby's ongoing growth. Some practitioners do not take the fundal height until after week 12 or even week 20. It's important to remember that fundal height is used as a screening tool only; women who are overweight, carrying multiples, or have a fetus in the breech position may not measure accurately.

You may be told about the alpha-fetoprotein test or triple/quad screen this month. This blood test is typically given in weeks 15 to 18 and screens for the possibility of neural tube defects and/or chromosomal abnormalities in the fetus. Since the test is optional, many providers give an informational sheet to patients the month before so that they have time to consider whether they want to take it.

Baby's Heartbeat

Hearing the steady woosh-woosh of your baby's heart for the first time is one of the most thrilling and emotional moments of pregnancy. Your first chance happens this month as your provider checks for the fetal heartbeat, using a small ultrasound device called a Doppler or Doptone. If you have a retroverted uterus (tipped or tilted), it's possible the Doppler won't detect the heartbeat just yet. Don't be alarmed; by your next prenatal appointment you will probably be able to hear it loud and clear.

FORGETFULNESS

Have you walked around looking for your sunglasses for 20 minutes before finding them on your head? Lost your car keys for the fifth time this week? Like any mom-to-be, you've got a lot on your mind. That alone may have you forgetting details that used to be second nature and misplacing items. Although researchers have looked at the problem of memory impairment in pregnancy, there hasn't been a clear consensus on the definitive cause. Pregnancy hormones, sleep deprivation, and stress have all been suggested as possible culprits.

Some studies have suggested that impairments in working memory, the short-term spatial memory you use to remember things like where you parked at the grocery store, are related to excessive levels of estrogen that start in pregnancy and peak in the third trimester. In other words, your forgetfulness might be hanging around a few more months. Until then, think about carrying a small notebook with you as a memory crutch. This can keep you from losing your mind—and your car.

Whatever the cause, forgetting appointments and misplacing things can leave you feeling muddled and helpless. Try relying less on your memory by writing notes, sticking to a routine (for example, car keys always go into a basket by the door), and living by a written or electronic organizer. If you aren't the wired type, start requesting a 24-hour advance phone call reminder when you schedule service appointments such as in-home appliance repair or a salon appointment. Having a system—whatever it is—is the key to staying reasonably organized and mentally together during this hectic time.

Chapter 8
MAKING ROOM FOR BABY

During the second month of pregnancy, start thinking about where your baby will be sleeping (or not sleeping) and playing so you can coordinate logistics and gear. If you're torn about giving up your study for a nursery (after all, she's small—how much space can she need?), think about the baby basics—crib, changing area, and dresser—plus all the inevitable stuff you're bound to acquire—swing, stuffed animals, bouncy chair, baby books, and bathtub—and the choice becomes clear.

MODIFYING YOUR LIVING SPACE

If a nursery isn't an option due to the size of your home or financial considerations, there are several ways to give your baby a place of her own by separating out a part of a room, including:

- Using a folding screen (or two)
- Hanging curtains from a ceiling track
- Building a wall for a more permanent partition

Nursery Safety

Evaluate the area for safety hazards. Make sure that you have:

- No peeling paint
- No dangling blind cords
- No loose flooring
- No two-piece doorstoppers (the rubber bumpers on many models can be a choking hazard)
- No decorative crib features that could potentially catch on clothing or entrap the baby
- A crib that meets federal safety standards
- A mattress that fits snugly against the crib sides

. . . .

Pregnancy Pointer

You can find a virtual nursery design tool online to help you design your room at *www .happyhealthypregnancy.com/tools/vr.aspx*. Printing these out can give you a head start on deciding how you want the room arranged.

. . . .

Baby Proofing

Although your home safety efforts will undoubtedly pick up steam as your child gets mobile and starts exploring her surroundings, there are some basic things you can do now to protect her in infancy and beyond. Check off the following precautions as you complete them:

- ☐ **Register for recalls.** Take the time to fill out those registration cards for all the baby gear you receive, including your child's crib. If a safety recall of the product occurs, the manufacturer will be able to notify you. You can also register for e-mail alerts of new product recalls from the U.S. Consumer Product Safety Commission at *www.cpsc.gov*.

- [ ] **Ban cigarettes.** You already know how dangerous it is to smoke during pregnancy, but did you know that secondhand smoke, particularly in a closed home environment, is harmful to your baby's health?

- [ ] **Get the lead out.** Lead paint and lead solder, most frequently found in homes built before 1978, is a major hazard to small children. When ingested, it can cause central nervous system damage and developmental problems. Contact a lead inspector to test your home for the presence of lead and to advise you on abatement procedures.

  Rearrange the furniture. Block off electrical cords and buy plastic protectors to seal up open outlets. Pad sharp table corners to protect your baby from injury.

- [ ] **Move dangerous items.** Store medications, cleaning products, and plastic bags out of a child's reach.

- [ ] **Put the lid down.** Make sure all members of the household leave the toilet seat (and lid) down. Small children are top heavy; if they peer into the toilet, they can fall in, but aren't strong enough to get out.

- [ ] **Evaluate your home from a baby's-eye view.** Crawl around your home. Pay special attention to anything about three feet off the floor and move anything dangerous, expensive, or breakable to higher ground.

CAR SAFETY

Time to face the cold, hard facts: that sporty two-seater just isn't going to hack it once you have both a baby and all her associated cargo to carry about town. Cast a critical eye toward your current vehicle, and make sure it meets both the practical and safety concerns of your growing family.

Check to make sure your current vehicle meets the following safety standards and allows you to take suggested precautions when baby arrives. If you have not checked off the entire list, record below what remains to be done to make your car baby safe before your baby is born.

- [ ] **Sit back and be safe.** The best place for any child is the back seat. If you have the choice, avoid pickup trucks or other vehicles that don't offer one.

··

Pregnancy Pointer

Airbags can save lives, but when used improperly, they can also cause serious injuries. A rear-facing infant seat in the front passenger seat places your child's head just inches from the airbag, which deploys with tremendous force and speed—a potentially fatal combination. All kids under thirteen should buckle up in the back seat whenever possible.

··

- [ ] **Turn off the front air bag.** If your new baby must ride in the front passenger seat and there is an air bag, there absolutely must be a switch that allows you to disengage the air bag on that side. If your vehicle doesn't have a switch, obtain permission to install one from the National Highway Traffic Safety Administration (NHTSA). Check with your state's motor vehicle bureau for details.
- [ ] **Scrutinize the side air bag (SAB).** Chest and head/chest rear-seat side air bags can also pose a significant risk of injury to children, while roof-mounted head SABs are considered safe. If the vehicle has an activated rear-seat side air bag, check with the car manufacturer or the NHTSA to make sure it has been adequately tested for safe use with children. Otherwise, have it deactivated.
- [ ] **Choose the right seat.** Make sure your baby's car seat fits properly in the vehicle and there is adequate room if you have more than one child to secure. Remember, your little one should ride in a rear-facing car seat until she reaches the top height or weight limit allowed by the seat's manufacturer (between ages 1 and 3).
- [ ] **Use locking seat belts, tethers, or anchors.** Most vehicles built after 2002 accommodate a LATCH system (lower anchors and tethers for children)

that allows you to secure the top and side tethers on a LATCH-equipped child seat to anchors built into the car interior. If your car seat or vehicle is not LATCH equipped, cars built after 1996 should have belts that work with most car seats. Always check the owner's manual of your vehicle and car seat for proper installation instructions.

☐ **Check the interior trunk release.** If your car was manufactured after September 2001, it should have a release mechanism inside the trunk to prevent curious children from becoming trapped inside. Retrofitted release latches are available for cars without this feature.

☐ **Don't run hot and cold.** If your car's heating and cooling system is out of commission, now is the time to get it fixed. An infant's internal thermostat is not as efficient as an adult's, and your child can quickly become overheated or chilled.

☐ **Accessorize.** Car seat belts and buckles left in the sun can pose a burn hazard, so consider a car seat cover or window and windshield sun screens, which are also useful in preventing your car's interior from absorbing the sun's heat.

Other features that may be helpful but aren't absolutely essential include built-in child car seats and safety door and window locks.

PREPARING YOUR HOME

Getting ready for a baby can be a big logistical adjustment. Your home will now need to accommodate a baby, a whole new person who comes with a whole lot of stuff. Your baby will impact almost all your living space at some point in the future. You can begin to prepare things before the baby is born, but you will also find that you have to be ready to make changes as your child grows.

Putting Together the Nursery

The big secret about nurseries is that they're not for babies. Instead, their main purpose is to fulfill parents' fantasies. A baby is happy with a bed and somewhere to be changed. Parents are the ones who desire fancy furniture, murals, and accessories. Having a separate room for a baby isn't even strictly necessary. However, having a baby is a big event in your life, and it probably is the fulfillment of your dreams, so making a big to-do out of the nursery is absolutely your right.

When setting up an area for the baby, choose a warm space with natural lighting. Keep the baby's sleeping area away from a window. Child safety experts recommend that you do not use bumper pads, quilts, or heavy blankets in a crib. Hardwood or laminate floors are considered optimal because they don't trap dust and allergens, but many parents prefer carpeting, feeling it is safer should the baby climb out of the crib. If you have an overhead light in the room, install a dimmer switch to make those nighttime diaper changes less startling.

When planning a baby's room, it is helpful to draw out the room to scale on graph paper. Then you can move around cut-outs of the furniture pieces you'll be using to see where they will best fit.

Simplifying

Motherhood means juggling lots of things, and the best way to do that is to simplify. There are many things you can do now that will make life easier when the baby arrives:

- Set up a changing area on every floor of your home.
- Start a file to keep warranty information for all your new baby equipment.
- Set up automatic online bill paying and automatic deposit of paychecks if possible.
- Stash basic beauty items (lip gloss, comb, eyeliner, toothbrush, facial wipes) in the room in which you plan on receiving visitors.
- Double every main dish you make from now on and freeze half, so you'll have some meals at the ready.
- Stock up your pantry with nonperishables and create a stockpile of toilet paper, tissues, and other essentials.
- Create a folder of takeout menus and a stash of cash.

- Learn how to use your camera and video recorder before the baby arrives.
- Create a list on which to record baby gifts so you can send thank-you notes.

MAKING PLANS FOR HELP

Asking for help is something a lot of new moms have trouble with, but it makes sense to make plans now for assistance after the baby comes. There are lots of great options available to new moms these days.

Doula

Doulas don't just provide support and assistance during labor and delivery. Postpartum doulas now work for a new mother for weeks and months after birth. These doulas assist with breastfeeding and infant care, as well as episiotomy or C-section incision care. In addition to all of this, they cook, clean, run errands, and more. If your doctor writes a prescription for a postpartum doula, you may be able to get coverage under your health insurance plan.

Baby Nurse

If you would like to hire a nurse who will help with baby care and offer you some relief at night, ask your pediatrician for a recommendation. You can also contact local nanny agencies and ask about specialized baby nurses. Baby nurses will help you with daily baby care and breastfeeding, and they watch the baby during the day or at night so you can sleep or do other things. Note that there are different types of nurses. A registered nurse (RN) will be the most expensive, but if you have a child with special needs this may be necessary. A licensed practical nurse (LPN) does not have the same kind of specialized training as an RN but is well trained to help you with daily care.

Child Care

It's not too soon to begin thinking about child care. During your pregnancy you can evaluate day cares for your return to work and get on the waiting list if there is one at the facility you select. Most child-care centers will not take infants younger than six weeks. In addition to making these long-term child-care plans, you should identify friends or relatives who will come over to help so you can sleep or rest in the first months or so that you can have a well-earned parents' night out.

Day Care

Day care is an excellent child-care option. Most centers will accept infants over six weeks of age. It's important to research day-care centers during your pregnancy as many have waiting lists for infants. You also don't want to make this decision at the last minute, when you're under pressure to return to work soon. You need time to visit the centers and evaluate them before making a decision.

Important Considerations

When choosing a day-care center, it's important to listen to your instincts about the facility and the people who work there. In addition, there are other practical considerations to ask about and look for when you are evaluating a center:

- **Costs:** Ask about weekly rates, hourly rates, and additional charges for extra hours. Some centers have registration fees and yearly supply fees as well. Ask if you are expected to supply snacks or supplies.
- **Sanitary measures:** Find out what their policy is. Toys and equipment should be cleaned regularly, and after a toy is mouthed it needs to be cleaned. The diaper-changing area must be cleaned after each use, and staff should wear gloves and/or wash hands each time.
- **Sleeping arrangements:** Ask if all infants must follow the same schedule of naps or whether babies can sleep as needed. Make sure each baby has a separate crib. If the center provides linens, they should be washed daily.

- **Hours of operation:** Some centers only accept full-time enrollment, so ask about part-time if that is your interest. Learn the hours they are open, as well as holiday schedules and closings due to weather. Ask about vacation and sick day policies as well.

- **Safety standards:** All equipment should meet safety standards and be checked for safety regularly. Safety also includes windows and doors, which can be hazardous if windows are floor-length, doors are made of glass, or mini-blinds are used. Bookcases should be bolted to the walls, electrical outlets covered, and outdoor play areas fenced. Smoke alarms, emergency plans, and compliance with fire codes are essential.

- **Feeding:** Learn if breastfeeding is encouraged and if mothers are welcome to come feed their babies. Milk and formula should be labeled and stored in the refrigerator. Parents should supply bottles and be responsible for washing them at home. Learn if babies are fed on a schedule or on demand.

- **Staff information:** Make sure all staff is trained in first aid, that they can provide references, and that their backgrounds have been checked. They should also have current immunizations. A director should be on the premises at all times.

- **Age separation:** Children should be grouped by age, with infants cared for in a room separate from other children.

- **Sick policy:** Learn what symptoms indicate your child should be kept home. Immunization requirements should meet the ones created by the American Academy of Pediatrics. Learn if there is a nurse or physician on call.

- **Parent involvement:** Some centers require parents to participate a certain number of hours a month. At the very least, parent involvement should be encouraged and welcomed.

- **Contract:** Ask to see the contract in advance, and look for liability waivers in it that say the center has no liability at all for your child.

In-Home Day-Care Centers

Many women run day-care centers out of their homes. Often they are home caring for their own children and agree to care for several other children at the same time. These centers feel more home-like. However, there are likely to be fewer resources and not as much backup available.

When evaluating a home day care, learn where in the home the children will be cared for and if it is childproofed and separate from the rest of the home. Determine how the provider will ensure equal treatment among her own children and your child. If there are other staff members, get information about their qualifications, training, and background.

Relative Care

Having a relative care for your baby can be convenient and inexpensive. You also have the peace of mind of knowing that someone who loves your baby is providing care.

In the beginning, when your baby is small, it may make more sense for your relative to care for the baby at your home. After all, all the supplies and equipment needed are there. Eventually though, you may agree to take the baby to the relative's home.

When you work out the arrangement, have a frank talk about pay. Many grandparents don't want to be paid, but other relatives might expect payment. Don't forget to consider compensation for travel and expenses such as diapers and formula. If this is an older relative, talk about current recommendations, such as putting babies to sleep on their backs, not starting solid foods until six months, and other "modern" child-care concepts.

HIRING A NANNY

A nanny can be a great child-care choice, as she will work in your home and care solely for your child. However, hiring a nanny is more expensive than a day-care center and presents some tax difficulties.

Agency Nannies

When you hire an agency nanny, you contract with an agency that provides you with a nanny. The agency screens the nannies, handles all payroll taxes, and can readily supply another nanny should one not work out. When working with an agency, get details on their screening process and minimum qualifications for nannies. Make sure you have the right to turn down a candidate they offer. Ask if the agency does unannounced spot checks on nannies in their employ. Be sure to get references for the agency.

Au Pairs

An au pair is a child-care worker, similar to a nanny, who is often a young foreign woman in the United States on a visa. She lives with your family and provides full-time child care in exchange for room and board, transportation, and a small stipend. To find an au pair, you need to work with an au pair agency. Ask how the girls are chosen, how good their English must be, how many hours they are expected to work, and how long they are placed with you. Get references for the agency.

Sitters

If you hire someone yourself to act as a nanny or a babysitter in your home, make sure you get references and check them carefully. Find out how experienced she is with infants. Set clear guidelines for what you expect her to do in addition to child care, if anything. Make sure you stop in unexpectedly once in a while to see how things are going. You will be responsible for payroll taxes for the nanny or sitter.

FAMILY MATTERS

No matter what shape and size your current household, the arrival of a new baby in your home will touch your life in ways you never imagined. Just about every aspect of your daily routine is going to change—how you eat, sleep, play, and work. As you wait to welcome your child into the world, take advantage of this time to lay the foundation for your expanding family circle.

A Space of Her Own

Start thinking about where your baby will be sleeping and playing so that you can coordinate logistics and gear. Keep an open mind as to arrangements, however. Even if you can't wait to see your little angel peacefully dozing against his color-coordinated crib sheets, you might have second thoughts about having him all the way down the hall once he arrives (especially when the 2 A.M. feeding rolls around).

Some parents choose to keep their newborns in their bedrooms, either in a crib or bassinet or in the parental bed—a somewhat controversial practice known as co-sleeping. Proponents of co-sleeping say that it encourages breastfeeding, boosts mom's milk production, and provides a better bonding experience for parents and baby. Critics cite studies finding that bed sharing disrupts sleep patterns and increases the risk of SIDS. However, factors such as baby's sleep position, type of bedding, and parental smoking and alcohol consumption raise SIDS risk as well, and it isn't completely clear whether bed sharing in the absence of these risk factors still presents a significant hazard.

Pregnancy Pointer

Make sure baby sleeps safely on a firm mattress, without soft bedding or duvets. Always place him on his back to sleep, and never share a bed with a baby after you have been drinking or if you are under the influence of drugs that alter consciousness.

Whatever you decide regarding your baby's sleeping arrangements (and you may not decide until you actually have her in your arms), if you have the space you're probably already laying plans for the baby's room. If you're torn about giving up your study for a nursery (after all, she'll be small; how much space can she need?), think about the baby basics (crib, changing area, dresser) plus all the inevitable stuff you're bound to acquire—swings, stuffed animals, bouncy chairs, baby books, bathtubs—and the choice becomes clear.

If a nursery isn't an option due to the size of your home, there are several ways to give baby a place of her own. A folding screen (or two) or curtains hung from a ceiling track can be a creative way to close off part of a room. If you have the money but limited room, think of building out a wall for a more permanent partition.

Wherever it is, the baby's space should be well-ventilated and insulated. Evaluate the area for safety hazards such as peeling paint, dangling blind cords, and loose flooring. If there are door stoppers installed, make sure they are one piece; the rubber bumper on many models presents a choking hazard. When it comes time to purchase a crib, make sure it has no decorative features that could potentially catch on clothing or entrap the baby, and that the crib slats are a maximum of $2^3/_8$ inches apart. The crib should also meet the latest safety standards and not have drop-down side rails. The mattress should fit snugly against the crib sides.

THE HIGH COST OF HAVING A BABY

If you have substantial or full insurance coverage for your prenatal care and delivery expenses, you can breathe a sigh of relief. According to an Agency for Heatlhcare Research and Quality report released in 2010, average hospital charges for delivering a baby in 2008 were $3,400 for an uncomplicated delivery and $5,700 for an uncomplicated cesarean section. The average cost climbs to $9,400 for a vaginal delivery with an operating procedure. And prenatal care adds another several thousand to the bill; however, studies show that such expenses are more than offset by improved outcomes for both mother and child.

Insurance Issues

Review your insurance plan so that you are clear on the extent and nature of your coverage for both prenatal care and labor and delivery. If you have questions, call your insurance company or speak to the benefits coordinator at your workplace.

Keep on top of insurance problems. As any physician's or hospital's billing department can tell you, insurance companies do occasionally lose and mishandle claims. Whenever you call either your provider's billing department or the insurance company, take notes summarizing the conversation, including a date to follow up, and the name of the person you speak with. If you're trying to unravel a knotty insurance issue, being able to track it with someone who is familiar with your case will save you time and aggravation. And if you aren't getting action, it helps to document exactly who has dropped the ball as you move up the chain of command. Follow up with letters and request written documentation of any actions taken over the phone so that you have a paper trail as well.

Payment Options

If you have a large deductible to pay out of pocket, or are responsible for a hefty percentage of your physician's bill, don't panic. Work with your provider's office to negotiate a realistic payment schedule. Contact the business office of the hospital or birthing center where you will deliver for registration information and details on their billing terms. Some providers and hospitals may have maternity assistance programs, including sliding fee scales and prepayment discounts.

Ways to Save

According to U.S. Census Bureau estimates, 16.7 percent of all Americans were without health insurance in 2009. There are public aid programs available if you are uninsured and unable to meet the financial obligations of prenatal care and childbirth.

Medicaid is a state-run public assistance program that provides medical care to low-income families at little to no cost. For information on qualifying standards, see the federal Centers for Medicare and Medicaid Services' website at *www.cms.gov* or call your state social services department.

The Special Supplemental Nutrition Program for Women, Infants, and Children (WIC) is a federally funded, state-administered program targeted to nutritionally at-risk women (both pregnant and postpartum) and children up to age 5. WIC provides food vouchers to those who meet qualifying guidelines and have an annual gross household income that does not exceed 185 percent of the federal poverty level ($41,348 for a family of four in the forty-eight contiguous states in 2011; slightly higher in Alaska and Hawaii).

The Children's Health Insurance Program (CHIP) is a federal program that covers infants and children in families that are financially strained but earn income levels too high to qualify for Medicaid. If you're concerned about insurance coverage for your newborn, call 1-877-KIDS-NOW or visit *www.insurekidsnow.gov* for more details.

There may be other financial assistance available in your area. Contact your area social services agency for more details.

Bargain Hunters

Even if you've never been one to clip coupons, the expense of keeping baby in diapers and other essentials is a strong incentive to start looking for savings. Next time you're at the doctor's office, take a look around the waiting room for product offers. Many new-parent clubs have cropped up, supported by formula makers, diaper manufacturers, and other baby product companies, and they often recruit members right there at the source.

Some kid-focused retailers also have coupon clubs. Sign up if you'd like to receive free product samples and coupons. One caveat: putting your name on their mailing lists may open you up to a deluge of junk mail from so-called "valued partners." Check out the form you sign for its printed privacy policy if this is a concern; it may offer you an opportunity to opt out of such mailings.

There are several free magazines on the market geared specifically for new parents and moms-to-be, again often available right at your provider's office. Be aware that because the publishers make their money from advertisers rather than from subscribers, these publications are typically laden with product ads. However, they still have lots of useful new parenting information and an abundance of coupons and free offers.

Check your local library for other community or regional parenting publications that can point you toward useful family resources and, again, those handy coupons.

Although breast milk is the least expensive way to feed your baby (along with its many other extraordinary health benefits), if you are planning on bottle-feeding, freebies abound. Formula is expensive, and baby will eventually be putting away about 30 ounces a day (900 ounces per month). Acquiring a loyal customer through free samples and other incentives makes good business sense to formula manufacturers, who are big on the aforementioned new-parent clubs. They also provide a steady stream of samples to prenatal care providers and pediatricians. If you don't see samples or aren't offered any, ask your provider.

Finally, if you deliver in a hospital, make sure you get what you pay for. Chances are you'll be billed for all the items you and your newborn use—including the pacifier, nasal aspirator, sanitary napkins, alcohol swabs, open bags of diapers and wipe cloths, and even the little plastic comb for baby's hair (whether baby has any or not). By all means, take these with you when you leave! Ask the nurse what is fair game. Often the hospital staff can send you home with even more free product samples than you will find in your hospital room.

FINANCIAL PLANNING FOR A BIGGER FAMILY

Clueless about baby care costs? Take a reconnaissance mission to the grocery store to gather prices on diapers, wipes, and other essentials. If you're considering day care or an in-home babysitter, now is also a good time to get information and monthly cost estimates. As usual, other parents are an excellent source of tips and leads to the best resources in your area.

. . . .

Pregnancy Pointer

In 1 week, the average baby goes through about sixty to eighty diaper changes. That's a potential pile up of 4,160 diapers in the first year alone! If you're using disposable ones, price out cases of diapers at the local warehouse club or discount store because bulk purchases are typically cheaper.

. . . .

Don't forget to factor in pediatric care and additional health insurance premiums on your bottom line. If you belong to an HMO or other managed-care health plan, it's probable that well-baby visits are covered at 100 percent or with a minimal copay. You may want to review your health insurance options now so that when baby comes you can enroll her in the most appropriate and cost-effective program.

Setting Savings Goals

Now that you've figured out what you'll be spending on baby care, of what practical use is this? Lay out your current spending habits, including basic monthly bills like utilities and housing, debts that can be downsized (for example, credit cards and car payments), transportation costs, food and household goods, health-care, and discretionary/disposable income. Accounting for everything in black and white will give you a much clearer picture of where you're spending and the size of any gap between income and expenses. This can also help you figure out big-picture questions like whether you have the financial means to switch to a part-time schedule at work.

When it comes time to balance your home budget, be realistic in your planning and prudent when you eliminate discretionary purchases; brown-bagging it to work each and every day for the next 3 years is a noble goal, but a weekly or biweekly meal out with colleagues could pay off in other ways. Give yourself a little breathing room for unforeseen emergency expenses like an appliance meltdown or car repairs. A little scrimping here, one less latte a week there, and you'll find budgeting easier than you thought.

Some parents find it daunting to consider long-term expenses, like college, when the costs and responsibilities of child rearing itself seem so overwhelming. Just remember that early planning can net big returns over time. If you start saving just $50 a month in a savings account or other interest-bearing investment at a 5 percent interest rate when your child is born, you will have $16,026 by the time your child is ready to start college. If you don't know an IRA from the NRA, you might want to sit down with a financial advisor to discuss college savings options. She might also be able to assist you in re-evaluating your life insurance needs, something else that should be done periodically as your family grows.

LIFESTYLE CHANGES, OR STATING THE OBVIOUS

Your baby's arrival will transform just about everything you think, say, and do. This sea change is usually most evident with first-time parents, who up until now have been enjoying the child-free pursuits of quiet dinners, R-rated movies, and even the occasional wild night out with the girls or boys. Even those moms and dads who are expecting a second or subsequent child will have big adjustments ahead with new challenges like siblinghood and advanced parental multitasking (for example, encouraging one child to use his napkin while preventing the other from eating hers). Don't look on it as an end but rather as a new and infinitely more rewarding chapter in your life. You will even find some family pastimes you have never considered before.

Pregnancy Pointer

Strange but true: men can have pregnancy symptoms, too. Known as couvade syndrome, this sympathy-pain phenomenon may have your significant other experiencing nausea, fatigue, weight gain, and mood swings. What's behind it? Anxiety associated with impending fatherhood is suspected by some, but one Canadian study found that men experiencing couvade symdrome had distinct hormonal changes that mirrored their pregnant partners'.

Sharing Pregnancy with the Dad-to-Be

With the big focus on mom and her growing belly, it's easy for dads to get overlooked in the pregnancy drama. Remind your significant other that you're in this together. If he isn't quite sure of his role in this new adventure yet, he could be looking to you for cues. Encourage him to join you at prenatal checkups as well as share pregnancy education and experiences like the first kicks. You should also try to pencil in some special couple time to talk to baby, contemplate names, and share your hopes and dreams about your family's future.

From Two to Three

The new person in your life has already started competing for your attention, changing your eating and sleeping patterns, and perhaps slowing down your pace. Unexpected emotions may surface between you and your significant other as your pregnancy progresses. He may feel pangs of jealousy at the loss of your couplehood and your focus on the baby. On the flip side, you may be feeling as if you're playing second fiddle to your future child as the prospective father questions the safety of every move you make. Such growing pains are normal. Try to talk about your feelings and approach parenting (even now) as a team effort.

Some dads are intimidated by the size and vulnerability of an infant and as a result pass on most of the child care responsibilities to the mother, a potential lose-lose situation for both of you. If he is feeling uneasy about his lack of experience in the child care arena, suggest a few tag-team babysitting sessions for a niece or nephew or a friend's child to build his confidence.

The Bond of Parenthood

Pregnancy can bring a couple closer together than they ever imagined, but it can also present new frictions in your relationship. The aches and pains of pregnancy can push the most even-tempered woman to her limits. Add to that a healthy surge of estrogen and progesterone, and you have the recipe for major mood swings. Other stressors, like a tepid sex life and financial fears, can also stir the pot. Try to approach these temporary changes with understanding and empathy for your partner and a healthy sense of humor, if at all possible.

NOTES AND CHECKLISTS

Checklist for Months One Through Three

☐ Evaluate your doctor, midwife, or group practice and decide if it's right for you and your pregnancy.

☐ Discuss any possible on-the-job hazards with your doctor or midwife.

☐ Evaluate your diet and begin taking prenatal vitamins if recommended by your doctor or midwife.

☐ Get up to speed on your health insurance coverage for prenatal visits, delivery, and the care of your child.

☐ If you smoke or drink, quit now.

☐ Prepare a budget to save for when your baby arrives.

☐ Start developing a maternity wardrobe.

☐ Make room for your baby.

☐ Create a baby-safe car environment.

☐ Create ways to compensate for forgetfulness.

☐ Make sleep a priority; set a new early bedtime and stick to it.

When to Contact Your Doctor or Midwife Checklist

A lot will be changing during your first trimester. If at any time you experience any of the following symptoms, call your doctor or midwife immediately:

☐ Abdominal pain and/or cramping

☐ Fluid or blood leaking from the vagina

☐ Abnormal vaginal discharge (foul smelling, green, or yellow)

☐ Painful urination

☐ Severe headache

☐ Impaired vision (spots or blurring)

☐ Fever over 101°F

- ☐ Chills
- ☐ Excessive swelling of face and/or body
- ☐ Severe and unrelenting vomiting and/or diarrhea
- ☐ Fainting or dizziness, especially if they are accompanied by abdominal pain or bleeding (They could be symptoms of ectopic, or tubal, pregnancy, a potentially fatal condition where implantation occurs outside of the endometrial lining of the uterus, such as in the fallopian tubes.)

While a good dose of common sense should be used in contacting your doctor or midwife after hours, in most cases better safe than sorry applies. Trust your instincts. If something just doesn't feel right to you, make the call.

PART 3

SECOND TRIMESTER

Chapter 9

GROWING WITH YOUR BABY

If this is your second or third child, you may already recognize the familiar sensation of your baby's body flexing in your womb. For moms in their debut pregnancy with somewhat less stretchy accommodations, the first movements—known as quickening—may not be felt quite as early. By week nineteen, most women have felt that distinctive first flutter.

YOUR BABY DURING THE SECOND TRIMESTER

Once your baby starts moving regularly, the sensation becomes second nature. When you begin to feel your baby moving regularly, try to record how many movements you feel within a few hours to get an idea of your baby's average number of movements per hour.

Hour One_____

Hour Two_____

Hour Three _____

On average, you should feel four or more movements each hour from your passenger. Three or fewer movements or a sudden decrease in fetal activity could be a sign of fetal distress, so if you notice either, call your provider as soon as possible to follow up.

YOUR BABY DURING MONTH 4

Welcome to the second trimester—what many women consider "the fun part." Your energy is up, and your meals are staying down. Your pregnancy is now a visible fact, so indulge in the occasional daytime nap and take advantage of designated close-in pregnancy parking spaces without feeling guilty. You and your baby are headed into a period of rapid growth now, so hang on and enjoy the ride. Here's a look at what you can anticipate in month 4.

What's Your Baby Doing?

Snoozing, stretching, swallowing, and even thumb sucking, your fetus is busy this month as he tests out his new reflexes and abilities. He is losing his top-heavy look as his height starts to catch up to his head size. By the end of this month, he will measure about 6 to 8 inches in length and weigh approximately 6 ounces.

Now is a good time to begin singing to, reading to, and even playing music for your little one. The inner ear structures that allow him to hear are developing this month. He has grown eyebrows, eyelashes, and possibly even a little hair on top.

The long bones of his arms and legs are growing, as cartilage is replaced with spongy, woven, soft bone in a process called *ossification*. Skeletal development will continue long after birth and well into adolescence and young adulthood.

Your baby is inhaling and exhaling amniotic fluid, practicing his technique for his first breath in the outside world. The lungs are already generating cellular fluid and a substance known as *surfactant*. In later months the surfactant will assist the development of the fetal lungs by expanding the alveoli (air sacs) within them. These substances move out through the trachea and become part of the amniotic fluid, along with the urine your unborn child is already passing.

The placenta is approximately 3 inches in diameter this month; the attached umbilical cord is about as long as the fetus and continues to grow. Fetal blood is being pumped through this little body at about 4 miles an hour, exiting through the two large arteries in the umbilical cord and on to the placenta. In the placenta, baby's waste products (urine and carbon dioxide) are exchanged for oxygenated, nutrient-rich blood that is returned to the fetus via the umbilical cord vein. Pressure from the blood pumping within the cord helps straighten it out and keeps it from becoming knotted or getting in the way of your unborn baby's kicks and somersaults. Total time for this complex exchange? About 30 seconds.

YOUR BODY DURING MONTH 4

In pregnancy, feeling is believing. Although hearing baby's heartbeat or seeing fetal movement on an ultrasound monitor are milestone moments, the first time you actually sense your child inside of you—proof positive that you are indeed nurturing an actual human being—is a humbling and life-affirming experience.

Your Body Changes

If you weren't showing last month, chances are you will have a definite pregnant profile by the end of this month. Your uterus is about the size of a head of cabbage, and its top tip lies just below your bellybutton.

Your appetite may start to pick up this month, especially if you've been too sick to enjoy a good meal until now. You'll need a healthy craving or two to fuel fetal growth: About 60 percent of your total pregnancy weight (about 11 to 15 pounds) will be gained in this trimester.

Belly Basics

The thin line of fine hair that runs from your navel down to your pubic bone—the linea alba—may turn dark in pregnancy, again thanks to hormonal changes. If you do develop this little stripe, now called a linea nigra, it will most likely lighten again postpartum.

Heartburn may start to become a persistent problem as your uterus crowds your stomach and the smooth muscles of your digestive tract remain relaxed due to the hormone progesterone. Some tips for putting out the fire:

- Avoid greasy, fatty, and spicy foods.
- Stay away from alcohol and caffeinated drinks (for example, cola, tea, coffee); these can relax the valve between the stomach and the esophagus and exacerbate heartburn.
- Keep a food log to determine your heartburn triggers.
- Eat smaller, more frequent meals instead of three large ones.
- Drink plenty of water between meals to reduce stomach acid.
- Don't eat just before you go to bed or lie down to rest.
- Rest your head on a few extra pillows in bed to assist gravity in easing heartburn while you sleep.

If heartburn symptoms won't relent, there are several over-the-counter antacids and medications available that are considered safe to use in pregnancy. Speak with your doctor to find out which one may be right for you.

As if heartburn weren't enough to deal with, pregnancy might start to become a real pain in the rear, literally. Many women develop hemorrhoids, which are caused by increased pressure on the rectal veins. Your growing uterus places pressure on the inferior vena cava, the vein that services the lower body, while pregnancy hormones cause veins to dilate (widen), encouraging swelling. And by straining to have a bowel movement, you may put undue stress on the rectal veins, which can become blocked—trapping blood, turning itchy and painful, and perhaps even protruding from the anus. Exercise, a high-fiber diet, and plenty of water can help to avoid constipation and straining with bowel movements that may aggravate the condition. Try easing the pain with an ice pack, a soak in a warm tub, wipes with witch hazel pads, or a topical prescription cream as recommended by your doctor.

Hemorrhoids do have the potential to become more than just a minor discomfort, so be sure to speak with your provider if they do occur. Although they typically resolve after pregnancy, in some cases clotting occurs and surgery is necessary.

Other symptoms of second-trimester pregnancy that you may start or continue to experience this month include:

- Nausea
- Fatigue
- Frequent urination
- Tender and/or swollen breasts
- Bleeding gums
- Excess mucus and saliva
- Increase in normal vaginal discharge
- Mild shortness of breath
- Lightheadedness or dizziness
- Gas and/or constipation
- Skin and hair changes
- Feeling warm or easily overheated

On Your Mind

You're now hitting your stride as the wooziness and uncertainties of the first 3 months fade away and the discomforts of late pregnancy still lie relatively far ahead.

Pregnancy Pointer

Varicella infection (chickenpox) can cause serious complications in pregnancy. If you have never had chickenpox or the vaccine and are exposed to the virus, contact your health-care provider immediately. If your blood tests negative for varicella antibodies, immediate treatment with varicella-zoster immune globulin (VZIG) can prevent or lessen the severity of chickenpox.

Feeling better and having more energy, you might be ready to conquer the world (or at least the nursery). Yet coworkers, friends, and family now starting to recognize you as "a pregnant woman" may be handling you with kid gloves.

The pampering is nice, within limits. Accept the small favors that ease the discomforts of pregnancy—such as a closer parking space or the cushy chair in the conference room. But don't hesitate to be firm with those who pressure you to cut back on tasks you're perfectly capable of handling or who treat you like a porcelain doll.

YOUR BABY DURING MONTH 5

At 10 to 12 inches long and around 1 pound in weight, your baby is about the size of a regulation NFL football. How appropriate, considering you've reached the halftime of pregnancy.

Your little linebacker is starting to bulk up a bit as she accumulates deposits of brown fat under her skin. This insulation will help regulate her body temperature in the outside world. She's using her bulk to make her presence known; if you weren't feeling her last month, you likely are now. A look at her through ultrasound might reveal a wave of her clenched hands, which open and close freely now and have their own unique fingerprints.

The fetus is now covered in an oily white substance known as *vernix caseosa*, a sort of full-body fetal ChapStick that keeps her fluid-soaked skin from peeling and protects against infection. Some of the vernix will remain on the baby at birth, particularly in the skin folds (more if she is early, less if she is post-term).

YOUR BODY DURING MONTH 5

As baby grows, your muscles and ligaments stretch to support this new weight. The result can be a new set of aches and pains as your body adjusts to the load.

By this time, you might be feeling like you're turning inside out. Your "innie" may have already become an "outtie" as the skin of your belly (and accompanying button) is stretching, tightening, and most likely itching like crazy. A good moisturizing cream can relieve the itching and keep your skin hydrated, although it won't prevent or eliminate *striae gravidarum* (stretch marks). Whether you develop stretch marks is largely a matter of genetics, although factors such as excessive weight gain and multiples' gestations increase your odds of having them.

The red, purple, or whitish striae are created by the excess collagen your body produces in response to rapid stretching of the skin. They may appear on your abdomen, breasts, or on any other blossoming body part right now. Don't be too alarmed; striae typically fade to virtually invisible silver lines after pregnancy. If you do feel self-conscious, there are options for postpartum treatment of severe cases.

The band of ligaments supporting your uterus is carrying an increasingly heavy load. You might start to feel occasional discomfort in your lower abdomen, inner thighs, and hips, called *round ligament pain*. Pelvic tilt exercises are useful for keeping pelvic muscles toned and for relieving pain.

The pelvic tilt can be performed while standing against a wall, although it might be more comfortable done on your hands and knees following these steps: Keep your head aligned with your spine, pull in your abdomen, tighten your buttocks, and tilt the bottom of your pelvis forward. Your back will naturally arch up. Hold the position for 3 seconds, then relax. Remember to keep your back straight in this neutral position. Repeat the tilt 3 to 5 times, eventually working up to 10 repetitions.

Pregnancy hormones, the root of discomfort, are also contributing to the lower-back pain you could be experiencing. Progesterone and relaxin, the hormone responsible for softening your pelvic ligaments for delivery, are also loosening up your lower-back ligaments and disks; combined with the weight of your growing belly, your back is feeling the strain. Women who are having twins or more are especially prone to lower-back pain, which occurs in up to 50 percent of all pregnant women.

A few tips to help you ease your aches and pains:

- **Stand tall.** Perfect posture can go a long way toward easing back pain. Don't lead with your belly. Try to keep your center of gravity in your spine and pelvis. Check yourself by contracting your abdomen and buttock muscles at the same time, which should align your posture perfectly. Keep your head straight and your chin level. Your ears, shoulders, and hips should all be aligned.
- **Sit up straight.** Use good posture when you're sitting as well, and choose a chair with good lower-back support. You can purchase a special ergonomic support pad for your chair back, but a small pillow can do the trick just as easily.
- **Avoid twists and turns.** With your back so loose, a sudden move as simple as quickly turning at the waist to get out of bed may strain your back. Use your arms as support for a slow takeoff when rising from a chair.
- **Practice your pickups.** If you have small children who still need to be lifted occasionally, it's essential to use correct form. To avoid injury, bend and use your leg muscles to lift weight rather than bending from the waist and lifting with your back.

- **Warm up.** A warm pad on your back, hips, or other sore spots can help relieve pain.
- **Sensible shoes.** Avoid high heels! They will place further stress on your spine, and they're anything but comfy these days.
- **Foot rest.** Use a low stool or step to rest your feet when sitting. If you must stand for long periods, alternate resting each foot on a step.
- **Massage.** You now have a medical excuse to indulge in a regular back rub from your significant other. A licensed massage therapist who is experienced in prenatal massage would also be helpful.
- **Fluff and stuff.** Sleep on your side with a pillow placed between your legs. This will align your spine and improve your sleeping posture. A full-size body pillow can help support your back as well as belly.
- **Exercise.** If you aren't doing them already, some stretching and flexibility exercises may be in order. Check with your health-care provider for approval and recommendations; if the pain is troublesome enough or if you have a history of back problems, she may suggest a physical therapist to work with.

Feeling hot and bothered? Pregnancy-induced changes in your metabolism and added weight can have you cranking the AC. Dress comfortably, cool off in the shower or tub, and invest in an extra fan if you don't have air conditioning.

Other symptoms that you may start or continue to experience this month include:

- Nausea
- Fatigue
- Frequent urination
- Tender and/or swollen breasts
- Bleeding gums
- Excess mucus and saliva
- Increase in normal vaginal discharge

- Mild shortness of breath
- Lightheadedness or dizziness
- Headaches
- Gas, heartburn, and/or constipation
- Skin and hair changes

At Your Doctor Visit

Beyond the usual weigh and measure routine, your doctor will screen for gestational diabetes toward the end of this month. If she hasn't discussed counting fetal movements before, she might mention it now.

Now that you're halfway through pregnancy, you are perhaps thinking more about labor and delivery issues. It's never too early to ask your doctor questions about what's on your mind. It's also a good time to start gathering information on childbirth classes from your local hospital or birthing center. There are several different methods of childbirth education; researching them now will give you and your partner time to learn more about which one is right for you. Even if you have experience in the delivery room, you can still benefit from a refresher course. Register early, but try to pick a class date that falls in your third trimester so that the information will still be fresh in your mind once the big day arrives.

YOUR MOOD

There's bound to be an uncomfortable episode or two while your emotions are so close to the surface. Couple this emotional tension with your ever-growing list of things to do, and meltdown is imminent. Try to defuse the situation ahead of time by having an action plan for coping with anger-provoking situations.

Irritability

Because of all the added demands on your body, mind, and emotional equilibrium, you could be finding yourself short on patience these days. In pregnancy the proverbial molehill quickly becomes a mountain. You have absolutely no tolerance for the idiosyncrasies of others, and people you found mildly annoying before pregnancy can become absolutely impossible to be around.

If you can't stand your coworker's endless prattle about who did what to whom and got away with it, tell her you need some quiet time. And the next time your neighbor launches into her 303 easy steps for making your home look as great as hers, politely excuse yourself for a rest rather than letting your boiling point rise. Pregnancy is the perfect excuse for steering clear of people who—let's face it—are just plain annoying. During this crucial time in which your emotional and physical balance are so important, it's good to have solutions for taking care of the little things and keeping your sanity intact.

If family and friends are getting your ire up as well, it might be a sign that you are feeling overwhelmed and undersupported. Take a look at what's really getting to you. When you blow up at your partner for forgetting to stop at the dry cleaner, is it because you really have to get your winter sweaters back posthaste, or because lately you feel like you have to either nag or do it yourself to accomplish anything? If the latter, sit down and tell your partner what you're feeling, and work out some strategies for easing the burden together.

Overwhelmed

Half of your pregnancy has passed you by, the baby's room is a sea of boxes, you can't decide on a name, and your office isn't even close to being ready for your maternity leave. Step back and take stock. Are you making work—and stress—for yourself through self-imposed deadlines? Look at your to-do list in terms of small tasks rather than as an all-or-nothing duty. Prioritize what's there and dare to cross off a few things that just aren't that important right now. It's nice to have everything "just so" for baby's arrival, but your new son is only going to care about three things—being warm, well fed, and near his mom and dad.

Also remember that you aren't in this alone. If you're single, enlist family or close friends to help out. And if you are married but still aren't getting the help and support you need from your husband or family, ask for it. Although it's nice when others anticipate your needs and pitch in voluntarily, they may be wrapped up in their own preparations and anxieties about the new family addition. Don't feel guilty about reminding them that their help is needed now.

Belly Basics

Having a planned C-section? You'll still benefit from prepared childbirth classes, which offer a comprehensive look at the entire birth experience, including hospital policies and procedures, newborn care, and a sneak peek at the birthing facilities. Mention your cesarean when you call for information; some programs offer special classes just for moms who are having C-sections.

YOUR BABY DURING MONTH 6

Feeling a rhythmic lurch in your abdomen? Your little guy probably has the hiccups, a common phenomenon thought to be brought on by his drinking and/or breathing amniotic fluid. They'll go away on their own eventually; in the meantime, enjoy your little drummer boy and take advantage of the beat to let your partner feel the baby move.

The once-transparent skin of your fetus is starting to thicken, and sweat glands are developing below the skin surface. He's over a foot long now and by the end of the month will weigh up to 2 pounds.

Your unborn baby might now startle (react) to a loud noise or other stimulation. Because his auditory system (the cochlea and pathways in the CNS) has developed enough to sense and even readily discriminate among sounds, he is becoming accustomed to your voice and that of others who talk to him frequently. Studies have demonstrated that newborns show a clear preference for their mothers' voices and for songs they heard while in the womb. Now is a good time to brush up on your lullaby repertoire.

Some clinical studies have found an association between exposure to excessive noise during pregnancy and high-frequency hearing loss in newborns. And while you can wear earplugs, your baby doesn't have the luxury. To stay on the safe side, it's best to avoid concerts, clubs, and other high-volume environments now. If your job involves heavy noise exposure, talk with your doctor about possible risks.

Belly Basics

Strange but true: if you're having a girl, your uterus also holds the origins of your grandchildren. By week 24 of gestation, your fetus has already developed an estimated seven million eggs in her ovaries. The eggs are enveloped in small sacs called follicles as pregnancy continues, and by birth the number of eggs will have decreased to around a million.

YOUR BODY DURING MONTH 6

Your uterus extends well above your navel now. You may actually be seeing fetal movement across your abdomen as baby gets comfortable in his shrinking living space. As baby seems to get more nimble, you feel exceedingly klutzy— breaking everything that isn't nailed down, tripping over your own swollen feet, and upsetting low-lying knickknacks with your burgeoning belly. Blame it on your shifting center of gravity, and be careful if you're walking in slippery or icy conditions.

Your Body Changes

If the shoe fits . . . consider yourself lucky. Few women are able to fit into all their prepregnancy shoes for 9 whole months. What's behind all the swelling? The dramatic increase in blood volume you've experienced in order to nurture your child is feeding excess fluids to surrounding tissues, resulting in edema (water retention). To make matters worse, the weight of your uterus is requiring the veins in your legs to work double time to pump all that extra blood back to the heart. And, of course, another culprit is (say it together, everyone) pregnancy hormones, as estrogen increases the amount of fluid your tissues absorb.

The result of all this is puffy and sometimes aching feet. Putting your feet up when you can, wearing comfortable low-heeled shoes, and soaking your feet in cool water are all good ways to ease the discomfort. Special compression stockings, available at medical supply stores, can also be helpful.

Pregnancy Pointer

If you experience sudden and severe swelling of the face and hands, call your doctor immediately. It may be a sign of preeclampsia (toxemia), a condition that is potentially hazardous to both you and your baby. Other signs of preeclampsia include high blood pressure, headaches, visual disturbances, and protein in the urine.

Don't restrict fluids or sodium. Although avoiding excess sodium intake is fine, you actually need slightly more sodium in your diet in pregnancy to maintain your electrolyte balance. Fluids are crucial as well, to prevent dehydration and keep you and baby well.

What You Feel Like

You might have added leg cramps to your laundry list of pregnancy complaints. Stretching out your calf muscles can often quash a cramp, so the next time one hits, extend your legs and point your toes toward your head. Some providers suggest calcium supplements to ease cramping, but clinical studies are inconclusive as to whether this treatment is effective (although it can't hurt, given your increased calcium needs right now). A number of studies have found, however, that oral magnesium supplementation can be useful in alleviating cramps in some women. Check with your health-care provider to see what she suggests.

Leg cramps can also be triggered by compression of your sciatic nerve—a condition commonly known as *sciatica*. Sciatica can also cause numbness and burning pain down the length of your leg and in your lower back and buttocks. Try stretching, a warm compress, or a tub soak for relief. If sciatica becomes more than a minor annoyance, talk to your health-care provider. A date with a physical therapist may be in order.

If your leg pain is accompanied by swelling, redness, and skin that is warm to the touch, call your health-care provider to report your symptoms. You could be experiencing deep vein thrombosis (DVT), a blood clot in your leg that impedes circulation and has the potential to embolize (break off and block a major blood vessel). Pregnant women are five times more likely to develop DVT than their nonpregnant peers due to a slowdown of blood flow and an increase in clotting factors. However, DVT itself is relatively rare, occurring in less than one of every 1,000 pregnancies. If DVT is diagnosed, intravenous anticoagulant drugs are typically prescribed to treat the clot, and bed rest is advised.

Pregnancy Pointer

CAN THE SEAT BELT IN MY CAR HURT THE BABY?

Definitely continue to buckle up for safety throughout your pregnancy. The lap belt should fit snugly under your belly bulge, and the shoulder belt should be positioned between your breasts. Don't worry about the belt hurting the baby; the uterus and fluid-filled amniotic sac are excellent shock absorbers.

Other symptoms on the menu yet again this month include:

- Nausea
- Fatigue
- Frequent urination
- Tender and/or swollen breasts
- Bleeding gums
- Excess mucus and saliva
- Increase in normal vaginal discharge
- Mild shortness of breath
- Lightheadedness or dizziness
- Headaches
- Forgetfulness

- Gas, heartburn, and/or constipation
- Skin and hair changes
- Round ligament pain or soreness
- Lower-back aches
- Mild swelling of legs, feet, and hands

At Your Doctor Visit

There is more of the same this month as your provider checks your weight and fundal height, listens to baby's heartbeat, and finds out about any new pregnancy symptoms you are experiencing. If you're reporting swelling, your provider may check your feet and hands. And, of course, no prenatal visit is complete without a urine sample and blood pressure check. If you weren't given a glucose challenge test to screen for gestational diabetes last month, it will probably be administered now.

ON YOUR MIND

Now that your belly is too big to not notice, it becomes a conversation piece. At first you may be surprised to find women you don't know asking about your due date or the gender of your baby. The next question will inevitably be "Is this your first?" Welcome to the sisterhood of motherhood.

Take advantage of all the attention. As you get closer to your baby's birthday, you could find your questions (and possibly your anxieties) about labor and delivery multiplying. Other moms are usually more than willing to share the unvarnished truth, so when someone engages you in conversation about your pregnancy, ask questions back. Just keep in mind that every birth is different, so your experience will be unique.

The "What If" Game

Every new-mom-to-be spends some time worrying about the health of her unborn child, especially if she's in a high-risk pregnancy. Take comfort in the fact that you've almost made it to the third trimester and your chances of delivering a healthy and happy baby are increasing each and every day. Obsessing over what could go wrong rather than focusing on living well will accomplish nothing but add stress, insomnia, and anxiety—three things that are bad for you and baby. Read on for some stress-busting techniques to release your worries and relieve your mind.

Chapter 10

WORKING THROUGH PREGNANCY

Pregnancy is a great time to take a step back and reassess where you are, and where you're headed, on your career path. Take the opportunity to align your professional goals with the new challenges of parenting. You might be anxious about functioning well on the job during your pregnancy. Recognize your value as an employee and as a woman. Don't let anyone make you feel guilty about being pregnant. Know your legal rights, stick to your guns, and realize you don't have to settle for the status quo when it comes to the workplace.

YOUR RIGHTS

Unfortunately, it's sometimes easier to change the legal structures of the employment landscape than alter prevalent workplace attitudes and prejudices. Too frequently, pregnancy is construed as a personal indication that you have no need for professional fulfillment.

Even if you do consider work nothing more than a way to pay the bills, your rights are still important. Intolerant and illegal practices concerning pregnancy in the workplace can result in financial loss as career advancement screeches to a halt, you get the minimum salary bump at your next annual review, and bigger and better job offers dry up. Fortunately, federal and state statutes are in place to minimize the chances that you will be professionally or economically punished for your choice to become a mother.

The Pregnancy Discrimination Act

The Pregnancy Discrimination Act is a 1978 amendment to Title VII of the Civil Rights Act of 1964. The act requires that your employer provide you with the same rights, resources, accommodations, and benefits as other employees who are on temporary disability due to illness or injury. It also dictates that your employer must allow you to work as long as you are physically able to do your job. Keep in mind that the act only applies to businesses with more than fifteen employees; and, if your employer does not provide disability benefits to injured or ill employees, there will be no benefits for your pregnancy either.

Pregnancy Pointer

If you belong to a union, talk to your union representative about maternity and paternity leave under your contract. You may have additional rights and benefits that aren't available to nonunion employees at your workplace, and in some cases these can exceed the benefits covered by state and federal law.

If you're searching for a new position while pregnant, the Pregnancy Discrimination Act protects you from prejudice on the basis of your pregnancy. Still, legalities aside, pregnancy may make your interviewer look for other viable reasons not to hire you. It's illegal for a potential employer to ask if you're pregnant or not in the interview, and you certainly aren't required to volunteer the information. However, if the job is offered to you, it is probably in your best interest to mention your pregnancy during final negotiations. You want to start your working relationship off on the right foot and address up front any concerns your prospective employer has.

The Family and Medical Leave Act (FMLA)

If you or your spouse works for a public agency, a private or public elementary or secondary school, or a company with more than fifty employees for a period of at least a year, you have coverage under the Family and Medical Leave Act (FMLA). The FMLA provides for up to 12 weeks of unpaid leave within a 12-month period for medical and family caretaking reasons, including the care of a newborn child. Both moms and dads are eligible as long as they meet the employment criteria.

Pregnancy Pointer

New parents who have been denied FMLA leave from their employer and believe they are eligible can file a complaint with the U.S. Department of Labor (DOL). The complaint must be filed within 2 years of the incident. Call the DOL at 1-866-4USWAGE for further information.

The FMLA also enables you to take unpaid time off if you experience health problems during pregnancy and your employer does not provide disability or sick-day benefits. The same goes for extended time off that you might require to care for your child should she have any health problems at birth. Again, the total time off provided for under the FMLA is not to exceed a total of 12 weeks in 12 months.

State Law

Depending on where you live, your state may mandate certain employee rights related to pregnancy and maternity benefits under workers' compensation laws. Check with the labor department or other applicable organization in your state to find out more.

OCCUPATIONAL HAZARDS

Depending on your position and work environment, you might have to alter your duties temporarily or request a change in location or accommodations. If your job involves any of the following conditions, talk with your human resources department about your options:

- **Weight lifting.** Lifting heavy packages, boxes, or other items (for example, shipping and receiving clerks, warehouse work) is not recommended in pregnancy, especially past week 20.
- **Secondhand smoke.** Women who work in the hospitality industry (for example, bartenders, waitresses) expose their fetuses to toxins in secondhand smoke.
- **High heat.** Excessive temperatures (for example, summer construction, factory environment) can be harmful to fetal development, particularly in the first trimester.
- **Teratogen exposure.** Jobs that involve working with certain chemicals and hazardous substances (for example, welders and lead exposure, dry cleaners and benzene exposure) are linked to birth defects.
- **Standing and repetitive movement.** Line work or other jobs that keep you on your feet all day (for example, factory jobs, assembly work, piece work) can exacerbate circulatory problems.
- **Ionizing radiation exposure.** Pregnant pilots and flight crew may be exposed to excessive ionizing radiation, another known teratogen. Radiographic imaging technicians who work with X-rays, CT scanning equipment, and nuclear medicine are also at risk.

BREAKING THE NEWS

In an ideal world, the news of your impending motherhood would be greeted with congratulations and reassurances at the office. Instead, reality may find you strategizing to prevent a negative employer reaction and determining the right time to drop the pregnancy bombshell for minimal fallout to your career. That pregnancy should be considered a handicap to be overcome rather than the positive, life-affirming force it is remains a glaring reminder of how far women still have to go to achieve equality in the workplace.

Belly Basics

According to the American Academy of Family Physicians (AAFP), the maximum safe fetal radiation dose during pregnancy is 5 rad. If you require X-rays or other radiological tests during pregnancy, the benefits of imaging need to be weighed against the potential risk to the fetus. If at all possible, tests involving radiation should be avoided during pregnancy. If the test is needed, however, radiology staff will do everything possible to minimize your exposure.

When you do inform your employer, make sure he hears it directly from you and not by way of the water cooler. Accompany the news with your tentative schedule for maternity leave so that your manager can plan accordingly. Offering suggestions for a replacement in your absence or ways to temporarily reassign workload will reflect well on you and your perceived commitment to your employer.

AVOIDING THE "MOMMY TRACK" TRAP

Once you share your news, you may suddenly find yourself on a slow road to nowhere at work—last in the information loop and out of the running for promotions and job advancements you were previously an easy pick for. Goodbye fast track and hello mommy track? Is it unavoidable?

Not necessarily. Employers who realize that a happy employee is more likely to be a productive employee won't punish you for pursuing a personal life. And if you continue to perform well and make it clear to your supervisors that you'd like to have a career path with the company rather than just a job, you're more likely to avoid the so-called "mommy track." Still, whether the mommy track exists in your organization or not depends on the corporate culture and the attitudes of upper management. Do they support family-friendly policies? Do they lead by example and make use of benefits like paternity and maternity leave themselves? And are efforts made to institute initiatives that benefit employees across the board, from the security staff to the CEO?

The Ideal versus the Real

In the real world, some organizations reward those who invest themselves more fully in the workplace than in family. The result is an atmosphere in which pregnancy is construed as a choice against company and career, a choice that may be tolerated for the sake of political correctness but that certainly isn't supported through policies and reward systems. The good news is that there are family-friendly employers who put their benefits packages where their mouth is. See where your company lies between these two extremes:

The ideal . . . a fully equipped lactation facility.
The real . . . a bathroom stall with a broken lock.

The ideal . . . paid time off for prenatal appointments.
The real . . . isn't that what lunch hours are for?

The ideal . . . expectant-mother parking spaces near the entrance.
The real . . . unless you are a VIP, it's first come, first served.

The ideal . . . a pregnant supervisor to commiserate with.
The real . . . your bachelor boss is a freshly minted MBA who thinks "family-friendly policy" means Christmas off with pay.

The ideal . . . a flexible schedule for your unpredictable pregnant body.
The real . . . don't forget to punch out for bathroom breaks.

The ideal . . . 4 months of maternity leave with full pay and benefits.
The real . . . with luck, that partial disability pay should arrive before your child's first birthday.

Defining Personal and Professional Goals

What do you want out of life, both personally and professionally, now that your family is changing? If this is your first child, it can be hard to fully assess the new direction you're taking. But there are probably some basic decisions you can make with a degree of certainty. For example, late shifts and working double overtime may be out of the picture for you now.

....

Pregnancy Pointer

If you work in an environment that isn't healthy for you or your growing baby, talk to your human resources department about a temporary reassignment to a more appropriate position. Jobs that involve chemical exposure, heavy manual labor, or staying on your feet all day with no opportunity for rest should all be reconsidered during pregnancy.

....

Perhaps you have career goals that you'd like to keep on target. Should they be mutually exclusive of motherhood? No. Might they be, depending on where you work? Yes. If you wanted to move into a supervisory position at your next review but see your company promoting only those who work excessive overtime, you have choices to make. Such is the delicate balance of motherhood. Fortunately, you always have the option to look for a workplace that is more in harmony with your personal and professional goals—or to take your own path, whatever it may be.

Realize Your Value

Think of full-time motherhood as another job offer on the table for your employer to stack up to. Your company could be willing to sweeten the pot with flextime, telecommuting, or other family-friendly working arrangements to keep you happy. Remember, in most cases it has poured a significant amount of money and resources into your training. The loss of that investment plus the cost of hiring and training a new employee is a big financial incentive for keeping you on board. Don't be afraid to rock the boat. Realize your value and use it as a bargaining chip.

Negotiate Toward Your Goal

Think about using your maternity leave as a launching pad for alternative working arrangements. For example, if you would like more than the 6 weeks of paid leave your company offers and would ultimately like some flexibility in your schedule, suggest a work arrangement like telecommuting for another 6 weeks following paid leave. If you're covered by the FMLA, your employer must give you 12 weeks off without pay to care for your newborn, if you request it. By offering an alternative to your complete absence, you appear flexible and dedicated, and your employer certainly has nothing to lose by trying such an arrangement. Even if you aren't prepared to take 6 weeks off unpaid should your employer turn you down, it's well worth the gamble to suggest the idea. You can always scale back your plans if your request isn't granted. And if it is accepted and works out well, you will have proven yourself for handling a more permanent arrangement down the road.

PRACTICAL MATTERS

No matter what your job, staying comfortable, relatively stressless, and economically secure during your pregnancy is essential.

Staying Comfortable

Pregnant women who do work on their feet should make a habit of changing positions often and moving when possible. Wear comfortable shoes and consider support stockings.

For jobs that require a lot of sit-down time, make sure you have an ergonomically appropriate chair that promotes good posture. A lumbar support pad can help ease pregnancy-related lower-back pain, and you can put up your feet under your desk on a small stool or even on a stack of phone books. If you work a desk job, look for opportunities to get up and about. Take a walk to speak with a coworker instead of picking up the phone, or hand-deliver a memo instead of using e-mail.

Scheduling Doctor Visits

With luck, your employer recognizes that good prenatal care translates to a healthier, more productive employee and, in the long run, to less time spent out of the office to care for sick kids. However, if you do face resistance in taking time off for doctor visits, remember that prenatal care is considered necessary medical care and is covered under the FMLA. If all else fails, you can invoke your legal rights.

Pregnancy Pointers

FMLA also allows work leave for an illness you have or to care for an ill family member. You or your spouse can therefore use it during your pregnancy as well as after the birth.

In the meantime, find out whether your provider has evening, weekend, or early morning appointments that might fit around your workday. If you must go during office hours and your supervisor isn't pleased, offer her the alternative option of taking the entire day off as vacation or unpaid leave instead. Perhaps she'll look upon your short absence in a new light.

If you're getting static for meeting basic prenatal care requirements now, just think what it will be like when you need time off to care for a sick child or to keep a well-baby appointment. File a mental note: family unfriendly. Companies that score poorly in supporting their pregnant employees will probably continue the trend postpregnancy. If too many red flags are raised during your pregnancy, once you reach maternity leave it's probably time to look for a company that recognizes the value of personal as well as professional fulfillment in their employees.

Controlling Stress

The workplace can be a stress hotbed. Deadlines, personality conflicts, difficult clients, quotas, overtime, and more make for a pressure cooker that's not good for you or baby. Try to maintain some perspective and peace of mind by realizing that petty office politics means little in comparison to the health and well-being of your child.

Remember that others don't control your feelings; you do. If work pressures and the attitudes of others are starting to wear you down, consider a yoga or meditation class to keep yourself balanced. And when possible, take a short mental health break during the work day to decompress. A regular lunchtime walk can help clear your mind and it's good exercise as well.

MATERNITY LEAVE

Your bonding time with baby should be free of workplace concerns. If you plan appropriately for your absence as early as possible, you'll get more out of your time off. It's a good idea to put all maternity leave plans in writing for your supervisor and appropriate managers and to make an extra copy for placement in your personnel file.

....

Pregnancy Pointer

According to a 2010 benefits survey performed by the Society for Human Resource Management, paid paternity leave was offered by only 17 percent of companies polled. If your workplace doesn't offer paid paternity leave, dads may qualify for unpaid time off under the Family Medical Leave Act.

....

Planning Ahead for Leave

Lay the groundwork for your maternity leave so that there won't be too many questions or crises in your absence. If appropriate for your position, delegate some tasks to coworkers and arrange coverage by others. Find out if your supervisor plans on hiring temporary help to fill in during your absence, and prepare training materials and checklists so that you won't face a mess upon your return to the workplace.

Check and double-check that all appropriate paperwork for benefits has been filled out, signed, and sent in well in advance of your planned departure. Maternity leave should be a low-stress time, not one that requires twice-weekly contact with human resources to find out the status of your disability claim.

How Many Weeks?

So, just how much, or how little, maternity leave should you take? Certainly the benefits your company provides will play a major factor in your decision. If you have quite a bit of seniority, you may be able to swing an even longer leave by tapping into accrued vacation time. Other factors to consider include:

- **Money.** How much time off can you afford if your maternity benefits are minimal or nonexistent? Don't forget to factor into your equation any money you'll be saving (that is, dry cleaning bills, lunches out, transportation expenses) by not working.
- **Management.** Even though you may be legally within your rights, in some organizations an extended maternity leave may be frowned upon by those above you. Consider what management might think and, more importantly, what kind of priority you should place on their disapproval.
- **Morale.** Are your coworkers and/or subordinates happy and motivated or disillusioned and resentful? Employees who work as a team and feel invested in their workplace are more likely to rise to the challenge in your absence.
- **Malleability.** Does employment have to be all or nothing? Think about offering some creative proposals for extending your leave, such as a reduced part-time schedule or the prospect of telecommuting.

Evaluating your leave options will reveal the pluses and negatives in your company's attitudes toward personal employee fulfillment. If morale is poor and management unyielding, once you've gotten past maternity leave it may be time to consider your work alternatives.

FULL-TIME AT HOME

Becoming a full-time mom is an exciting new venture for many women. If you can afford to stay home without working for someone else, go for it. Pouring your skills and knowledge into parenthood can be enormously fulfilling and in fact is probably the most rewarding job you'll ever have.

Finally, consider the possibility of forging your own family-friendly path. In today's wired world, many occupations lend themselves to home-based work; writing, income tax preparation, desktop publishing, and web design are naturals. If the field you currently work in is unfulfilling and you'd like to make a change, look to the hobbies you enjoy for some ideas. Refinishing antiques, creating crafts for retail, sewing, and painting are a few activities that might be a good fit for a new career. Starting something new is never easy, but just experiencing the miracle of your developing child can help you envision widening possibilities.

Work Leaves and Career Changes

No matter what your career, having a baby has some impact on you because you need to take at least some time off from work. How much time you want or need is an individual choice. Some women make plans, but then find that once the baby comes, their feelings have changed. They either want more time off or feel they are ready to return to work sooner than they thought. Nothing you decide is written in stone. Before you can make maternity leave plans, you must first find out your options.

Chapter 11
FEELING GOOD THROUGHOUT PREGNANCY

With the busyness and exhaustion of pregnancy, it is sometimes easy to lose sight of the one person who needs you the most—yourself. You should embrace your changing body and changing psyche throughout pregnancy. This is a life-changing experience, and one that you should enjoy, rather than simply tolerate, counting the days until it is over.

LOVING YOUR PREGNANT SELF

In a society that emphasizes appearance, and worships thinness, it can be difficult to watch helplessly as not only your abdomen expands but as you also see changes to almost every other part of your body. Learning to accept and love a larger body can be a challenge for many women.

Pregnancy can be difficult to adjust to for women who have struggled with body image all their lives, but it can be equally difficult for women who have never had conflicting feelings about their body. Whether you've always been thin, have always been overweight, or have yo-yoed, it can be difficult to embrace your new shape. Perhaps the thing that is most frustrating is that suddenly your body is out of your control. People are used to controlling and shaping their bodies through exercise and diet, but in pregnancy, you can't prevent change.

Some women are really displeased with the changes in their body and think themselves to be fat, misshapen, or unattractive. Other women thoroughly enjoy pregnancy, reveling in their new shape and enjoying the fact that for once in their lives they do not have to struggle to retain their figure.

Pregnancy Pointer

If you have an eating disorder, it is essential that you tell your health-care provider. Failing to eat enough, or eating and purging, can deprive your baby of essential nutrients, and you could face miscarriage, preterm labor, birth defects, or a low birth-weight baby. If you are an overeater, it is also important that you work with your health-care provider to limit your weight gain.

If you are feeling uncomfortable with your burgeoning body, or the prospect of pregnancy changes yet to come, there are things you can do to continue to feel good about yourself and your physical changes. First, take positive steps for your health. Doing things that are good for your body, such as exercising and eating healthy foods, will make you feel good physically and will give you a mental and emotional boost.

Take the time to remember that your body is performing a miracle. Appreciate the miracle, even if you aren't so pleased with the outward consequences. Remember that every pound you gain is another important benefit to your baby and that as your body changes, so does your baby. Your baby loves you and your body exactly the way it is.

Try to focus on the pregnant glow you're giving off, and accentuate the parts of your body that you appreciate. Many women are excited to see their breasts get larger, for example. Touching your own body will help you feel more comfortable with it, and the tactile connection will bring together your body and your mind. Try to be accepting and appreciative of the changes you experience, and remember there are many women who cannot ever experience this. Pregnancy is giving the gift of your body to another human being. Once the pregnancy is over, you can start to regain your body—the gift is not permanent.

ACCEPTING THAT YOU MUST DO LESS

For many women who have lives that are happily full with careers, relationships, friends, activities, and interests, it can sometimes be difficult to let pregnancy step in and slow them down. It's easy to say to yourself that pregnancy won't change anything and while having a baby may require some minor adjustments, everything in life can go on as it did before. However, the truth is that pregnancy does require changes, and being a mother is more life-altering than you think it will be.

Just because you are pregnant you don't need to quit your job, cancel your gym membership, and relegate yourself to the recliner all day. It's important to stay active, do the things you love, and follow your interests during pregnancy. However, the simple fact is that there will be days when you're tired, sick, puffy, cranky, weepy, or just huge. And on these days, you will find that your previous schedule just doesn't cut it.

If you try and push yourself, refusing to yield to the needs of your changing body, you will probably find yourself extremely tired and overwhelmed. Your body has taken on a gigantic project of its own, and it needs some of your focus and energy to complete it. Thinking that pregnancy doesn't have to have an impact on your life at all is not realistic.

Pregnancy Pointer

A study done in Poland found that heavy physical labor at work during pregnancy was linked to low birth-weight babies, whereas simply expending a lot of energy at work was not as clear a risk factor for low birth weight. The study showed that pregnant women need to be careful when it comes to heavy work, but there is no danger in using a lot of energy during pregnancy.

You can continue to do everything you want to do, but in moderation. Or you may find there are some things you want to cut out of your life to make more room for other things that are more important to you. For example, you may sign up for prenatal yoga and decide to drop your book club. During pregnancy your body is making adjustments, and you will probably find that you need to make adjustments in your daily life as well.

It's essential to continue to do the things that make you happy, keep you healthy, and keep you fulfilled. If you listen to your body, you'll find ways to trim back, find shortcuts, or make substitutions that will adjust things for your pregnant needs. You need to find a balance that works for you during pregnancy. Keep in mind that your life will always be changing from this point on, as your newborn baby grows and goes through different stages. Motherhood is all about change. You need to be prepared to be flexible so that you can adjust your life to your child's needs and your needs.

To continue to do things you love during pregnancy, consider making some adjustments such as these:

- Decrease the amount of time spent on the activity, such as half an hour gardening instead of an hour.
- Take a lighter approach to the task, such as baking one batch of Christmas cookies instead of five at a time.
- Rely on conveniences, such as delivery, Internet shopping, or free carry-out service.
- Decrease the frequency, such as working late only one night a week instead of two.
- Quit sooner, such as heading home to bed at 11 P.M. instead of staying out till 1 A.M.
- Sit down more often throughout any task.
- Come prepared with food and water to any activity so you don't get hungry and thirsty.

CHANGING YOUR PERCEPTION OF WHO YOU ARE

Becoming a mother doesn't have to change who you are. Still, it is likely that your pregnancy has started to create a paradigm shift inside you, and you're changing your priorities. This can be a bit nerve-wracking and uncomfortable, but it is the beginning of becoming a mother and is something that will soon come more naturally.

Once you become pregnant, you suddenly change from being a person who is responsible for herself to being a mother with a baby to care for. This can be a dramatic shift. It can feel frightening to suddenly give your body and your life over to someone else. You may feel a bit lost in all the changes and uncertain of who you really are anymore.

As your life starts to change and you begin to see yourself as a mother, don't lose your perception of who else you are and what else is important to you. If you have a full and active life before getting pregnant, it's unlikely that you'll feel satisfied if you relegate the rest of your identity away so you can be "just a mother." Take the time to enjoy your newfound motherhood, though. Pregnancy is fleeting, as are the newborn days. Remind yourself to simply enjoy each day as it comes, even as you are balancing motherhood with the other parts of your life.

Now that you're adding "mom" to your list of responsibilities, it may be time to take stock of who you really are and who you really want to be. For example, some women decide that as much as they have enjoyed their career, a baby means a change to becoming an at-home mom, even if only for a few years. Other women find that the prospect of becoming a mother makes them rededicate themselves to a goal or a way of life, such as finding time to create art or becoming more spiritual. Take the time to explore who you are at this stage of your life and where you want to go from here.

LISTENING TO YOUR BODY

You often hear people recommending that you listen to your body during pregnancy. This may be easier said than done. Learning to home in on the signals your body sends you is an important way to monitor your pregnancy.

The first thing to remember is that although it certainly affects your mental state, pregnancy is something that happens in your body, not your mind. You aren't in control of it, and you can't direct it. It may even seem like you are at its mercy. Because it is a physical condition, you need to learn to interpret the clues your body sends you and determine what they mean.

One important thing to remember during pregnancy is that your body really means business. When you're not pregnant, you may be able to work through fatigue, ignore thirst, bypass hunger, or push through discomfort. During pregnancy, however, you need to learn to pay heed to these signals. When you're thirsty, drink. When you're hungry, eat. Rest when you're tired. Those rules may seem obvious, but many women who have had years of experience controlling their bodies find it can be difficult to unlearn those controlling impulses.

Belly Basics

If you want to take the advice to listen to your body literally, you can purchase or rent a handheld Doppler that will allow you to listen to your baby's heartbeat. Dopplers are considered safe during pregnancy and can be a great way to bond with your baby, but they do not work well until the fourth or fifth month. Additionally, it can be hard to find the heartbeat when the baby is very active.

Fatigue is another important signal from your body. There may seem to be absolutely no reason why you should feel so tired, but what you must remember is that your body is working extremely hard building and supporting a new life. This takes vast amounts of energy. Here are some other signs that should not be ignored during pregnancy:

- **Bleeding or spotting:** While many women bleed or spot without consequences, it is always something you should be aware of and, if your health-care provider indicates, may be a sign you need to slow down. It is always a good idea to call your provider any time you have bleeding during pregnancy.

- **Pain:** Always consult your health-care provider about any pain during pregnancy, and always stop any activity that causes you pain.

- **Contractions:** While Braxton-Hicks contractions are normal in late pregnancy, painful, ongoing, or strong contractions are not, and they should be reported to your health-care provider. This kind of contraction means you need to stop whatever activity you are doing and rest. The key is that contraction sensations have a rhythm; they come and go. If you are in doubt, lie down quietly and put your hand over your uterus. If it is a contraction, you will feel the uterus become hard and then relax. If these increase in frequency, duration, and intensity, it may be preterm labor. If you are in doubt, always call your provider.

- **Swelling:** Edema, or swelling, is common in pregnancy, but it should be discussed with your health-care provider. Continued swelling is a sign you need to elevate that part of your body. Sudden and progressive swelling of the hands and face or rapid weight gain of three to five pounds may be a problem. You should call your provider and have your blood pressure checked and urine tested for protein.

- **Faintness:** Feeling dizzy or faint is something you should let your health-care provider know about, but when you experience it you need to sit or lie down. If you haven't eaten recently, do so.

- **Nausea:** This is the most common pregnancy complaint and is something you have to pay heed to. If a food makes you feel nauseous, don't eat it.

- **Discomfort:** While there's no getting around discomfort, particularly in late pregnancy, use your discomfort as a clue. If your groin muscles hurt, learn about exercises to strengthen them. If your feet hurt, put them up more often and wear more comfortable shoes.

- **Intuition:** Some women sometimes have a sense that something simply is not right with their bodies or their pregnancy. If you feel this way, don't ignore it. Tell your health-care provider, and find out if there is a basis for this warning sign.

NOT LETTING PREGNANCY TAKE OVER YOUR LIFE

If you're worried about getting a mommy brain, you're not alone. Many women, particularly those who are older and have careers, are loath to let themselves be defined by their growing uterus, or later by the baby they hold in their arms.

It can be a struggle to keep your pregnancy from taking over every aspect of your life—your health, your home, your job, your relationship, and more. It's important to remember that you will be a better mother if you continue to have a sense of self and continue to live a life that satisfies your own unique needs. Resting and taking care of yourself now is important, just as spending lots of time with your baby will be important once you're a mother. At the same time, refusing to let yourself be entirely defined by your parenthood status can help you keep your head screwed on straight.

Sometimes it's easy to get completely caught up in the pregnancy whirlwind. You're buying maternity clothes, comparing baby monitors, deciding between cloth or disposables, rearranging your schedule, interviewing nannies, trying to understand breastfeeding basics, and more. It's okay to delve into these new and exciting things. After all, how will you ever fully understand them and come to grips with them if you don't? But at some point you may find you need to take a step back and realize that the choice between green or yellow crib bedding may not be as crucial as it can sometimes come to seem.

There are also times when you may need to remind people that there is more to you than that bump growing out in front of you. You shouldn't be sidelined from important work projects or passed over for an important role in your favorite charity's next event just because you're pregnant. Sometimes you have to make the extra effort to let people know you're still interested in being yourself and doing the things that you've always done. Often people think they are helping you by making things easier. They may not realize that you don't want your condition to be a deciding factor.

While achieving balance is so important in keeping you sane and happy, it's also important to realize that there are times when things *should* be out of balance. For example, as you get closer to your due date, more of your thoughts and energy will turn to the baby and the upcoming delivery. This is normal and good. Similarly, it is terrific if you have a very busy week at work during your second trimester and get very wrapped up in a deadline and don't think much about the pregnancy or the baby. Let your priorities naturally set themselves, and you will find that you can achieve a long-term level of balance in your life.

DRESSING THE PART

Baby on board? Although you definitely have a baby on board, you probably are looking for maternity clothes that fit your own sense of style and meet your daily needs. It is possible to dress like a grownup and be pregnant at the same time.

You will probably want to continue to wear your own clothes for as long as possible. You can stretch their usefulness by buying waistband expanders. There is also a product called Bella Band that allows you to wear your pants unbuttoned and partially unzipped by slipping a large fabric elastic band over it. You can buy expanders for your bras as well to give them a little longer life.

There are more choices than ever before for well-designed, quality maternity clothes. The first rule of dressing for pregnancy is to stick to what works for you. If you didn't like jumpers before you were pregnant, you're not going to like them now, so don't even consider them. Remember who you are and choose clothes that reflect that. Select colors and fabrics that appeal to your taste. Don't feel like you have to veer off into unfamiliar territory just because that's what your local maternity store is showing. You can maintain your sense of self by relying on accessories you like and that work well for you.

Some women like to purchase regular women's clothes (non-maternity) in larger sizes. This is a great way to find fashionable clothes, but they may not last to the end of your pregnancy. Your belly will grow so large by the end that normal shirts are too short in the front and normal pants will not fit over it. It is, however, a good way to shop for basics such as T-shirts, pantyhose, and other items that you can wear underneath other clothes. Additionally, some women like to wear some of their partner's clothes, at least around the house.

Shop online for the biggest selection of maternity clothes. Remember that many pregnant women find they get hot easily, especially in the last trimester, so avoid items that are very heavy. Tight clothes can be especially uncomfortable during pregnancy. Pants and skirts that are expandable are a good bet so that you can wear them smaller in the beginning and open them up to full size at the end.

Maternity clothes in general are not made to last. Most women wear items for about five months total. If you're working full-time and are trying to limit what you're spending, you're going to be wearing the same pieces over and over, so buy quality clothes that will last. If you have friends or family members with children, they may be able to lend you some of their better items, adding to your wardrobe. There is also a very brisk business for maternity clothes at secondhand stores and on eBay.

You may find you need to purchase new shoes during pregnancy. Very high heels are not recommended in pregnancy because coupled with a large uterus, they can throw your balance off.

If you experience a lot of swelling, your current shoes may no longer fit. In addition, some women find that their feet actually grow during pregnancy. This is due to the hormone relaxin, which helps relax your joints during pregnancy and can cause your feet to become longer. Foot swelling usually goes away within a month after delivery, but any foot stretching due to loose ligaments is permanent. Don't wear tight shoes. Not only do they hurt, they can also cause a lot of problems such as ingrown nails, calluses, or corns. Additionally, very uncomfortable shoes make it harder to walk and can seriously affect your balance.

FEELING GOOD THROUGHOUT YOUR PREGNANCY

Pregnancy is an ever-changing condition. One minute you're sick, the next you're not. One minute you're excited, the next you're terrified. Staying focused and remaining positive will help you feel better mentally and physically throughout your pregnancy.

Managing Stress

During your pregnancy, you're dealing with a lot of changes, as well as the thought of many more changes to come in the future. You are probably thrilled to experience these changes. At the same time, it can be very stressful to manage all of these new things and cope with the physical limitations you may be encountering.

Several studies have shown that very high levels of stress can contribute to preterm birth and low birth weights in babies. Note that we're not talking about everyday momentary stress, such as getting a little upset in traffic or feeling bad because you flubbed a presentation. This is ongoing high-level stress, the kind that is unhealthy for anyone. Ongoing stress during pregnancy can cause fatigue, problems sleeping, lack of appetite, overeating, headaches, and backaches. While some stress is unavoidable, controlling the stress levels in your life can help you feel better during pregnancy.

Physical Stresses

Pregnancy is all about your changing body. It can be very frustrating to suddenly feel as though your entire life is ruled by your physical condition. You do have to listen to your body during pregnancy, but you don't have to let it stop you from doing the things that are important to you. Pregnancy stress and mood swings are often caused in part by blood sugar changes, hormonal fluctuations, and even water retention. Mood swings tend to even out midway through pregnancy, but many women experience them until the baby is born.

Learning to manage the physical demands of pregnancy means changing your expectations. You can still do almost all of the things you enjoy, but you may need to modify them. For example, if you've always loved hiking, you can still do it, but you may need to take more frequent breaks, go shorter distances, or choose less-challenging paths. Make compromises with yourself and your pregnancy that you can do the physical things you want to do in a way that keeps your body comfortable and healthy.

Surprise Stressors

Pregnancy can make your emotions unpredictable and unstable at times. Things that have never bothered you can suddenly become unbearable. For reasons you can't explain, or even understand yourself, a small annoyance can erupt into what feels like a crisis. While these unexpected upsets can definitely keep you on your toes, they can also make you feel like a giant heap of uncontrolled hormones.

Accept that sometimes you will unexpectedly find yourself crying or angry about things that previously might not have made a hill of beans of difference to you. Part of the difficulty in these situations is that you feel frustrated at yourself for reacting in a way that might seem uncharacteristic. It can be difficult to relinquish control of your emotions to your pregnancy, but struggling against it can actually create more internal stress. You're not losing your mind or becoming out of control if you find that your emotions overwhelm you during pregnancy; you're simply reacting to the signals your body is sending out.

....

Pregnancy Pointer

If you and your partner do not share a last name, you may be wondering what name your baby can have. You can choose either name, a combination, or a completely different last name for your baby. You do so simply by entering this on the birth certificate application.

....

Stress Relief Techniques

One of the keys to coping with stress is to pinpoint what exactly is bothering you. Many times there may be nothing specific because your hormones are simply making you weepy, but sometimes there are specific triggers that you can identify and then work on. Whether you are worried about a project at work, upset because the nursery hasn't been painted, feeling neglected by your partner, or are overtired, you can best cope with the stress if you're able to first isolate its cause. Once you have done that, work to reduce, resolve, or eliminate the problem. Of course, many problems can't be made to go away, and so there are some things you have to learn to cope with.

To help relieve and reduce your stress during pregnancy, do the following:

- Eat healthy meals and snacks regularly, and drink enough water.
- Exercise regularly, if your health-care provider approves.
- Get enough sleep, and rest when you need to.
- Avoid caffeine and alcohol, which are not considered acceptable during pregnancy and can add to your stress.
- Try soothing techniques, such as yoga, massage, meditation, baths, or other activities that bring you joy and pleasure. Breathing exercises or medication can also be very relaxing.
- Talk to friends and family about the things that are bothering you. Bottling stress up inside of you only makes it worse.

Remember that all pregnancy-related stresses are temporary. Pregnancy doesn't last forever, and your life is in an intense period of change. What seems unbearable today may become a mere blip on your radar tomorrow. Remind yourself that you will get through this, and you will work through anything that is troubling or bothering you.

DEALING WITH WORRIES AND FEARS

At some point, just about every pregnant woman worries about whether her baby will be okay, and she feels nervous about birth. These are normal reactions to pregnancy. While they can make you feel unsettled, they are not something you should dwell on.

The whole point of your pregnancy is to have a healthy baby, and most women are well aware that there are many things that can go wrong. However, the odds are that you will have a healthy baby. Your health-care provider can help ease your fears. It's his job to help make sure that your baby grows well and comes into the world healthy. Some health-care providers tell their patients to let them worry about the unlikely possibilities and ask the patient to keep her mind focused on enjoying pregnancy.

If you've never given birth before, labor and delivery is a new thing for you. New experiences are always a little frightening simply because you can't completely know what to expect in advance. If you are fearful or nervous about birth, the best thing you can do is take a childbirth preparation class. The class will provide you with a lot of information and help you talk through your fears. You will also learn techniques that will put you in control during labor and delivery and help you manage your fears at that time.

Pregnancy Pointer

Some studies have shown that women with extremely stressful jobs are at a higher risk for preeclampsia, a dangerous high blood pressure condition in pregnancy. If you have a job that is very high pressure, talk to your health-care provider about what you can do to ensure a healthy pregnancy.

Talking to other moms may help with your fears, or it may make them worse. Don't talk to people who are intent on sharing their horror stories with you.

Remember that each woman is different. Your experience will be your own, not a re-enactment of someone else's. Talking to your health-care provider can also ease your worries. Let her know what aspect of birth you are most worried about, and she can talk you through it and help you understand that she will be there to help you get through it.

SEX AND INTIMACY

It's ironic that intercourse is what begins a pregnancy and then becomes something many women aren't very interested in. There are lots of ways to stay connected to your partner during pregnancy, and intercourse is only one of them.

....

Pregnancy Pointer

Talk to your health-care provider about any restrictions on your sex life. If you experience vaginal bleeding, leak amniotic fluid, have an incompetent cervix, are having preterm labor, have a history of miscarriages, or are having problems with your pregnancy, intercourse is not recommended.

....

Sexual intimacy and sex are safe throughout pregnancy, all the way to the end. It cannot hurt the baby, who is not aware of what you are doing. Having orgasms does not cause you to go into labor or have a miscarriage. Orgasms can sometimes cause uterine contractions, though. In an otherwise-normal pregnancy, this poses no risk. However, if your pregnancy is at high risk for premature labor or delivery, it is not clear if orgasms that cause contractions may pose a risk; you should speak with your health-care provider.

However, just because sex is safe doesn't mean it's at the top of the list for some women. In early pregnancy, nausea and fatigue can play a big part in reducing a woman's interest in sex. During the second trimester, interest in sex often returns, sometimes very strongly. During the third trimester, backache, fatigue, and the size of the uterus can make sex again become complicated. Many moms will tell you that sex can work to relieve some of your symptoms and can be a great way to relax during pregnancy.

Some women feel nervous about sexual intercourse during the first trimester because they worry it may cause miscarriage. This may especially be true for women who have a problem with repetitive miscarriages or who have had fertility problems. Although there is no evidence that intercourse causes miscarriage, many women still are apprehensive. If this is something you are worried about, it's perfectly fine to hold off on intercourse until you have an ultrasound or until the first trimester is over.

Oral sex is safe during pregnancy, as long as your partner does not blow air into your vagina. The air may enter the large blood vessels that supply the vagina and cervix and travel to the heart; this is called an air embolism, and can be fatal. Anal intercourse during pregnancy is not dangerous, but due to engorgement of the hemorrhoidal veins or hemorrhoids during pregnancy, it may be uncomfortable or may cause bleeding.

Sex toys are something many women wonder about and on which there is no clear consensus. If sex toys are not cleaned meticulously, they can cause infection. If they are inserted too deeply or too forcefully, they can cause injury. If you would like to use sex toys during pregnancy, it's a good idea to talk with your health-care provider first. Don't be embarrassed to discuss this. Any health-care provider will be happy to talk about this and would much prefer to have a frank, unembarrassed conversation than have a patient sustain an injury.

No sexual activity (penile penetration, sex toy, or oral sex) should ever involve going from the anal orifice to the vagina since this can introduce infection. Some women find that pregnancy greatly increases their sex drive. If you experience this, it is completely normal. The hormonal fluctuations of pregnancy play a part in how interested you are in sex.

Because there is increased blood supply to vaginal and cervical tissues during pregnancy, mild vaginal bleeding or spotting may occur after intercourse, especially if the penis bumps against the cervix during sex. If this occurs after sex, don't panic; it does not hurt the baby. You should, however, always contact your health-care provider immediately if any bleeding occurs during pregnancy regardless of the circumstances.

Nipple stimulation can definitely cause contractions and even induce labor in the third trimester. The effect can be as powerful as the drug oxytocin which is used to induce labor. Because of this, excessive nipple stimulation should be avoided during pregnancy. This is especially important in pregnancies already at risk for premature delivery.

If you find you're not interested in intercourse, you and your partner can satisfy each other in other ways. It's important to remember that you can find ways to feel close to your partner that do not involve intercourse or sexual behavior. Just spending time together, holding hands, having him rub your back, or doing things together to prepare for the baby can give you a sense of closeness and connectedness.

Belly Basics

In a survey done by Babycenter.com, 40 percent of women surveyed said that pregnancy drastically reduced the amount of sex they were having. For tips and good advice, read *Hot Mamas: The Ultimate Guide to Staying Sexy Throughout Your Pregnancy and the Months Beyond*, by Lou Paget.

Some women worry that their partner will no longer find them to be attractive as their body changes throughout pregnancy. Usually this is an unfounded worry. A loving and caring partner loves you for who you are and is thrilled to watch as the child develops. Many men find pregnant women beautiful and attractive at every stage. If this is something you're worried about, talk about it with your partner. Find out how he is feeling, and share your own concerns or worries. It is likely you will be able to find a way to keep both of you satisfied and happy throughout your pregnancy.

Another concern of many women is that giving birth will permanently change their vagina so that sex will never be the same again. The vagina is able to stretch and retract. While having a baby does change your body, it does not mean you'll never enjoy sex again or that your partner will not find as much pleasure in you after you have a baby. Wait until after your postpartum checkup before having sex.

COPING WITH PREGNANCY PROBLEMS

Hopefully, your pregnancy will go smoothly, but even if you encounter some problems, you can still get through them and have a healthy baby. A wide variety of problems or complications can arise in a pregnancy. Your health-care provider can manage and control most of these.

It's important to remember that most pregnancy problems are minor. Puffy ankles might not be fun, but most of the time they aren't extremely serious. Because you're getting good medical care, your health-care provider will be able to spot problems and take steps to reduce any risks.

Blame

It's not uncommon for women to blame themselves for things that go wrong during pregnancy. "I must have done something to cause this," or "There are things I could have done that would have prevented this from happening" are common thoughts. What you must realize, though, is there is most likely nothing you did or didn't do that brought about whatever problem you are experiencing. Remind yourself of all the things you've done to stay healthy—seen a health-care provider, eaten healthy foods, and avoided drugs, tobacco, and alcohol.

Belly Basics

After the fourth month of pregnancy, a woman should not lie flat on her back because the weight of the uterus places pressure on blood vessels. Because of this, the missionary position is not recommended for sex after the fourth month of pregnancy.

Blaming yourself is not helpful. It doesn't really matter what exactly caused your complication to arise since you can't change what has happened. What you can do, however, is move forward with your health-care provider to resolve the complication and ensure that you will have an uneventful end to your pregnancy.

Bed Rest

According to the *Online Journal of Health Ethics*, 20 percent of women are placed on bed rest for at least one week of their pregnancy. Being put on bed rest is difficult and worrisome. The first thing you need to do is find out exactly what activities are permitted and which are not. There are many different degrees of bed rest, and it is important to get details about what is safe for you to do. Ask your health-care provider about these possibilities:

- Working from home
- Lifting children
- Performing daily household activities
- Climbing stairs
- Walking around and mobility in general
- Showering and bathing
- Sitting versus lying down
- Driving a car
- Having sex and experiencing orgasm
- Stretching and light exercise
- Watching for warning signs

If you are restricted and told to stay home and put your feet up, or stay in bed, there are some things you can do to make it more bearable. Set yourself up in a room that provides everything you need within arm's reach. A bed and a recliner may be allowed. You will probably want access to a TV, DVD player, CD player, computer, and telephone. Stay in touch with friends and family by encouraging them to visit and by talking on the phone. This is a good time to read books you've had on your nightstand for a while or to take up a hobby such as knitting, scrapbooking, or learning to play chess. Look at this time as a time of rest and rejuvenation and a chance to focus on your pregnancy and your baby.

Managing Health Problems

If you experience a complication in your pregnancy, the most important thing to do is to follow your health-care provider's instructions. It's very easy to go online and do research yourself. While educating yourself is a great idea, self-diagnosis and treatment are not. If you come across things online that concern you, ask your health-care provider about them before doing anything.

Remember that health-care concerns are a physical situation but also a mental and emotional one. It takes time and mental and emotional effort to cope with a complication. You cannot expect yourself to not feel any effects, no matter how minor a complication you are experiencing. You need to give yourself time and space to think things through, ask questions, and care for yourself.

Belly Basics

The risk for preeclampsia is higher for women having their first baby at an older age. For this reason, your health-care provider will always check your blood pressure and test your ankles for swelling. Rapid weight gain (more than two to three pounds in a week) may also be a warning sign of preeclampsia.

Finding Support

The good news about pregnancy is that lots and lots of women are going through it or have gone through it. You are by no means alone. Talking with other moms or pregnant women can help you feel less anxious and can offer important connections. The nurses, midwives, or physicians at your health-care provider can also offer support and information.

There are lots of ways to get in touch with other pregnant women, if you are interested. Joining a prenatal exercise or yoga class can help you get to know other pregnant women in your area. When you take your childbirth education class, you will meet other women who have due dates close to yours. Since you are all roughly at the same stage of pregnancy, you can go through it all together and learn from and support each other.

Many women find support online. There are myriad bulletin boards and listservs for pregnant moms. You can join due-date clubs, where all the women on a board or list are due in the same month. Many of these lists stay together for years, as the women support each other through different stages of motherhood. There are also many boards and lists for particular interests—over 35, plus-size, pregnant again after a loss, gestational diabetes, and so on.

Don't forget to rely on your partner, family, and friends for support. Although they may not be going through a pregnancy, they love you and are there to listen and help you. Your health-care provider's staff is not only very educated about pregnancy but also very interested in helping women through all aspects of it. There is sure to be someone there who can help you with almost any problem.

NOTES AND CHECKLISTS

Checklist for Months Four Through Six
- ☐ Treat yourself to a special day out.
- ☐ Begin keeping a food log.
- ☐ If you don't have one, shop for a crib that meets current safety standards.
- ☐ Create a prenatal exercise routine.

- ☐ Plan a special night out with your partner.
- ☐ Choose a method of childbirth instruction.
- ☐ Tour childbirth centers.

- ☐ Take a day off and pamper yourself.
- ☐ Start putting together your birth plan.
- ☐ Think about who you want in the delivery room.
- ☐ Begin listing baby names.

Career Future Sheet

Ask yourself the following questions to assess the career direction you may want to take and decide what are feasible goals for your job future. Write your answers in the space provided so you can reread your goals at any time during your pregnancy.

1. Do you want to move into a supervisory position at your next review? Do you see your company promoting people who work excessive overtime? If so, are you capable of committing to working extra hours after your baby is born?

   _____

   _____

   _____

   _____

2. Will you require an extremely or moderately flexible job?

   _____

   _____

   _____

   _____

3. Is your partner's job flexible enough to allow your job to be less so?

_____

_____

_____

4. Do you intend to advance in your current career and become or remain the primary earner in your family, or will your partner take on that role?

_____

_____

_____

5. Are you a single parent who will be relying on your own income after your baby is born?

_____

_____

_____

6. Do you have options for affordable child care for when your baby is born? How does this affect your postpartum working schedule?

_____

_____

_____

7. Is your job adaptable so that you can work from home? If not, would you like a job that is?

_____

_____

_____

_____

Second Trimester Notes

Use the space below to write down any notes about your second trimester.

_____

_____

_____

_____

_____

_____

_____

_____

_____

_____

_____

_____

_____

_____

_____

_____

_____

_____

_____

_____

_____

_____

_____

_____

PART 4

THIRD TRIMESTER

Chapter 12

WHAT TO EXPECT IN YOUR THIRD TRIMESTER

It's the homestretch, the final act, the big countdown—the third trimester. You've made a lot of decisions so far, and there are even more to be made this month. Full speed ahead with labor-and-delivery preparations as you sort through your options for childbirth classes and start to assemble a birth plan. You may feel some Braxton-Hicks contractions as your body starts prepping for the hard work of labor. Consider them a dress rehearsal for the big event.

YOUR BABY DURING MONTH 7

Weighing in at 4 pounds and measuring about 16 inches long, your baby is growing amazingly fast now. Her red, wrinkled skin is losing its fine lanugo covering as more insulating fat accumulates. And her eyelids, closed for so long, can now open and afford her a dim view of the place she will call home for just a few more months.

Dramatic developments in the brain and central nervous system are also occurring, as baby's nerve cells are sheathed with a substance called *myelin* that speeds nerve impulses. A 7-month-old fetus feels pain, can cry, and responds to stimulation from light or sound outside the womb.

Her gymnastics may subside as her space gets smaller, but you're feeling her more intensely now; her movements might even be visible to both you and your partner. Periodically tiny elbows and feet will turn your belly into an interactive relief map. Gently pushing back can provide endless entertainment for all three of you.

Even though your fetus is producing lung surfactant, a liquid mixture of lipids and proteins that coats the lungs and makes it easier to breathe, and developing alveoli (air sacs), her lungs still aren't developed enough to breathe in the outside world. If complications require an early delivery now, steroids might be administered intravenously to boost surfactant production. Chemical surfactants can also be used after birth.

YOUR BODY DURING MONTH 7

You're likely feeling perpetually stuffed and slightly out of breath as your uterus relocates all your internal organs. The relief and energy felt in the second trimester can start to fade now. Just remember, you're almost there!

Your Body Changes

The top of the fundus is halfway between your bellybutton and your breastbone, displacing your stomach, intestines, and diaphragm. Your expanding abdomen has formed a shelf, handy for resting your arms on and balancing a cold beverage at the movies. On the down side, you'll be catching a lot of crumbs, and your napkin just doesn't seem to stay on your lap anymore.

Not only are your breasts heavier, but also they are more glandular and getting ready to feed your baby. In this last trimester your nipples may begin to leak colostrum, the yellowish, nutrient-rich fluid that precedes real breast milk. You may find the leaking more apparent when you're sexually aroused. To reduce backaches and breast tenderness, make sure you wear a well-fitting bra (even to bed, if it helps). If you are planning on breastfeeding, you might want to consider buying some supportive nursing bras now that can take you through the rest of pregnancy and right into the postpartum period.

Belly Basics

If you're picking up some nursing bras, be sure to test-drive the clasps for easy nursing access. Try to unfasten and slip the nursing flaps down with one hand. This may seem unimportant now, but when you're in a crowded shopping mall juggling packages and trying to discreetly put baby to breast single-handedly, you'll be thankful you had the foresight.

What You Feel Like

Your body is warming up for labor, and you may start to experience Braxton-Hicks contractions. These painless and irregular contractions feel as if your uterus is making a fist and then gradually relaxing. If your little one is fairly active, you might think that she is stretching herself sideways at first. A quick check of your belly will reveal a visible tightening.

Braxton-Hicks can begin as early as week 20 and continue right up until your due date, although these contractions are more commonly felt in the final month of pregnancy. Some first-time moms-to-be are afraid they won't be able to tell the difference between Braxton-Hicks and actual labor contractions. As any woman who has been through labor can attest, when the real thing comes, you'll know it. Rule of thumb: if it hurts, it's labor.

Starting at week 20, the uterus has a basic rhythm. The smooth muscle of the uterus is similar to your intestinal tract in that both involuntarily contract in a wavelike pattern designed to facilitate movement of what's inside (be it breakfast or your baby). These early rhythmic and generally painless contractions are called Braxton-Hicks when they do not cause any changes to the cervix and are occurring at irregular intervals. They can even be uncomfortable at times but will usually subside if you change positions, another way to distinguish Braxton-Hicks from the real thing. The actual definition of labor, even when it is premature, is the onset of regular, painful, uterine contractions that lead to a change in the cervix.

If your contractions suddenly seem to be coming at regular intervals and they start to cause you pain or discomfort, they could be the real thing. Lie down on your left side for about a half hour with a clock or watch on hand, and time the contractions from the beginning of one to the beginning of the next. If the interludes are more or less regular, call your health-care provider. And if contractions of any type are accompanied by blood or amniotic fluid leakage, contact your practitioner immediately.

The list is growing. Other symptoms that may continue this month include:

- Fatigue
- Frequent urination
- Tender and/or swollen breasts
- Bleeding gums
- Excess mucus and saliva
- Increase in normal vaginal discharge
- Mild shortness of breath
- Lightheadedness or dizziness
- Headaches
- Forgetfulness
- Gas, heartburn, and/or constipation
- Skin and hair changes
- Round ligament pain or soreness
- Lower-back aches
- Mild swelling of legs, feet, and hands
- Leg cramps

At Your Doctor Visit

Starting with this initial third-trimester visit, your trips to the doctor might start to step up to twice monthly. Your provider will probably want to know whether you've been experiencing any Braxton-Hicks contractions, and he will cover the warning signs of preterm labor and what you should do if you experience them. If you're unsure about what type of childbirth class you'd like to take, you might want to bring your questions to your provider for his take. Just remember, the decision is ultimately up to you and your partner.

Pregnancy Pointer

People are fascinated with the life force of pregnancy, and you're radiating it, big time. Most people will ask permission before touching, but to stop the belly rubbers who strike without warning, take a step back or turn away. Hopefully, they'll get the hint.

Women who are Rh-negative will need treatment this month with Rh immune globulin (RhIg; RhoGAM). An injection is typically given at about week 28 to protect the fetus from developing hemolytic disease—a condition in which the mother's antibodies attack the fetal red blood cells.

This month will bring new questions and uncertainties as you ponder your ideal birth experience. Are you looking forward to a completely chemical-free birth, or are you already exploring your painkilling options? Is your provider open to your needs and willing to make reasonable accommodations to meet them? Do you want only your partner in attendance, or would you like additional support? Whatever your idea of perfect labor and delivery is, make sure the direction of your birth plan is driven by the needs of your partner and you and not by the expectations of others.

Keep in mind that you don't want to create such incredibly high expectations of yourself and of the birth experience that you're bound to be let down. Try to build room for flexibility into your conception of the ultimate birth. Your little one might not be following the same game plan as you, and last-minute strategy changes are often required. Fortunately, if you work on your birth plan now, you can build in allowances for complications and save yourself unnecessary angst later.

Don't miss the boat on insurance. Many childbirth classes, sibling classes, and breastfeeding classes are completely covered by your health insurance provider. If cost is holding you back, check out your coverage. Even if you aren't covered, courses are usually relatively inexpensive, and many facilities offer sliding-fee scales for those who qualify.

YOUR BABY DURING MONTH 8

You are a pregnancy pro now, deftly handling all the aches and pains that come with the territory. Even if you're one of the lucky ones who sail through pregnancy feeling just fine, you've still faced down plenty of lifestyle challenges by now. You have learned to adjust to the fashion hardships, the changes in your home and routine, and the logistical struggles that your baby and belly have brought to the forefront. It's not much longer now.

Gradually shifting to the position in which approximately 95 percent of all babies are born, your fetus starts to move into a head-down pose, known as the *vertex position*. The small but stubborn percentage that don't assume the vertex position are considered breech. Feel a lot of kicking on your pelvic floor? It could be a clue that baby is still standing or sitting tall. She might also be lounging in the transverse (sideways) position in the womb.

Your little one is now up to 18 inches long and as heavy as a 5-pound sack of flour. The rest of her body is finally catching up to the size of her head. Although it may feel like she's constantly up and about, she's actually sleeping 90 to 95 percent of the day, a figure that will drop only slightly when she is born.

If your child were born today, she'd have an excellent chance of surviving and eventually thriving outside the womb. However, she'd still be considered preterm or premature, as is any birth before week 37 of gestation.

YOUR BODY DURING MONTH 8

Can you still remember your prepregnancy body? The little things—like being able to zip up your coat, wear your rings, and sit on the floor without requiring adult assistance to stand again—may be a distant memory. You will not be pregnant forever, of course, although it might sometimes feel that way.

Your Body Changes

Weight gain should start to slow down this month. If it doesn't, however, don't cut your calorie intake below 2,600 to try to stop it. You need the extra energy for both of you.

As baby settles firmly on your bladder, bathroom stops step up once again. You may even experience some stress incontinence: minor dribbling or leakage of urine when you sneeze, cough, laugh, or make other sudden movements. This will clear up postpartum. In the meantime, keep doing your Kegels, don't hold it in, and wear a panty liner.

....

Belly Basics

Amniotic fluid is clear to straw-colored and has a faintly sweet smell. Less commonly, it may be tinged green or brown. If you think you're leaking amniotic fluid, no matter how small the amount, contact your care provider. If your membranes have ruptured, you risk infection if you don't deliver soon.

....

What You Feel Like

Your Weeble-like physique has you off balance and generally klutzy. Be careful: you wobble, and you can fall down. And, of course, those (say it together, everyone) pregnancy hormones have loosened up your joints and relaxed your muscles to make you a bit of a butterfingers.

Now is not the ideal time to be fitted for new contacts or glasses. Pregnancy-related fluid retention can actually change the shape of your eyes and trigger minor vision changes. Also at work is estrogen, which causes your eyes to be drier than normal and can make contact lenses uncomfortable right now. Unless you want to invest in new eyewear again postpartum, you should hold off on any such purchase for now.

Although you may not relish the thought of air travel in your current wide-body state, for most women in low-risk pregnancies, flying is safe through week 36. Obviously, if something happens while you are in the air or away from home, you would need to get care from providers you don't know, and that can be very stressful. If you do need to fly late in your pregnancy, consider taking a copy of your prenatal chart in case any problems do arise. Some airlines restrict air travel after a certain point in pregnancy because they don't want to deal with any complications, while others require a doctor's note for travel. Check with individual airlines regarding their policies when booking your flight.

Dehydration due to the low humidity in airplane cabins can be avoided by drinking fluids during the flight. Skip the soda and stick with water or juice; the low air pressure in the cabin also makes gas expand and can make carbonated beverages and other gas-producing foods an uncomfortable choice.

There is a theoretical concern about developing blood clots while immobilized on a flight, but this has not been well documented; moving around in your seat and walking to the bathroom will probably be enough to prevent their occurrence.

It's increasingly easy to get winded as your little one pushes up into your diaphragm. Take it slow, breathe deeply, and practice good posture. To ease breathing while you sleep, pile on a few extra pillows or use a foam bed wedge to elevate your head.

Other symptoms that may continue this month include:

- Fatigue
- Frequent urination
- Tender and/or swollen breasts

- Colostrum discharge from nipples
- Bleeding gums
- Excess mucus and saliva
- Increase in normal vaginal discharge
- Mild shortness of breath
- Lightheadedness or dizziness
- Headaches
- Forgetfulness
- Gas, heartburn, and/or constipation
- Skin and hair changes
- Round ligament pain or soreness
- Lower-back aches
- Mild swelling of legs, feet, and hands
- Leg cramps
- Painless, irregular contractions (Braxton-Hicks)

If you experience blurry vision or visual disturbances (for example, spots), let your provider know immediately. Either one could be a sign of high blood pressure, which is dangerous to both you and your child. These are also symptoms of preeclampsia, which can be dangerous for both you and your baby.

At Your Doctor's Visit

You'll see your provider twice or more this month as you continue your every-other-week routine. She will check the position of your baby to determine whether he has turned head down in preparation for birth.

If your practitioner brings up the possibility of a breech birth (bottom- or foot-first), it's because she has felt the head of your unborn baby up near your ribs, or an ultrasound has confirmed that your child is in the breech position. Don't panic. Your fickle fetus is likely to change position again in the next few weeks. If she doesn't, your practitioner may try to turn the baby once you're closer to term, using a technique known as *external cephalic version*: manually attempting to turn the fetus in the uterus. ACOG recommends that an external cephalic version be attempted in most breech cases, typically between weeks 36 and 42.

....

Belly Basics

External cephalic version (or simply version) is successful in turning a breech baby in about half of all instances where it is attempted. However, if it is done too far in advance of the estimated delivery date, there is a possibility that the fetus may flip back to the breech position.

....

Babies can be delivered vaginally in breech position in some instances, but the procedure is more difficult and carries a higher risk for the infant. If your provider has not been adequately trained to perform vaginal breech delivery (and many are no longer so trained), you could be offered a C-section. Currently, C-section is the method of choice for a safe breech delivery. If you really want a vaginal birth and a cephalic version is unsuccessful in turning your breech, some practitioners may agree to a trial of labor to see if your contracting uterus helps to turn the child.

There are three classifications of breech: frank, complete, and incomplete. In frank breech, your baby uses your pelvic bone as a seat and stretches his legs up close to his chest. In a complete breech, your baby has his bottom on your pelvis again, but legs and arms are crossed in front of his little body. A footling breech is not a good candidate for vaginal delivery because the diameter of the legs will be smaller than the head, resulting in an increased risk of entrapment (the head being too large to move through the cervix). With incomplete breech, one or both legs will drop down during delivery and will arrive before the rest of the body. This is also called a *single- or double-footling breech birth*.

LABOR ON YOUR MIND

As labor looms closer, your thoughts turn to the task at hand. Going into labor and delivery with as much knowledge of the process as possible can make the difference between a positive childbirth experience and a long and arduous one.

"Am I Up to the Task of Labor?"

Women have been doing this since the beginning of time and under much more difficult circumstances. Yes, in most cases labor will be hard work, but if you prepare yourself by learning what to expect, you will be ready to face whatever comes your way. You'll also find that your spouse or labor partner and coach will be a huge asset in helping you through childbirth.

"Am I Up to the Task of Motherhood?"

Great mommies are made, not born. Although some aspects of mothering will seem to come to you instinctively, practice and trial and error will make up the better part of your parenting education. Use the tools around you—your pediatrician, other mothers, and research and reading—to build and sharpen your skills. In the final analysis, listen to your inner voice in the application of what you learn.

Dealing with Stress

As pregnancy winds down, your patience goes with it. The belly rubbers, advice givers, urban-legend spreaders, and comedians seem to be everywhere and completely unaware of the dangerously thin ice they are treading on. Rather than biting heads off, take a deep, deep breath and remind yourself that though insensitive, most are well meaning. In the meantime, photocopy the following list of no-nos for your coworkers and hang it in the break room; maybe it will sink in.

Belly Basics

The average labor lasts 12 to 14 hours, plenty of time to get to the hospital. To avoid any unforeseen delays, work out a route in advance, keep your gas tank full, and have cash on hand for a cab in case your car conks out with the first contraction.

Top ten things not to say to a pregnant woman:

- Haven't you had that baby yet?
- Are you still here?
- Wow, you're HUGE!
- You really should avoid pain medication when you go into labor; it will hurt the baby.
- Labor is hell! Take all the drugs you can get!
- So, how much weight have you gained?
- You don't mind if we call you at home while you're on maternity leave, do you?
- Are you having twins?
- You look terrible; why don't you take a nap?
- Sorry—our restrooms are for employees only.

STAYING SANE WITH BED REST

At first that bed may seem like a welcome oasis, particularly if you've been getting little sleep as of late. A prescription to snooze! What more could you ask for?

That feeling will likely be short-lived, however. There's only so much you can do horizontally (or even slightly tilted). Yet there are ways to make the time pass a little faster. Some ideas to keep busy beyond the usual TV and movie fare:

- **Baby shopping by mail or web.** Get on your laptop or leaf through some of those catalogs your mailbox has been inundated with. Shopping has never been so easy on your feet.
- **Get crafty.** Creating something special for baby—embroidered, crocheted, or knitted—is a good way to pass the hours. Even if you are a rookie, a beginner's kit can get you started. You may not have the time again for years, so go for it.
- **Feed your mind.** Read, read, read. Not just baby books (although feel free to keep this one handy), but classics, new fiction, and anything else you can get your hands on.
- **Catch up.** All those pictures you've been meaning to put into photo albums, the scrapbooks that are half finished, letters on your list to write, and other assorted undertakings are perfect bed rest projects that have the added bonus of imparting a sense of achievement.
- **Be game.** Dust off some of those old board and strategy games you haven't played in years, and recruit your partner or kids to play, too. A rousing game of Risk can be a lot more entertaining than another evening spent channel surfing.

NESTING

Ah, nesting—that overwhelming urge to turn everything in your house upside down and rearrange it just so. Your mad dash to finish the nursery and squirrel away a year's supply of diaper wipes is an instinctive reaction to baby's upcoming arrival. You're preparing a safe haven for your little one and assuring yourself that all his needs and wants will be adequately met.

Stocking Up on Essentials

Don't go crazy buying supersized cases of baby supplies. You may not like the brand or configuration you purchase, which leaves you with a lot of unwanted merchandise on your hands. Instead, buy small so that you can sample. Once you've decided what works best for you and baby, you can stock up at the warehouse store.

And now is the time to start thinking about whether you want to go cloth or disposable with diapers. If you're thinking green, cloth diapers have the advantage of not ending up in a landfill, although they do require additional fossil fuels and water resources to wash and transport (if you use a service). Cost can be an advantage, but it's probably a slight one if you use a service. Call local diaper services to get estimates and a rundown of what's included. You can wash them at home, of course, but be sure you have the time and the strength to be doing laundry daily. If your baby has sensitive skin, you might find cloth less irritating. Like most things in parenting, it's trial and error; have a supply of both and see how each works for you.

YOUR BABY DURING MONTH 9

Your child is packing on about a half-pound per week as he prepares to make his big exit. He's fully formed and just waiting for the right time now. If you're having a boy, his testicles have descended and may be visible in any 9-month ultrasound images. His lungs, the last organ system to fully mature, now have an adequate level of surfactant in them to allow breathing outside the womb.

···

Belly Basics

A pregnancy is considered full-term from weeks 37 to 42. Only 5 percent of expectant women actually give birth on their estimated date of delivery, and first-time moms are more likely to go past their due date. If you've delivered a baby before, however, statistically you are more likely to give birth within 4 days of your EDD.

···

A dark, tarry amalgam of amniotic fluid, skin cells, and other fetal waste is gathering in your baby's intestines. This substance (called *meconium*) will become the contents of his bowel movements during the first few days of life.

Fetal movement will naturally slow down as you get closer to your due date and the baby is pressed for space, but a healthy baby should still be making his presence known. Your provider may ask you to count fetal kicks. Pick a typically active time of day for your little one, and start counting his moves. Your provider will let you know how many movements you should feel in what period of time (usually around eight to ten in a space of 2 hours).

Pregnancy Pointer

If your baby's movements aren't as frequent as your provider has told you they should be, it's possible she is sleeping. Try drinking a glass of juice to get her going. Be sure to call your provider immediately if fetal movements are notably decreased or absent.

YOUR BODY DURING MONTH 9

While baby is still growing, your weight gain tapers off this month. Groin soreness and backaches are more persistent as the musculoskeletal system strains to support your abdomen. The good news: you can't get any bigger.

Your Body Changes

Engagement (lightening), the process of the baby dropping down into the pelvic cavity in preparation for delivery, can occur any time now. In some women (particularly those who have given birth before), it may not happen until labor starts.

Your cervix is ripening (softening) in preparation for baby's passage. As it effaces (thins) and dilates (opens), the soft plug of mucus keeping it sealed tight may be dislodged. This mass, with the appealing name of *mucous plug*, may be tinged red or pink; it is also referred to by the equally explicit *bloody show*.

What You Feel Like

If the baby has dropped, you could be running to the bathroom more than ever. He also may be sending shockwaves through your pelvis as he settles further down onto the pelvic floor. On the up side, you can finally breathe as he pulls away from your lungs and diaphragm. Braxton-Hicks contractions can be more frequent this month as you draw nearer to delivery. How will you recognize them?

Real contractions will:

- Be felt in the back and possibly radiate around to the abdomen.
- Not subside when you move around or change positions.
- Increase in intensity as time passes.
- Come at roughly regular intervals (early on, this can be from 20 to 45 minutes apart).
- Increase in intensity with activities like walking.

Other signs that labor is on its way include amniotic fluid that leaks in either a gush or a trickle (your "water breaking"), sudden diarrhea, and the appearance of the mucous plug. Keep in mind, however, that for many women, the bag of waters does not break until active labor sets in.

AT YOUR DOCTOR'S VISIT

You'll see your doctor on a weekly basis from now until you deliver. Unless you are scheduled for a planned cesarean, your provider will probably perform an internal exam with each visit to check your cervix for changes that indicate approaching labor.

Tests This Month

The CDC recommends that your provider administer a group B strep (GBS) test in weeks 35 to 37. This culture is performed by swabbing a sample from both your vagina and your rectum. If the cultured sample comes back positive for GBS, you may have intravenous antibiotics administered during delivery to prevent group B strep bacteria transmission to the baby.

Checking Your Cervix

Your provider will be checking your cervix for signs that it is preparing for your baby's passage. She'll also be taking note of any descent or dropping of the baby toward the pelvis, called the *station*. Take the numbers you hear with a grain of salt, however. Although you may start effacing and dilating now, it's still anyone's guess as to when labor will begin, and it could be a few more weeks yet.

MOOD CHANGES

You are so ready to have this baby. Nothing fits, not even your shoes. You can't sleep for more than a few hours at a time. Your belly itches and your breasts ache. You look toward your due date like a long distance runner approaching the end of a marathon. As you waddle toward the finish line, enjoy these final sensations of your child moving inside of you—the funny little hiccups, the elbow and knee bumps parading across your belly, and the subtle nudges that remind you you're not alone even if no one else is around.

When your cervix hasn't budged and your due date has come and gone, you may be tempted to try one of those sure-fire homemade labor inducers that every pregnant woman hears about. Castor oil, herbal concoctions, spicy food, breast massage, and sex are just a few methods bandied about in pregnancy chatrooms everywhere.

···

Belly Basics

Massaging the areola and gently rolling the nipple mimics the action of a nursing baby and stimulates the natural release of oxytocin, which triggers uterine contractions. Several clinical studies have shown that this method can be useful in labor induction and also helpful in reducing postpartum hemorrhage.

···

Unfortunately, some "natural methods" might only succeed in making you nauseated, while others can pose a real danger. Even if you're embarrassed, you need to run these by your doctor or midwife before taking matters into your own hands. A good provider will listen and won't laugh, letting you know what's safe and what isn't.

Irritable and Anxious

As sleep gets more and more elusive and your discomfort ratchets up, you may find yourself easily provoked. The best short-term solution to keeping your cool? Stay clear of encounters with people you just know will irritate you (whether they mean to or not), and ask your significant other to be the point person on all those "Anything yet?" questions.

First-time moms may find themselves overwhelmed with anxiety now that birth is so near. Take a deep breath, go over what you learned in childbirth class (repeatedly, if it helps ease your mind), and talk with your partner or labor coach about ways to relax and get past the anxious feelings. It's perfectly natural to be fearful of the unknown, but don't let fear wrest control of your labor from you.

Even if you have been through pregnancy already, you might still be anxious about baby's arrival. Perhaps you're following a different kind of labor and birth plan, or you're concerned about how your other child will react to his new sibling. Again, talk it out with your partner, ask your provider any questions that are still on your mind about labor and delivery, and remember that you've been through this once and you'll make it through again.

Excited and Happy

How could you not be excited? You're finally going to meet the little one you've known only through kicks, hiccups, and grainy ultrasound images. Will she look like you? What will you do when you get to hold her for the first time? Relish these final days of exhilaration and anticipation; they are unique.

GEARING UP FOR THE BIG EVENT

Since baby's timetable is somewhat unpredictable, start getting your affairs in order at the beginning of this month. Cover all personal, professional, and family bases to ensure a smooth transition from home to hospital and back home again.

Finalize Maternity-Leave Plans

If you're right up until your due date, start clearing the decks early in the month. Make sure coworkers and managers are regularly apprised of where outstanding projects stand, and try to treat every day as if it might be your last before you leave. The more you enable matters to flow smoothly in your absence, the less likely you are to get calls at home.

....

Pregnancy Pointer

Having a cesarean section? You'll be recovering from major surgery as well as going through new-mom adjustments. It's essential that you have adequate rest and support so that you can heal and care for baby. Federal law mandates that health insurers cover at least 4 days of hospitalization following an uncomplicated C-section birth. Stay as long as you can.

....

Talk with your supervisor about communication during your absence. If you want to remain incommunicado (and you have every right to do so), make your feelings known. You might think about setting a limit on any contact you do agree to, such as e-mails only, which may be easier to answer at your leisure when baby is asleep, or phone calls only in a certain window of time each day. Be sure to outline circumstances that you would consider important enough to be disturbed for. Remember—this is your time off, both to recuperate and to get to know your child. Your workplace will survive.

HURRY UP AND WAIT

You've finally reached that magic EDD number and . . . nothing. No fanfare, no contractions, and definitely no baby. Disappointed, you resign yourself to yet another day of pregnancy. Don't be too depressed. Instead try to stay busy, and if you feel up to it, get out and about. A nice long walk may be just what your little one needs for inspiration. Sitting at home, analyzing every twitch of your abdomen, and watching the hours crawl by will only make the waiting longer.

Unless you have a precise 28-day cycle and are positive of the exact day that sperm met egg, gestational dating can be fuzzy at best. If you are a week or more past the EDD, your provider will order additional tests, including a biophysical profile, which includes a nonstress test and ultrasound assessment of amniotic fluid levels and fetal activity. These tools will give her a much better picture of whether or not baby is ready to arrive.

Babies who stay in the womb 42 weeks or longer are considered postdate. Postdate pregnancies can develop macrosomia, or large body size of 4,000 grams (8 pounds 13 ounces) or more that could make it difficult to pass through the birth canal. A postdate fetus may also pass meconium, the black tarry stool that is baby's first bowel movement. If meconium is released into the amniotic fluid, it has the potential to cause lung problems after the baby is born. It may also be a sign of current or past fetal distress. Postdate pregnancies are also associated with an increased risk of stillbirth and placental insufficiency (when the placenta can no longer provide enough oxygen and nutrients to the baby). That's why regular assessment of a postdate pregnancy is extremely important.

Chapter 13
YOUR BIRTHING PLAN

By your third trimester, you should have your birthing plan ready to go. If your medical provider does not have a copy of your birthing plan, be sure to send one over. You'll want to be sure you are prepared for a variety of birthing possibilities. This chapter will help you get ready for anything.

CHILDBIRTH CLASSES

The beginning of your third trimester is a good time to start gathering information on childbirth classes from your local hospital or birthing center to give you and your partner time to decide which class is right for you. Pick a class date that falls in your third trimester so the information will still be fresh in your mind once the big day arrives. While hospital policy will dictate a lot of what's covered in prepared childbirth classes, here's a general idea of what you will experience:

- **Commiseration:** You'll interact with other pregnant couples and demonstrate that misery (and joy) truly does love company.
- **Reality:** Through lecture and (in many cases) actual video footage, you'll get the full scoop on what really goes on in labor and delivery.
- **Guided tour:** If your class is at the birthing center or hospital, you will probably get a tour of the facilities and some basic instructions on when and where to show up when labor hits.

- **Teamwork:** Your husband, partner, or labor coach will learn more about his or her role in this process, and you may even be given homework to try out techniques at home.
- **After-birth instruction:** Many classes offer valuable information on breastfeeding basics and baby care. Don't be surprised if the instructor brings in a bag full of baby dolls for practice.
- **Seasoned support:** Most prepared childbirth classes will be conducted by a trained childbirth educator.
- **Paperwork:** A lot of literature, brochures, pamphlets, handouts, forms, photocopies, and leaflets will come your way. Bring a bag.

Following are some of the most popular childbirth educational offerings for you to consider as you research your options.

Lamaze

While rhythmic breathing exercises are stressed for each stage of labor in Lamaze, helpful laboring and birth positions, relaxation techniques, and pain management are also covered. In addition to massage, water therapy, and hot and cold compresses, you're taught how to focus on a picture or object to diminish your discomfort.

Lamaze also stresses the empowerment of the mother-to-be and her right to the birth experience and environment she wants.

Bradley Method

Denver obstetrician Robert Bradley, MD, was a big advocate of fathers helping their partners through the birth process. Bradley Method classes teach couples how to relax and breathe deeply, but the emphasis is on doing what comes naturally—such as father as coach, proper nutrition during pregnancy, and knowing all the options beforehand. They also emphasize the "natural" in natural childbirth, suggesting that pain medication be used as a last resort rather than a front-line tool.

HypnoBirthing

British doctor and natural childbirth pioneer Grantly Dick-Read, who authored the classic *Childbirth Without Fear*, is the inspiration behind HypnoBirthing education. Dr. Dick-Read believed that a woman's labor pains were magnified by her fear and anxieties. HypnoBirthing emphasizes slow abdominal breathing and other relaxation techniques that teach you how to focus on the feelings and signals your body sends during labor.

Childbirth Class Follow-Up Sheet

If you are still confused about different types of childbirth classes, call your hospital or birthing center and ask for printed schedules and descriptions of upcoming classes. Once you get a basic feel for what is offered, you can call with follow-up questions. Use the questions below to gain as much information as you can.

1. What are the instructor's credentials and training?
2. What methods are taught in the class?
3. What is the typical class size?
4. What does the curriculum consist of?
5. How much does enrollment cost?
6. Are there additional costs beyond the enrollment fee, such as for study materials or learning aids?
7. Are there couples that can be contacted as references?

TOURING THE HOSPITAL/BIRTHING CENTER

Even if you don't choose a childbirth class sponsored by the facility at which you'll be giving birth, you should try to arrange a tour. On the tour, you can:

- Find out where you must park when you and your partner arrive at the center.
- Get a sneak peek of the labor and birthing rooms.

- Get a feel for the staff's attitude and level of friendliness and approachability.
- Tour the nursery and maternity ward.
- Observe newborn care.
- Acquaint yourself with hospital/center policy and procedures.

WRITING YOUR BIRTH PLAN

A birth plan is a road map for your entire childbirth experience, beginning to end. It's your chance to let everyone involved (doctors, nurses, partners) know what you want the experience to be. Anything you have definitive expectations about should be outlined in your birth plan, from your wishes regarding pain relief to specifications for how your newborn is fed and cared for in the hospital. Use it to chart the course of labor and delivery, but remember that you might have to take alternate routes occasionally depending on conditions.

Why Have a Birth Plan?

The process of talking through and creating a birth plan helps you and your partner establish what you want out of childbirth (aside from the child, of course). Having it down as written word can ease your anxieties about labor and delivery. And when things get crazy as the big day arrives, a birth plan can be your calm in the storm, something solid to grasp when you suddenly seem to have forgotten just about everything you've learned.

A birth plan also serves the very important purpose of letting your provider know just what kind of experience and what level of interventions you're looking for. Because the plan can tread on some sensitive and controversial medical territory, it's important that you include your doctor or midwife in the process.

Preparing Your Provider

Once you and your partner have your birth plan together, you should present it to your provider for his comments and questions. Communicating your wishes and being receptive to feedback can make the difference between a birth plan that works and one that doesn't.

Many physicians and midwives will set up a separate office visit dedicated to discussing the birth plan you've come up with. Consider the plan you initially take to her to be a first draft. You can then incorporate your provider's input into your final plan.

Unfortunately, not all practitioners are thrilled about the prospect of a birth plan. This can be a hot-button issue for physicians who either feel as if their patients don't trust them or don't want to have a disappointed patient if the actual birth strays from the plan. For these reasons, birth plans have the potential to set up an adversarial situation in some doctor-patient relationships.

How can you prevent your birth plan from becoming a bone of contention? First, be willing to really listen to any suggestions or issues your provider has and make an effort to work toward a resolution together. Also, try to keep your expectations grounded in reality and not overly restrictive. Wanting your three-year-old to be nearby so that she can meet her sibling shortly after birth is great, but insisting she be front and center the moment baby's head emerges is unrealistic.

Pregnancy Pointer

Once you have reviewed your birth plan with your practitioner and made your final changes, ask him to place a copy in your chart and hospital record. Make sure your labor coach and other support people who will be present at the birth have one as well, so everyone is playing by the same game plan.

Make It User Friendly

If you hand your doctor a birth plan the size of *War and Peace*, she might start to wonder what she's gotten herself into. While covering all your bases is important, you simply can't control every possible aspect of what does or doesn't occur during labor and delivery. Medical emergencies do happen, which is why you have signed on a practitioner to begin with. You need to trust your provider to follow the spirit of your birth plan while making adjustments for your health and that of your baby. Establishing a good communicative relationship is the best way to ensure this.

Conciseness is better from a logistical viewpoint, too. The medical staff attending your birth and aftercare should be able to easily access and reference the information. Think brevity and bullet points—the CliffsNotes of your thoughts on how you'd like birth to proceed. Keep the plan under five pages, if possible; fewer than that is even better.

Try to use language that is cooperative and communicative. Your birth plan should not read like a ransom note. Filling it with demands and absolutes leaves your provider very little room to make appropriate medical suggestions should birth go off course.

The bottom line is that labor is very unpredictable and rarely do birth plans get followed to the letter. Outlining your wishes in terms of preferences and giving your provider alternatives in case complications arise will make your birth plan more useful to everyone involved, especially to you and baby.

ATMOSPHERE

Comfortable surroundings will help both your mind and body relax during labor. Whether you're giving birth in a hospital, at home, or somewhere in between, outlining your preference for what you'll be seeing and hearing around you is an important component of the birth plan.

The Perfect Place

First, know what you have to work with. Hospital birthing facilities are starting to recognize the value of a homey, warm atmosphere. You may find that yours is already set up to suit your needs well.

However, if the setting looks a little sterile and spartan, there are ways to make it more welcoming. Easy and acceptable additions include a cozy blanket and pillow from home, a picture or two (which can serve as focal points during contractions), and fresh flowers. You might also be able to adjust the lights and sounds to make the environment more relaxing.

Home birth is an option if you feel strongly about giving birth in familiar surroundings and among family. However, home birth doesn't mean you should opt out of a health-care professional's help; in fact, this is even more important since you won't have access to the medical monitoring and diagnostic equipment that a hospital offers. In many uncomplicated pregnancies, a home birth can be a completely safe and emotionally rewarding choice. However, women who might experience high-risk deliveries for any reason need to seriously contemplate the benefits and safety of a hospital birth.

Pregnancy Pointer

Be aware that professional and insurance restrictions may prohibit your doctor from attending a home birth. If your provider can't be there and your mind is set on a home birth, find out if he can refer you to a midwife or doctor who can attend.

An in-between alternative for some women is a birthing center, which is equipped to handle some medical problems that may occur yet can offer some less conventional labor and delivery methods, such as a water birth.

Music and Lighting

Music is one of the easiest ways to change the mood. Just bring a portable stereo and a few diverse musical selections, in case you need a change of pace, and you're all set. Classical music can help to soothe and center you, while something fast and furious can get the adrenaline going for the hard work. Just be conscious of the fact that other moms will likely be laboring nearby and that your baby is not wearing earplugs. Keep the volume down, or use headphones if you don't mind yet another line hooking you up.

As far as lighting goes, you might not have a lot of choices beyond off/on if you're giving birth in a hospital setting. Even if you can dim the lights, you want your provider to be able to see what she's doing. But requesting that the drapes be drawn and the lights be turned down during early and active labor is not unreasonable.

Photo Finish

Chances are you will want pictures, and lots of them. Your birth plan can outline your audiovisual expectations (for example, video of the delivery, pictures of a C-section in the operating room, live webcast of baby's first breath). The plan also serves as a good checklist for you and your partner when packing for the hospital.

If you want to capture your little star's debut on video, it's best to check with your provider to make sure there's no policy against an amateur videographer being underfoot. Even if there is, in some cases you might be able to work out a compromise, such as setting up the camera in advance on a stationary tripod.

FAMILY, FRIENDS, AND SUPPORT

So, who will be at the big event? This is perhaps one of the most crucial parts of a birth plan: to prepare for adequate support during this very difficult job that lies ahead. Is this a personal experience for just your partner and you, or do you want additional family, friends, or doula support there? The decision is even tougher for first-time moms, who may have some misconceptions about exactly what will happen and who will be there when they hit the maternity ward.

Many women think that their provider or, at the least, a dedicated staff nurse will be available to assist them with the entire labor and birth. In most places that simply isn't true, for a variety of reasons. Shift changes, the number of patients in labor, and other factors may have you and your partner spending a lot of the time alone. Having a doula on your labor team is a great way to ensure continuity of care.

Why enlist a doula's assistance if a dad or coach is present? Many doulas will provide early labor support at home, a benefit that most practitioners can't match. It's also reassuring to many dads to know that they have a backup and aren't forced to remember everything they learned in their 6-week childbirth class during this emotionally charged time.

If you will have people waiting at the hospital who won't be participating in your birth but whom you would like to introduce to the baby as soon after delivery as possible, indicate your wishes in the birth plan. And don't forget about a caregiver for any younger children present, who will need supervision and support.

LABOR PREP

You have the people and the place set. Now for some decisions that will affect your comfort and mobility during labor.

Labor Prep Preferences

Shaving, enemas, and intravenous lines are just a few of the ways the nursing staff may get you ready for the rest of your labor and for delivery. You have the option of doing some of these steps yourself and forgoing others completely. Whatever you decide, make it a part of your birth plan.

Food and Drink

Some hospitals and providers put a strict ban on lunching during labor, for several reasons. First, if events don't go as planned and you end up having to have a general anesthetic for a C-section, having food in your stomach puts you at risk for aspiration (inhaling vomit). Second, your stomach and gastrointestinal tract will have to digest that food when clearly there is more important action happening right next door.

That said, labor is a marathon that lasts exceedingly long for many women, who may need some sustenance to make it through. Simple, liquid-based carbohydrates such as a glass of juice, a Popsicle or juice bar, broth, or tea or lemonade with honey are easily digested and can give you the boost you need. Outline what you'd like to have access to so that you can discuss it with your doctor. If your provider or hospital believes a light snack of food and drink is an absolute no-no in labor, intravenous lines will probably be used to take care of any risk of dehydration. However, a dry mouth is annoying and uncomfortable, so see if you can at least get ice chips to suck on, and bring your lip balm.

Monitors and Mobility

Being tethered to a bed can make handling contractions and labor difficult. Yet checking the fetal heart rate and your contractions is important to ensure that baby isn't encountering any stress. To give yourself room to move through the contractions while ensuring your little one's safety, ask for intermittent monitoring. Unless you require internal monitoring, which is sometimes the case in higher-risk pregnancies, having the freedom to move at least part of the time shouldn't be an issue. Wireless fetal monitors can let you cut the cord altogether; ask your hospital or birthing center if they use them.

PAIN RELIEF BASICS

One of the biggest decisions of childbirth is whether you will want or need pharmaceutical pain relief. Your provider and anesthesiologist can also shed more light on the use of painkillers if you have additional questions.

Going Natural

If you intend to go completely drug free, this section of your birth plan will be a bit more detailed than others. You'll want to outline the access you'd like to drug-free pain relief strategies. Practices like hydrotherapy (shower or whirlpool), massage, and birth balls might be on your list. Requesting to go natural doesn't close the door on changing your mind. If you're a first-time mom, you can't predict whether or not pain medication will be necessary.

Timing of Pain Relief

Some practitioners have policies about how late (or how early) in labor they will permit an epidural (an injection of drugs into the spinal column that decreases pain in the lower half of the body). Whether her policy is grounded in research, experience, or preference will probably make the difference in whether your provider is willing to be flexible on this point. If you have strong feelings about when you want access to an epidural or other pain relief option, outline your wishes in your birth plan.

....

Pregnancy Pointer

A birth ball is a large, inflatable rubber ball that you can sit on, drape yourself over, or do just about anything else that feels comfortable during a contraction. It is available in different sizes and in oblong or ridged versions for more stability. When used in the sitting position, the natural give of the ball encourages perineal relaxation.

....

WHEN TO CHANGE COURSE: INTERVENTIONS

Your doctor will warn you up front that unforeseen circumstances will mean a deviation from your birth plan. Sometimes women feel as if they have failed if matters do not go precisely according to their concept of the ideal birth—which is certainly not realistic. The best way to avoid disappointment is to build alternative scenarios into your birth plan regarding interventions that might be required. For example, if you really don't want an episiotomy (an incision between the vagina and the anus performed to widen the birth canal), you should indicate that in your birth plan and suggest perineal massage with vitamin E oil or another lubricant, warm compresses, or another acceptable alternative. But be prepared to work with your doctor during labor if your alternative plan just doesn't do the trick. And don't be too prescriptive—when you start instructing your physician in the type of sutures to use, you're forgetting that you've hired her because of her medical expertise, not in spite of it.

Some possible interventions that come up in labor and delivery include:

- Induction
- Forceps use
- Vacuum extraction
- Episiotomy
- Artificial membrane rupture

OTHER CONSIDERATIONS

The choices continue after labor and delivery and include decisions not just about your own care, but also about the care of your new son or daughter.

Cutting the Cord

You or your partner will probably be given the option to cut the baby's umbilical cord if you want to. Keep in mind that if your baby needs immediate medical attention at birth, it's possible the cord will be cut swiftly by the attending doctor or midwife instead.

The issue of when exactly to cut the cord could require some negotiations if you have strong feelings about delaying it. If your provider disagrees and believes a swift snip is in order, find out the reasons and research behind his opinion so that you can explore the issue further and come to a meeting of the minds, if possible.

First Contact

Every woman wants her first encounter with her baby to be just perfect. After all, you've had a 9-month buildup to this moment, so wanting to stage and execute it seamlessly is natural.

Belly Basics

Even with a cesarean birth, there are many choices along the way. Will dad cut the cord? Can video be taken? Will you get to hold your baby right after the procedure? A birth plan will help you clarify these issues with your doctor ahead of time.

If you're giving birth in a hospital, find out whether there are strict procedures that must be followed with the baby's care immediately following the birth. Will you be able to nuzzle with her for as long as you'd like, or will she be whisked away for cleaning, fingerprinting, and the rest after a quick hello? Will your other children be able to meet her immediately, or will they have to wait until visiting hours? Contact your birth facility before you create this part of your plan so that you aren't in for an immediate letdown if your wishes for the first encounter are against hospital policy. If you find the policies are just too restrictive, you still have time to explore other options for where you deliver.

Creative thinking may be required to make some rules and regulations acceptable to you. If you can only hold your baby for a few minutes before she goes for her after-birth tune-up, perhaps your partner can assist with those duties and use this special time to bond with baby himself.

POSTPARTUM PLANNING

Adding a postpartum section to your birth plan can be a tremendous help in getting organized after you and your baby are back at home. Will you have live-in help for a few days or weeks? Are you and your partner both taking time off? Will baby have a whirlwind schedule of introductions to friends and family or just a few exclusive engagements?

Outline your maternity leave timetable, if you know what it is, and tentative plans after it's over. Include baby's 2-week doctor visit so that you won't forget to schedule it when she arrives.

Even though your health-care provider won't need to put his stamp of approval on this portion of your plan, it's a good idea to run this by him. He can give you feedback on whether you'll be physically capable of doing what you've set out to do in order to ensure that you have a sufficient recovery period.

Chapter 14
FINAL DECISIONS

You're almost there! Only a little while longer and you'll have your baby in your arms. There's a lot to get done leading up to the big moment, so plan accordingly and give yourself enough time to make some last minute big decisions.

CHOOSING A PEDIATRICIAN

Your pediatrician will look in on and care for your newborn in the hospital, so getting one lined up now is important. Some things to inquire about beyond the basic office hours and insurance questions include:

1. Do ill children have a waiting room separate from the one for well-child visits?
2. Will the doctor support your feeding choice?
3. Are lactation consultants available?
4. How are calls into the office triaged and returned?
5. Additional questions or concerns:

ARRANGING CHILD CARE

Now is also a good time to begin scoping out potential child care providers. Your best source of leads for good child care is other moms in your life who share your values and viewpoints on child rearing. Then narrow down your list of facilities based on the answers to the following questions. You should visit and observe children at any facility you are considering for your own child.

- Does the facility have adequate staffing? (For infants, this is generally a minimum of one provider to every three babies.)
- Does the facility provide a stimulating and child-friendly environment?
- What is the staff like? (Are they caring and nurturing, or do they seem to be distracted or overburdened?)
- Is the facility properly licensed and accredited? (See the website of the National Association for the Education of Young Children, *www.naeyc .org*, if you are unsure.)
- Is an adequate number of the staff specially trained for early childhood care?
- Do the children in the program seem comfortable and happy?
- Are parents allowed to observe when their child is in the program?
- Does the program focus on emotional, cognitive, and physical development in activities?
- Does the staff provide adequate individual attention to infants?

THE DIAPER DEBATE

Deciding whether you'd like to use cloth diapers or disposable diapers is a choice many new mothers go back and forth on. Some moms swear by the old-fashioned and eco-friendly use of cloth diapers, while others find the convenience of disposable diapers a necessity. Your decision may depend on a variety of factors, including your concern about the environment, the amount of time and labor you are willing to devote to maintaining a supply of clean diapers, and the level of convenience that would work best for you from day to day.

Below you will find a list of pros and cons to help you decide where you stand in the cloth versus disposable diaper debate.

USING CLOTH DIAPERS	
Pros	**Cons**
Biodegradable	Requires electricity and water to wash
Cheaper than plastic	Can become expensive if you hire a service to wash diapers
Can be less irritating for baby's skin	Labor intensive if you wash them yourself

PACKING YOUR BAG

You'll have a lot on your mind in the few days before your baby's birth, so pack early. Essentials you should pack for your delivery include:

Overnight Bag Checklist

Essentials you should pack for your delivery include:

- ☐ **Pain-relief tools for labor:** Include things like massage balls, a picture for focusing on through contractions, a water bottle, and so forth.
- ☐ **Music to labor by:** Check with your hospital or birthing center in advance to see if a small portable stereo is acceptable. If not, you can always bring personal headphones.
- ☐ **Snacks:** If your hospital or birthing center allows food and/or drink in labor, pack yourself a small cooler with supplies. And don't forget about a little something for your coach.
- ☐ **Stopwatch, clock, or watch with a second hand:** This will come in handy for timing contractions.

- ☐ **Phone numbers:** Make sure your partner has names and numbers of the folks you'll want to clue in immediately on the new arrival.
- ☐ **Several nightgowns:** Bring some with button or snap fronts if you're going to nurse.
- ☐ **Extra underwear:** Make them comfortable but not your best. They'll probably end up with some postpartum bloodstains.
- ☐ **Sanitary pads:** The hospital will provide you with some, but extras are good to have on hand.
- ☐ **Picture of the kids:** If you have other children, taping a picture of big brother or sister to your newborn's bassinet is a good way to emphasize your first child's important new role in the family.
- ☐ **Glasses or contacts:** Make sure you can see the baby after he's finally here.
- ☐ **Warm socks and/or slippers:** Those hospital floors can be cold.
- ☐ **Bathrobe:** You'll want this for hallway walks to the nursery.
- ☐ **Toiletries:** Remember toothbrush, toothpaste, and other basics.
- ☐ **Shower supplies:** You'll be given an opportunity to shower at the hospital, so pack shampoo and other necessities.
- ☐ **Going-home outfits for both you and your baby:** Pack a set of newborn clothes and make sure you bring something loose and comfortable to wear yourself.
- ☐ **Baby blanket:** You'll want to swaddle your baby for his return home. Let your partner bring the car seat on discharge day so you aren't overwhelmed with luggage.

If you're breastfeeding, you might also pack:
- ☐ **Nursing bras:** If you don't have any yet, a bra with a front fastener will work well as a stand-in for now.
- ☐ **Box of nursing pads:** These will be handy for when your milk comes in.
- ☐ **Vitamin E oil or lanolin ointment:** Pack them for sore or cracked nipples.

Use the additional space to add other items you want to have with you.

_____

_____

_____

_____

_____

_____

_____

_____

_____

OUTFITTING YOUR BABY

In addition to some of the other products you may have purchased in anticipation of baby's arrival (diapers, wipes, car seat, alcohol swabs, baby shampoo, baby soap, bottles, and a thermometer), make sure you have the following before you bring your new baby home:

- Three undershirts that snap
- Ten onesies and/or one-piece sleepers (depending on the season and climate you live in)
- Five bibs with waterproof linings (e.g., rubber)
- Three hooded bath towels
- Seven pairs of booties or socks
- Ten+ towels or cloth diapers for dealing with spitup
- Four+ snap-up jumpsuits for daywear
- Two+ baby hats
- Nightlight
- Baby monitor

- Four+ crib or bassinet sheets
- Four+ receiving blankets
- Baby nail clippers
- Four+ face cloths
- Q-tips and/or cotton balls
- Baby oil
- Diaper rash ointment
- Changing pad

THINKING OF NAMES

You and your significant other have no doubt been thinking about the potential name you will choose depending on the gender of the baby. To get you started on ideas, below are the most popular names for babies born in 2012.

BOYS' NAMES	GIRLS' NAMES
Jacob	Isabella
Ethan	Sophia
Michael	Emma
Jayden	Olivia
William	Ava
Alexander	Emily
Noah	Abigail
Mason	Madison
Aiden	Elizabeth
Liam	Mia

Source: U.S. Social Security Administration

NOTES AND CHECKLISTS

Baby Names—Boys

Here you can record boys' names that you and your partner like.

_____

_____

_____

_____

_____

_____

_____

_____

_____

Baby Names—Girls

Here you can record girls' names that you and your partner like.

_____

_____

_____

_____

_____

_____

_____

_____

_____

Checklist for Months Seven Through Nine

- ☐ Make a date with yourself to relax, read, or just catch up on sleep.
- ☐ Interview pediatricians.
- ☐ Sign up for childbirth classes.
- ☐ Contemplate the breast versus bottle decision.
- ☐ Set up an appointment to discuss your birth plan with your provider.

- ☐ Take five and de-stress; it's good for you and baby.
- ☐ Lay out your baby's essentials.
- ☐ Compare and decide on cloth versus disposal diapers.
- ☐ Discuss circumcision with your pediatrician and your partner.
- ☐ Start wrapping up projects at work.
- ☐ Finalize your child care plans for after maternity leave.
- ☐ Preregister at your hospital or birthing center.

- ☐ Make sure that your other children's teachers and care providers are aware of your impending hospital stay.
- ☐ Pack your bag and compile a call list for your partner.
- ☐ Line up postpartum assistance.
- ☐ Stock up the freezer with heat-and-eat meals or recruit postpartum kitchen help.
- ☐ Make a plan, and a backup plan, for getting to the hospital.
- ☐ Put your feet up, relax, and take a deep breath. The rest is up to your baby!

Birth Plan Checklist

Now is a good time to go through a birth plan checklist. A birth plan is a road map for your entire childbirth experience, beginning to end. It's your chance to let everyone involved (doctors, nurses, partners) know what you want the experience to be. Use your birth plan to chart the course of labor and delivery, but remember you may have to take alternate routes occasionally depending on conditions.

Where will the birth take place?
- ☐ Hospital
- ☐ Birthing center
- ☐ Home
- ☐ Other:

Who will be there for labor support?
- ☐ Husband or significant other
- ☐ Doula
- ☐ Friend
- ☐ Family member

Will any room modifications or equipment be required to increase your mental and physical comfort?
- ☐ Objects from home, such as pictures and a blanket and pillow
- ☐ Lighting adjustments
- ☐ Music
- ☐ Video or photos of birth
- ☐ Other:

Do you have any special requests for labor prep procedures?
- ☐ Forgo enema
- ☐ Forgo shaving
- ☐ Shave self
- ☐ Heparin lock instead of routine IV line
- ☐ Other:

What do you want to eat and drink during labor?

- ☐ A light snack
- ☐ Water, sports drink, or other appropriate beverage
- ☐ Ice chips
- ☐ Other:

Do you want pain medication?
- ☐ Analgesic, such as Stadol, Demerol, or Nubain
- ☐ Epidural
- ☐ Other:

What nonpharmaceutical pain relief equipment might you want access to?
- ☐ Hydrotherapy, such as a shower or whirlpool
- ☐ Warm compresses
- ☐ Birth ball
- ☐ Other:

What interventions would you like to avoid unless deemed a medical necessity by your provider during labor? Specify your preferred alternatives.
- ☐ Episiotomy
- ☐ Forceps
- ☐ Internal fetal monitoring
- ☐ Pitocin (oxytocin)
- ☐ Other:

What would you like your first face-to-face with your baby to be like?
- ☐ Hold off on all nonessential treatment, evaluation, and tests for a specified time.
- ☐ If immediate tests and evaluation are necessary, you, your partner, or another support person will accompany the baby.
- ☐ Want to nurse immediately following birth.
- ☐ Would like family members to meet the baby immediately following birth.
- ☐ Other:

If a cesarean section is required, what is important to you and your partner?

☐ Type of anesthesia (e.g., general vs. spinal block)

☐ Having partner or another support person present

☐ Spending time with the baby immediately following procedure

☐ Bonding with the baby in the recovery room

☐ Type of postoperative pain relief and nursing considerations

☐ Other:

Do you have a preference for who cuts the cord?

☐ You

☐ Your partner

☐ Provider

When would you like the cut to be performed?

☐ Delay until cord stops pulsing.

☐ Cord blood will be banked. Cut and stored per banking guidelines.

☐ Cut at provider's discretion.

☐ Other:

What kind of postpartum care will you and the baby have at the hospital?

☐ Baby will room-in with mom.

☐ Baby will sleep in the nursery at night.

☐ Baby will breastfeed.

☐ Baby will bottle feed.

☐ Baby will not be fed any supplemental formula and/or glucose water unless medically indicated.

☐ Baby will not be given a pacifier.

☐ Other:

What are your considerations for after discharge?

- ☐ Support and short-term care for siblings
- ☐ Support if you've had a cesarean
- ☐ Maternity leave
- ☐ Other:

PART 5

THE BIG DAY!

Chapter 15

LABOR AND DELIVERY

At last! The moment you've been waiting for, the birth of your child, is finally here. Getting ready for labor and delivery is an exciting time. You have a lot of choices and decisions to make, but all of them will lead you to the happy result of finally becoming a mother. Labor is hard work for sure, but with a good labor coach and a good understanding with your health-care provider, you will be prepared to do that work willingly.

LABOR COACH

No matter how and where you give birth, having a labor coach is one recommendation that does not change. Your labor coach will offer support, comfort, encouragement, and assistance all throughout labor and delivery.

Traditionally, a woman's partner has been her labor coach, but now many women make other choices. Some women choose a close female friend, mother, sister, or other relative. Other women rely on the services of a professional doula who is trained in offering support during labor.

Choosing someone other than your partner does not have to mean your partner is left out of the process. Most health-care providers have no problem with several people being present at a birth to offer support to the new mom.

Some women designate one person as the photographer and another as their personal coach. Whatever works for you is perfectly acceptable. Some partners simply do not do well in the role of labor coach, and recognizing that and making other arrangements is sensible.

Your coach should ideally attend childbirth classes with you, so you are both prepared. Make sure you are able to reach the coach day or night as your due date approaches. You may wish to arrange for a backup coach in case your first choice is unavailable for some reason. Some hospitals require that the coach attend classes while others do not, so be sure to check into this so you can meet requirements.

CHOOSING A BIRTH FACILITY

When you're deciding where you would like to give birth, you may think a hospital is your only choice. In fact, you have several options to consider. Where you plan to give birth is an important component of your birth plan, and it is something you need to discuss with your health-care provider.

Birth Center

A birth center is a facility that has some medical equipment but is more comfortable and homey-feeling than a hospital. Birth centers are staffed by midwives, but they also have physicians available. These facilities often offer a wide range of birthing alternatives, such as water birth, birthing balls, birthing chairs, and other choices. Birth centers are often located next to a hospital, yet they do not have that hospital feel.

Birth center rooms are designed to look like real bedrooms. They often have kitchens and living areas for family members to make themselves comfortable in. Birth centers afford more privacy than hospitals and usually allow you to wear your own clothing.

When choosing a birth center, make sure it is accredited by the Commission for the Accreditation of Birth Centers (*www.birthcenters.org*).

Birth centers have lower C-section and episiotomy rates than hospitals. While this is partially due to the approach taken in birth centers, it is also because higher-risk pregnancies are generally not accepted at birth centers because of the likelihood of complications. Epidurals are not available at most birth centers. Women who go to birth centers often receive their prenatal care at the center as well. Most insurance companies will cover the cost of a birth center birth.

When considering a birth center, ask the following questions:

- Do they accept your insurance?
- What training and certifications do attendants have?
- How many beds are available?
- Which OB or practice is on standby for complications?
- How long has the center been in operation?
- How many babies are delivered per month at the center?
- What percentage of births are transferred to the hospital?
- What kinds of pain relief are available, if any?
- If a birth is transferred to a hospital, can the midwife go with you?

Hospital

Many women feel most comfortable with a hospital birth. You have access to medical equipment if needed, and your physician or midwife can deliver the baby. When selecting a hospital, talk to your health-care provider about the level of risk you face. If you are at high risk, your health-care provider may recommend you give birth at a hospital such as a children's hospital or perinatal center, where advanced medical care is available for your newborn.

Hospitals that handle obstetrics are designated by levels one through four, with level one approved only for low-risk pregnancies and level four for the highest risk pregnancies. It is important to realize that obstetrical and neonatal care is a highly competitive business. In some instances, hospitals may attempt to market themselves as being capable of managing high-risk pregnancies when in fact the claims may be exaggerated. Health-care providers may also be partial to a particular hospital, and their decisions on the site of delivery may be based more on political than health-care considerations. If you have a high-risk pregnancy of any kind, you should ask your provider about the level of care appropriate for you. You should also ask about the hospital's capabilities. For example, a level three obstetrical hospital may have the capability to care for a problem pregnancy or premature baby, but it may not have a maternal-fetal medicine specialist or neonatologist on site twenty-four hours a day. If your baby may require pediatric specialty care, it would be best if the baby were born in a facility where that is available.

If your baby needs to be transferred after birth to a higher-level facility, you may not be able to be transferred with the baby, or if you are transferred, your insurance company may not pay for the transfer or stay at the other facility. This can be particularly problematic if you have undergone a C-section and cannot be discharged earlier. Most pregnancies can be managed in level-one or level-two facilities. Pregnancies at moderate risk (for example, premature birth over thirty weeks) can usually be managed at a level-three facility. However, the highest risk pregnancies (serious medical complications of pregnancies, birth defects, or extreme prematurity) are best managed in level-four or regional perinatal centers. Do not let community hospital politics or fancy marketing dictate the best place for your delivery.

Some physicians practice in teaching hospitals where residents and medical students are present. Many patients are concerned about having medical students and residents involved in their care. In fact, in a teaching environment where residents and medical students are well supervised, the care is actually better. However, you may have reservations about the number of individuals in the room when you are laboring and delivering or the number of people involved in your care. You should speak to your obstetrical provider about these issues during your prenatal visits. Remember, it is always your right to control these types of issues.

Pregnancy Pointer

Labor is divided into three stages. The first stage, cervical dilatation, is subdivided into the latent phase (contractions without cervical dilatation) and the active phase (cervical dilatation occurs). The second stage is after full cervical dilatation, when the baby descends in the birth canal and finally delivers. The third stage is delivery of the placenta after the baby is delivered.

You should also ask your obstetrical caretaker if he has a covering caretaker(s) who will take over care should your original caretaker be on vacation, ill, or unavailable. Some physicians practice out of more than one hospital, which may create a conflict if there is a patient in more than one facility. You should also ask if there is an in-house obstetrician (or "doc in the box," as they are called). Many hospitals require or provide an obstetrician on-site twenty-four hours per day, seven days per week. The job of these obstetricians is to act in an emergency if your doctor is not available or to assist your doctor should a complicated situation come up. In many places this individual will assist your physician at a cesarean section if required.

You may also want to ask about the availability of obstetrical anesthesia coverage and epidurals in the hospital you deliver in. Though not absolutely necessary, the ideal is to have on-site twenty-four-hour anesthesia coverage for obstetrics should a problem develop. Many smaller hospitals do not have this. You should also inquire about the pediatric backup availability and credentials of those available, should the baby develop a problem in the delivery room or after birth. You should make sure that the hospital where you deliver has a transfer agreement with the regional perinatal center should the baby need additional treatment. Ask about the policy of the hospital where you are to deliver. Under what circumstances, and at what gestational age of the baby, is the mother transferred to a regional perinatal center, and which center is it? In some communities you have a choice of one or two centers. Some obstetrical care providers may make such decisions based on personal bias or convenience. You should insist upon the center that provides the highest level of care both for yourself (if you are transferred) and the baby (if the baby is transferred). Ideally, the center should have board-certified neonatologists and maternal-fetal medicine specialists as well as pediatric specialists, and they should be available twenty-four hours a day, seven days a week.

Home Birth

Giving birth at home offers you the comfort of being able to labor and deliver in surroundings that are comfortable, with family present. Some families choose home birth because they want their existing children to be present. If you give birth at home, you should use a trained midwife.

....

Belly Basics

Home births are not recommended for high-risk pregnancies, women who want pain medication, or women who live more than fifty miles away from a hospital.

....

Home births are a controversial area in obstetrics, and most states have laws governing home deliveries. There are several considerations. First, you should remember that the purpose of the pregnancy is to have a healthy baby and mother. All other considerations must be secondary. You should also check the regulations in your state governing home births and make sure you are in compliance. Make sure that the midwife is in compliance with state regulations, is complying with safe guidelines to determine pregnancy risk, is licensed in the state where she practices, and has an obstetrical backup and plan should problems arise.

PAIN-RELIEF OPTIONS

Many women want to know about the pain-relief options available during labor and delivery. Pain-relief options are highly evolved and can offer a lot of relief to women who choose to use them. They range from using simple breathing techniques to different types of medication. Some women decide well in advance what kind of pain-relief options they want to use. The best advice is to educate yourself about all available kinds and make your decisions as you go through labor.

Nonmedical Solutions

First, have plenty of pillows on hand. Experiment with different positions, such as on all fours, against a wall, and leaning against someone or something while bent forward at the waist.

Pregnancy Pointer

If you don't want to be bound to your bed during labor, find out whether your birth facility has fetal monitors that use telemetry. These wireless monitors strap on like a regular external device so that you don't have to remain plugged into anything. There are even telemetry units that are waterproof, if you plan on easing labor pains with hydrotherapy.

Back labor, which occurs when baby's face is toward your abdomen rather than toward your spine, can cause severe lower-back pain. Ask your partner to try massage or a warm water bottle to ease contractions. The soothing jets of a whirlpool tub can do wonders, if you have one. If your water has broken, however, never take a soak without approval from your provider.

Keep positive, supportive people around you. Let your coach be your buffer and clear out any distractions. Try to remain focused on riding through and past the contraction. Fix your eyes on something that relaxes you and practice the breathing exercises you learned in childbirth class to keep the oxygen and blood flowing. Don't hyperventilate. Talk or groan through the peak of the contraction if it helps.

It's difficult to relax while you're in the midst of a really big, really uncomfortable contraction. However, letting go in between contractions can help ease your mind and body and loosen you up for impending delivery. You probably learned a few relaxation exercises in childbirth class. If so, now is the time to try them, as they can make the pain more manageable.

Progressive relaxation, a series of muscle tightening and releasing, is a good way to release your stress. Make sure you're in comfortable clothes in a soothing atmosphere (that is, quiet and perhaps dim). Recline with your head and back elevated, then start tensing and releasing each muscle group, from your head to your toes. Breathe in with the tension, and blow out with the release. Try to clear your head of everything but the sensation at hand. If you practice this prior to labor, it can be a good tool for managing some of the early pain when contractions are still relatively far apart.

Analgesics and Narcotics

These medications provide temporary pain relief during labor through an intramuscular injection. Common medications are Demerol, Nubain, Stadol, and Sublimaze. These dull pain but do not remove it. These drugs are useful for relieving anxiety as well as pain.

Epidural

An epidural is the continuous injection of pain-relieving medications into the epidural space in the spine. The catheter is taped to your back, and the amount of medication delivered can be dialed up or down depending on your sensation or need to push. A low-dose epidural, also called a walking epidural, allows full movement while reducing pain. Pain relief with an epidural can be uneven, with more sensation on one side than the other. Pain relief is not immediate and may take time to work. More than 50 percent of all U.S. births involve epidurals. The risks involved with an epidural include low blood pressure and slowed labor.

There is considerable controversy regarding epidural anesthesia during labor, as to whether it poses risk to mother and baby, or whether it slows down labor and increases the need for vacuum or forceps delivery and C-section. In skilled hands, epidural anesthesia can be extremely beneficial and safe. As with any medical intervention during labor, the decision on its use should be individualized according to the mother, baby, and the situation. It is probably a good idea to discuss epidurals with your health-care provider. This topic is also covered in childbirth classes.

Spinal Block

A spinal block is the injection of pain-relieving medication into the spinal fluid. A spinal provides complete, immediate numbing of the middle and lower body; however, it is temporary and wears off within an hour or two. Spinals are generally reserved for C-sections.

Combination Epidural and Spinal

A combination of an epidural and spinal can provide benefits of both: the immediate relief of a spinal and the lasting effects of an epidural.

....

Belly Basics

A study in the medical journal *The Lancet* found that low-dose epidurals resulted in fewer interventions during birth, with 43 percent of women being able to give birth on their own without forceps or vacuum extraction, compared to 35 percent of women who were given higher-dose epidurals. However, those with low-dose epidurals took longer to recover from birth, and their babies were more likely to need breathing assistance.

....

Local Injection

If you need an episiotomy, you may be given an injection at the site to numb the area. If a forceps or vacuum assisted delivery is needed, a local block is given to numb the area.

LABOR INDUCTION AND AUGMENTATION

Sometimes labor does not start naturally on its own or does not continue at a normal pace. In these instances, your health-care provider may decide to either begin labor for you or urge it along using medical procedures or medication.

Induction

If you go past your due date, experience problems that necessitate delivery, or your water breaks but labor does not begin on its own, you may need to have your labor induced. Most elective inductions of labor are performed for postdatism (usually one or two weeks past your due date), or when continuing the pregnancy may pose an unnecessary risk to the baby or mother (such as preeclampsia, maternal diabetes, or fetal growth restriction). Your health-care provider will first perform a pelvic examination to determine the ripeness of your cervix. This is determined by evaluating the softness and thickness of the cervix, effacement (thinning) of the cervix, cervical dilation (if any), and station (how high the baby is in the birth canal). A numerical score called a Bishop score is then assigned. The higher the score, the higher the likelihood of a successful induction.

There are several methods your health-care provider may choose from or combine to induce labor:

- **Stripping the membranes:** Your health-care provider separates your membranes from your uterus, which causes the release of hormones that can begin labor. This can be done at your doctor's office and can be uncomfortable.

- **Breaking your water:** Your health-care provider breaks your bag of waters (this is called an amniotomy), causing the release of hormones that will get your labor started. An amniotomy should only be performed in a hospital setting.
- **Prostaglandin analogues:** These are drugs that can be taken orally or intravaginally for both cervical ripening and induction. These drugs can cause excessive contractions (called hyperstimulation) and need to be removed should that occur. Usually, you must remain in the hospital during cervical ripening, and the process may take up to twelve hours.
- **Pitocin:** This is the hormone oxytocin, which your health-care provider may give you intravenously to stimulate contractions. When Pitocin is used, your contractions and the baby's heart rate will be carefully monitored.
- **Cervical catheter:** Your health-care provider inserts a small catheter with an inflatable bulb on it into your cervix and expands it. This can cause the cervix to ripen and labor to start.

Belly Basics

A study in the *American Journal of Obstetrics and Gynecology* found that as the mother's age increases, so does her risk of needing labor augmentation, having a prolonged labor, and needing a forceps or vacuum extraction. The same study also showed that older mothers are more likely to have babies who experience shoulder dystocia, the shoulders getting stuck during birth. Pushing the baby back in (cephalic replacement) and then performing a cesarean section is a last resort if the shoulders can't be freed.

If your health-care practitioner induces labor, but you don't give birth within forty-eight hours, she may advise you that you need a C-section. The risk of infection increases the longer you wait to deliver, especially if your water bag has broken.

Augmentation

Labor augmentation is used when your body is in labor but you aren't progressing. If your water has not broken yet, your health-care provider will likely break it for you. If that is not successful or your water has already broken, Pitocin is given by IV to increase your contractions. Because older women tend to have longer labors, they are also more likely to receive labor augmentation to attempt to move things along.

VAGINAL BIRTH

Vaginal birth is what most mothers plan on and is considered the safest type of delivery. While the odds are that you will have an uneventful vaginal delivery, some situations are more likely to occur in older mothers. It's best to be aware of them just in case.

Prolonged Labor

Older women are more likely to have a cervix that is slower to dilate. The cervix must fully dilate and efface before you can deliver. If this process is slower than usual, your labor can go on for a long time, not only increasing fatigue but also increasing the chance of infection.

Dysfunctional or prolonged labor means the labor is not progressing at an appropriate rate. First babies tend to be slower at every stage of labor. Older women are more likely to need Pitocin augmentation, have vacuum or forceps delivery, experience prolonged labor, and have a greater chance of a C-section. The exact reason for this is not known.

Belly Basics

Your physician can increase the odds you will deliver in a normal time frame by carefully managing your labor and using Pitocin. As a general rule, older mothers, especially those who have had more than one child, can expect to have a normal vaginal birth, but they may expect to need Pitocin to augment their labors more frequently. An important thing to keep in mind is that a longer labor is really expected for older mothers and is nothing to be overly concerned about if it happens to you. Your health-care provider will manage your care to help you deliver in a time frame that is considered normal by the medical establishment.

Breech Presentation

In normal deliveries, the head is delivered first. A breech presentation is when the baby's feet or buttocks are closest to the cervix, instead of the head. Breech births are more difficult because the legs or feet can bend and get stuck. They occur in 3 to 4 percent of all deliveries. Age increases your risk of breech birth 1.3 times for every five-year age increment. The risk at age 40 is 11 percent. The highest risk group is older mothers who are having their first baby. The exact reason for the increase in risk for older moms is not known. Some have theorized that uterine fibroids, which are more common in older women, may distort the uterine cavity.

If your baby is in breech presentation, your health-care provider may try what is called an external version, in which she tries to turn the baby by applying pressure to your abdomen. This should only be attempted by an experienced health-care provider. The overall chance of success for an external version is about 70 percent, and it is usually done around thirty-seven weeks. In the United States and Canada, breech deliveries are generally not performed vaginally any longer. Many health-care providers have no experience with breech deliveries, and there is some evidence that a C-section is a safer option. Breech deliveries with twins are somewhat different. Some health-care providers will perform a vaginal delivery of a twin breech if the breech is the second twin (first twin head down, second twin breech) and the gestational age is not extremely premature.

Large-for-Gestational-Age Baby

A large-for-gestational-age (LGA) baby is one who measures over the ninetieth percentile for the gestational age of the baby, which at term is nine pounds. Large babies are common in mothers who have gestational diabetes (an increased risk for older moms), are obese, or moms who gain too much weight during pregnancy. An LGA baby can be difficult to deliver vaginally and is at a higher risk for shoulder dystocia (having shoulders that become stuck during delivery). These babies can also have low blood sugar, especially if the mother has gestational or pregestational diabetes. If a baby is still large for its age when it is six months old, it is at a higher risk for obesity. Listen to your health-care provider's recommendations for weight gain during pregnancy to try to avoid these problems.

Placenta Previa

This condition occurs when the placenta covers the cervix. A vaginal delivery is not possible in this situation. This is a condition that is usually diagnosed well before you go into labor and is usually not a surprise.

Your Attitude

A 1999 study in the journal *Birth* found that older mothers seemed less likely to believe their babies' lives were in danger during labor and were happier with the way staff handled labor problems. Based on this study, it seems that older mothers tend to come away from the birth experience feeling more comfortable and secure than younger moms.

Even if you've read everything ever written about labor and delivery, taken copious notes in childbirth class, watched hours of birth stories on cable TV, and questioned all your friends on their birth experiences, you'll still find your labor is different in some way from that of others. Because every woman's labor is unique, comparisons of length, progress, and pain perception can be inaccurate and even discouraging. Follow your own path, and you'll do fine.

YOUR BODY IN LABOR

Labor is hard work (don't let anyone tell you otherwise), but it's also the most rewarding work you'll ever do.

Contractions

The first signal of labor is contractions—the tightening and release of your uterus that helps propel your baby down the birth canal. These contractions are different from the Braxton-Hicks ones you've possibly had in that they occur at regular intervals, are painful, and are slowly but surely opening the door (that is, cervix) for baby's exit.

You don't need to rush to the hospital or birthing center after your first contraction. But you should call your doctor or midwife to let her know labor has started and how far apart contractions are. Remember, contractions are timed from the beginning of one to the start of the next. Your provider will let you know at what point you should head for the hospital or birthing center. Until then, you can labor in the comfort and privacy of your own home. However, if the pain from contractions starts to be more than you can handle without professional help, have your coach call your provider back and let her know you're heading for the hospital early. Read on for early pain relief options you can try at home.

Prep

When you do arrive at your birthing center or hospital, the nursing staff will prep (prepare) you for labor and delivery. What prepping involves depends on facility policy and doctor preference, but here are some procedures you might encounter.

You'll change into your hospital gown or nightgown from home. Try not to wear a lot of jewelry or other extraneous items that can get lost in the shuffle from room to room. You could be getting a partial shave of your perineal area or, less commonly, a full shave of both your abdominal and pubic area.

Poking and Prodding

It's possible that your hospital requires an enema to clear out your bowel so that baby will have a smoother passage down the neighboring birth canal. It's not very common in today's hospitals and birth facilities, but it is a possibility. Find out in advance if this is required; you might be able to administer it at home if it makes you more comfortable. If contractions have had you on the toilet all day and you've got nothing left to give, let your nurse know and staff might bypass this step.

Your nurse may insert a needle with a heparin lock and secure it to your arm with surgical tape. If intravenous (IV) medication is suddenly needed during labor, it can be easily hooked up. Other hospitals will hook you up to an IV line as a matter of course and administer a glucose solution to keep you hydrated. Other medications can be added to the line as necessary.

Baby Monitor

Chances are good that you've experienced the fetal and uterine monitors during a visit to your provider, so this part of the procedure should be familiar to you. The monitor will give you a visible and audible look at your contractions and the fetal heart rate; it will allow you and your coach to see when a contraction is coming and, more important, when it seems to be almost over. It will also pick up fetal heart sounds and alert you to any stress the baby may be experiencing from oxygen deprivation or problems with the umbilical cord. An internal monitor might be used if you are considered to be at high risk.

Other anesthetic blocks that are used less frequently include:

- **A caudal block** is administered into the bony area right at the end of your spine; it affects the abdominal and pelvic muscles.

- **A saddle block** is a type of low spinal anesthesia that numbs a more limited area of your body—your perineum, inner thighs, and buttocks.
- **With a paracervical block,** the anesthetic is injected into either side of your cervix during labor to numb the area.
- **With a pudendal block,** the anesthetic is administered to the nerves around the vagina and pelvic floor to help control pain when the baby's head bulges into your cervix.

LABOR IN THREE ACTS

Labor is a series of three distinct stages, aptly called *first, second,* and *third stages.* For most women the longest span is the first stage, which lasts from the earliest signs of labor right through baby's descent into the birth canal, in preparation for stage two—pushing. Stage three consists of delivering the placenta; mothers usually feel this is a cakewalk after all the hard work involved in baby's arrival.

First Stage

The first stage of labor begins with early (latent) labor and ends with active labor. Your provider probably uses the term "transition" (descent) to refer to the end of first-stage labor.

During the early phase the cervix effaces (thins) and dilates (opens). This ripening process perhaps started several weeks ago, well before the regular contractions of early labor began. Now your cervix will dilate to about 4 or 5 centimeters. Contractions will arrive every 15 to 20 minutes and last 60 to 90 seconds. If your partner or coach isn't around, now is the time to contact him so that he can be by your side. Then touch bases with your provider, who will tell you at what point you should head to the hospital or birthing facility.

Try to stay up and moving through contractions as much as you can to let gravity help your baby descend. Consider a light liquid snack (for example, broth or juice) to power up your energy reserves for the long road ahead. Rest if possible. Try the breathing and relaxation techniques you picked up in childbirth class as well as the coach-assisted massage or showering to get you through these first few hours. Then leave for the hospital and the next phase—active labor.

In active labor your contractions are coming closer together regularly, perhaps 3 to 5 minutes apart, and they can be intense, lasting 45 to 60 seconds. These strong contractions are dilating your cervix from about 4 or 5 centimeters to around 8.

Belly Basics

If your birthing center or hospital has whirlpool tubs or showers available for laboring moms, you might find the pulsating water welcome relief for getting through contractions. This pain relief method (called hydrotherapy) is not the same as a water birth, in which a baby is actually born submerged in a pool of water.

Once you reach the birthing center or hospital, you'll be quickly prepped as described earlier and given an internal exam to check the dilation of your cervix. The baby's position will be checked, and you will probably be hooked up to a fetal monitor to assess the baby's well-being.

Other signs that active labor is in progress:

- **Your membranes rupture.** If the amniotic sac hasn't already broken, it will now or very soon.
- **You bleed from your vagina.** More of the mucous plug is being expelled.
- **You need air.** Put those cleansing breaths and other breathing techniques into practice. Your hard-working uterus needs oxygen.
- **Your back really hurts.** The baby's head is pushing on your backbone. Massage can help.
- **You have muscle cramps.** Again, massage can help the ill-timed charley horse.

- **You're exhausted and physically spent.** Remember what you're working toward. Let your coach know how you're feeling so that she can motivate you and get you whatever she can to keep you moving forward.

Don't feel inadequate or guilty about asking for pain medication at any point if you want it. You wouldn't hesitate to take Novocain if you were getting a wisdom tooth pulled, yet having an 8-pound child pulled through a 10-centimeter opening doesn't qualify? Pain medication is a tool, just like your breathing exercises. Wisely used, it can result in a better birth experience for both you and your child.

Once your cervix reaches 8 centimeters and contractions start coming one on top of another to get you to full dilation, the end of the first stage (transition) has arrived. Because of the frequency of contractions and the overwhelming urge to push, this is the most difficult part of labor. Fortunately, it culminates in your child's delivery, once you bridge those final 2 centimeters to become fully dilated.

As you begin to transition from first- to second-stage labor:

- You can become nauseated and may even vomit.
- You have chills or sweats, and your muscles twitch.
- Your back *really*, *really* hurts.
- Contractions are just minutes apart, if even that.
- There is pressure in your rectum from the baby.
- You are absolutely exhausted.
- You may feel like pushing even though your cervix is not yet fully dilated.

Although every fiber of your body is probably screaming "PUSH!," you need to hold back just a few moments more. Your cervix is almost, but not quite, open far enough for baby's safe passage. Take quick, shallow breaths and resist the urge to push until your doctor or midwife gives the go-ahead.

Second Stage, or PUSH!

Your cervix has made it to 10 centimeters, and you are finally allowed to push. This second stage can last anywhere from a few minutes (with second or subsequent babies) to several hours. Your contractions will still arrive regularly, but they aren't quite as close together—a welcome relief. Pushing is very hard work, but the sensations may change from the intense gripping you've experienced to more of a stinging or burning sensation.

Pregnancy Pointer

If possible, try to find a pushing position that makes you feel comfortable and in control. Use gravity to your advantage by kneeling, squatting, or sitting up with your legs and knees spread far apart. Stirrups are likely available, but don't feel forced into using them if they don't work for you.

Your birth attendant and/or coach will let you know when the peak of the contraction occurs, the optimum time for pushing effectively. Use whatever it takes to push effectively. If that means moaning, grunting, and emitting other primal sounds that make your prenatal snoring sound like a lullaby by comparison, go for it. The people attending your birth have probably heard just about everything. Don't be embarrassed, because the noise won't even faze them.

The emergence of the head at your vaginal opening starts with a small patch of skin visible during the peak of a push. The patch may recede when you rest but will reappear at the next contraction. Unless your baby is arriving in a breech position, the head will finally crown (bulge) right out of your vaginal opening. You may be asked to stop pushing momentarily as the baby's head is ready to emerge, in order to prevent perineal tearing. Panting can help you suppress the urge. The obstetrician or midwife may decide on an episiotomy if your skin doesn't appear willing to stretch another millimeter, or she may attempt perineal massage.

Finally the head slides face down past the perineum and is eased out carefully by the birth attendant to prevent injury to the baby. The attendant may wipe the eyes, nose, and mouth and suction any mucus or fluid from her upper respiratory tract. It's all downhill from here as the rest of the body slides out.

As your baby leaves the quiet, dim warmth of the womb for the bright lights and big noises of the outside world, his respiratory reflexes kick in and the newborn lungs fill with air for the first time. He'll probably test out those lungs with a full-fledged wail. Your doctor will place the baby on your stomach for introductions, usually with the umbilical cord still attached.

The cord will continue to pulse with blood flow for a few minutes. The timing of the actual clamping and severing of the cord will depend upon your practitioner, and this is a matter of some debate in childbirth circles. Some professionals believe that waiting until pulsation has stopped or even until after the placenta is delivered improves baby's circulation and blood pressure, reducing baby's risk of early childhood anemia and mom's chance of hemorrhage. Other practitioners still follow the traditional method of clamping and cutting the cord earlier. You may want to talk the issue over with your doctor in advance of delivery day if you have concerns about the timing of the cord cut. If baby requires resuscitation, or if the cord is tightly wrapped around a body part or is exceedingly short, it will be cut sooner.

Most practitioners will give dad (or even mom) the option of cutting the cord in an uncomplicated birth. Don't feel bad if it isn't your cup of tea, especially if either one of you is a bit squeamish. Better to spend the time cuddling your baby than being picked up off the delivery room floor.

Some parents choose to bank their child's umbilical cord blood and/or placenta blood after birth. This blood contains stem cells, those miraculous little blank slates from which all organs and tissues are built. Cord and/or placenta blood collected immediately after birth is placed in a collection kit and flown to a facility where it is cryogenically frozen and banked for later use, if needed. The theory behind banking this at birth is that if your child ever develops a disease or condition requiring stem-cell treatment, the blood can be thawed and used for her treatment. If it matches certain biological markers, it may be used to treat other family members as well. However, banking is cost prohibitive for many and requires an ongoing annual storage fee.

Third Stage

The third stage of labor is the delivery of the placenta. The entire placenta must be expelled to prevent bleeding and infection complications later on. Contractions will continue, and your doctor may press down on your abdomen and massage your uterus or tug gently on the end of the umbilical cord hanging from your vagina. You might also be injected with the hormone Pitocin (oxytocin) to step up your contractions and expel the placenta. You'll be given pushing directives again, but this part will seem like a piece of cake given the task you've just completed.

Pregnancy Pointer

If you are having a scheduled cesarean, try to arrange a few moments to consult with the anesthesiologist ahead of time. If you've had any poor experiences with anesthesia in prior C-sections, let her know so that you can improve the outcome this time around. She can also answer any questions you might have about her part of the procedure.

Once the placenta is out, any stitches you require to repair tearing or episiotomy incisions will be put in. A local anesthetic will be injected to deaden the area if you aren't still anesthetized from an epidural.

Chapter 16
CESAREAN SECTIONS (C-SECTIONS)

Many women deliver their babies by cesarean section (C-section); in fact, national averages show that C-section accounts for 29 percent of all births. C-sections are surgical procedures that are recommended when vaginal birth is not possible, labor is not progressing, the baby is in distress, multiples are being born, or the mother's health is in danger. For many women, a C-section is not an ideal birth and can feel like something of a disappointment, while other women request C-sections without a medical reason. Each woman has her own reaction to and opinion about C-sections and should be permitted to make her own choice after receiving medical advice.

C-SECTION BASICS

While C-sections are truly a lifesaver in many instances and highly recommended in others, in general, avoiding them is the way to go if at all possible. A CDC study published in the journal *Birth* found that for mothers that were low risk, the infant mortality rate is twice as high for babies delivered by C-section than vaginally. (Note that simply being over age 35 may be considered a factor that makes you high risk.)

C-sections are surgical procedures and carry risks that include the following:

- Reaction to the anesthesia
- Blood clots
- Wound infection
- Increased bleeding
- Injuries to the bladder or bowel during the surgery
- A longer recovery time
- Increased risk of hernias due to the weakened abdominal wall
- Adhesions (Fibrin, a natural defense to tissue damage, can adhere to organs, causing twisting and pulling in the abdomen and leading to infertility, pelvic pain, and bowel obstruction.)

In addition to these risks to the mother, babies born by C-section (especially if labor has not taken place prior to the procedure) are more likely to experience temporary breathing problems after birth. This condition, called transient tachypnea, requires medical attention. The labor and delivery process normally clears fluid from the baby's lungs and releases hormones that stimulate lung activity. Missing out on labor and delivery means these things don't happen, increasing the chances of problems. Babies born by C-section may be groggy due to the medication the mother receives during the surgery. There is also a small risk of scalpel injury to the baby.

Once you have one C-section, you are much more likely to need another one in a subsequent pregnancy. This is particularly true since evidence shows repeat C-sections may be safer than VBAC for many women and due to the fact that VBAC may not be available in all hospitals. Previous C-sections increase the risk of placenta previa and placenta accreta in the pregnancies that follow. The more C-sections you have, the more scar tissue you build up, which can make future conception more difficult. Multiple C-sections also make the surgery more technically difficult, increasing the risks of prolonged surgical time, infection, and damage to other internal organs such as the bladder or the bowel.

If you have a C-section, ask your physician to use adhesion barriers. These barriers, which are not common in C-sections although they are for other abdominal surgeries, prevent the growth of adhesions that can cause many problems. Another request to make is for suturing of the peritoneum, the membrane that covers the internal organs. Often in C-sections it is left to close on its own, but a recent study showed suturing it prevents adhesions.

Another risk of C-sections is that your baby may be born too early. If your C-section is not preceded by natural labor and is instead scheduled or follows an induced labor, your baby may be slightly premature if the calculations used for your due date were not accurate. Preterm babies face the risk of jaundice, breathing problems, feeding difficulties, and an inability to properly regulate body temperature. Generally, though, if your pregnancy is accurately dated, performing an elective C-section prior to labor can be done from thirty-nine weeks on without concern about fetal lung immaturity. If you need a C-section sooner, or if the dating of the pregnancy is in question, an amniocentesis can check the baby's lung maturity. Women who are HIV-positive and who are having a C-section to prevent transmission of HIV to the newborn may have an elective delivery at thirty-eight weeks, so that the C-section is performed before labor begins. The risk of the baby having respiratory problems is relatively low under these circumstances.

Patient-Choice C-Sections

Patient-choice C-sections (those done based on a patient's request, and not for any medical reason) have seemingly become popular in recent years. Many celebrities schedule them, and according to Health Grades, an independent health-care ratings agency, the number of women choosing patient-choice C-sections rose by 36.6 percent between 2001 and 2003. However, these procedures are not nearly as popular as the media has portrayed them. One study showed that approximately 96 percent of women preferred a spontaneous vaginal delivery. Of the 4 percent who said they would prefer a C-section, the majority either had some type of risk factor that they thought made C-section safer for the baby or had a bad experience with a prior vaginal delivery.

Women who choose patient-choice sections do so for a variety of reasons:

- Fear of the pain or embarrassment of labor and delivery
- A need to exactly plan the birth date for work or personal reasons
- A belief that avoiding delivery will prevent bladder control problems later in life
- A belief that delivery will change their vagina permanently, making sex different or less pleasurable
- A belief that delivery negatively impacts the pelvic floor muscle tone
- Fear that problems during delivery will harm the baby, causing problems such as cerebral palsy.

Belly Basics

The American College of Obstetricians and Gynecologists (ACOG) has issued a formal policy on patient-choice C-sections, saying it is ethical if it is in the best interest of the patient both physically and emotionally. Because of this policy, many physicians are willing to perform patient-choice C-sections.

Some of these reasons are valid, and some are not as valid. Some women are simply not able to face labor and delivery for a variety of reasons, and having the option of a C-section is important for them. Each woman has to make a decision about what is right for her personally, and she should be permitted to do so. Some women need to be able to plan an exact birth date due to pressing career, family, or personal reasons, and they should be supported in their need to do so.

It is also true that a vaginal delivery does stretch out vaginal tissue and that it can never be exactly as it was before. The vagina is designed to stretch, though, and any change is minimal. Most women find that they have normal, satisfying sex lives after a vaginal birth.

The information about pelvic floor changes causing a loss of muscle tone or leading to incontinence is conflicting. While there is evidence that vaginal birth can lead to these problems, the primary culprit is probably carrying a pregnancy. The weight of a baby on your pelvic floor for so many months is more likely to cause changes that lead to muscle tone changes or future incontinence.

While problems can occur during vaginal birth that can impact the baby, most problems are present before delivery, including increasing evidence that cerebral palsy is not caused by birth trauma. Some women see birth as a risky situation. While it is true that labor and delivery can be unpredictable, a competent physician can manage just about anything that happens. A C-section is not without risks either, so neither option is considered entirely risk-free.

Acceptance

No matter how you come to have a C-section, ultimately you have to accept the fact that you've had one and come to terms with it. Whether your baby exits your body through your vagina or through an incision in your uterus, you have still given birth and still have grown and nurtured a human being inside your body. You are a mother either way. The type of birth you have is a small part of your baby's history and does not mean you are any less of a woman or mother.

It is important to remember that both vaginal birth and C-section birth require stamina, courage, and commitment. Whichever you end up going through, you have accomplished something to be proud of.

REASONS FOR C-SECTIONS

Unquestionably, there are situations in which C-sections are the best and safest choice for both the mother and baby. If your health-care provider recommends a C-section for you, take her advice seriously.

A C-section might be recommended to you for a variety of reasons, including the following:

- Previous C-sections or abdominal surgeries
- A baby that is too large to be safely delivered vaginally
- Placenta previa (the placenta covering the cervix)
- Placental abruption (the placenta pulling away from the wall of the uterus)
- Failure to progress in labor, or labor that is too slow
- An infection such as genital herpes or HIV
- Gestational diabetes or preeclampsia (C-section not necessary but in some cases is recommended)
- Multiples
- Breech position
- Umbilical cord prolapse (the umbilical cord slips down into the vagina, possibly cutting off oxygen supply to the baby)
- Shoulder dystocia (the baby's head is delivered but the shoulders are stuck under the mother's pubic bone).
- Prior third- or fourth-degree tear in a previous delivery (if the muscle around the anus or the rectum tears, a subsequent vaginal birth can increase the risk of bowel problems)
- Nonreassuring fetal status, previously called fetal distress (a slowing of baby's heart rate, indicating a problem)

In some situations, an emergency C-section is necessary and there is no time for your physician to discuss the options and risks with you. In this instance, follow the medical advice you receive and let your trained professionals do what they are trained to do. There are other instances when you have time to agree to a C-section and ask questions.

HOW TO DECREASE YOUR CHANCES

Because a C-section is major surgery and carries risks, most women wish to avoid having one if possible. It's not always possible to avoid a section, but there are things you can do to reduce your odds.

Age

First of all, you have to realize that your odds of a C-section are simply higher because of your age. According to the March of Dimes, about 40 percent of women over age 35 will have a C-section. While this figure is high, it does not mean that you will need a C-section. If you actively work to avoid one, you may improve your odds. Keep in mind that your physician is also aware of these statistics. While most physicians do not prejudge a woman's ability to give birth solely based on age, some may be less inclined to work with you to avoid a C-section. Talk to your doctor about what you can do to reduce the chances of a C-section, and make clear your desire to avoid one.

Be Educated

Read and educate yourself about pregnancy, labor, birth, and C-sections so that you will understand whatever happens and will be prepared to deal with it. Arming yourself with knowledge is also likely to reduce anxiety and tension, and it may help you relax more during labor, leading to a successful outcome.

Belly Basics

Take a childbirth education class. If this is your first child, it is an essential step to take. You will not only learn about pregnancy, labor, and delivery, but also about breathing and relaxation techniques that will help you cope with labor more successfully. If you had a previous C-section and want to try for a VBAC, ask about a VBAC class.

Stay Healthy

Staying healthy during your pregnancy and following your health-care provider's recommendations are key. Eating a healthy, well-balanced diet and exercising will keep your body in good condition and help you prepare for labor. Also, not gaining excessive amounts of weight, or following your diet strictly if you have gestational diabetes, will reduce the risks of having an oversized baby that can't be delivered vaginally.

Stay Home

Once you go into labor, follow your health-care provider's instructions about when to contact him and when to go to the hospital. Remaining at home as long as possible during the first stages of labor can help you remain calm and relaxed and reduce the risk of medical intervention.

Epidurals and Labor Augmentation

Some studies show that epidurals slow down labor. If you are very concerned about this, you may wish to use alternative relaxation techniques during your labor. If your baby is overdue, the risk of the epidural slowing things is outweighed by the benefit of getting the baby delivered before size becomes an issue.

Having your labor induced or augmented also increases your chances of having a C-section, although this is most likely the result of the way your labor is progressing rather than the fault of the medication. The risk of needing a C-section from an induction increases if the cervix is not ripe. The use of cervical ripening agents reduces this risk. If the induction fails after two days, most patients will opt for a C-section rather than going home to wait for labor to start naturally. The take-home message is that unnecessary inductions (not medically or obstetrically indicated) should be avoided.

Ultrasounds

Medical opinion used to be that doing a late third-trimester ultrasound could help decide if the baby was large and if induction would reduce the risk of a C-section or shoulder dystocia. However, it has been shown that the risk of shoulder dystocia actually increased in women who were induced in these situations, and the risk of C-section also increased. It is now not recommended that nondiabetics have an ultrasound to help make this determination. For diabetic pregnancies, however, it is legitimate to base delivery decisions on ultrasound-estimated fetal weight.

Stay Mobile

Move around during labor. Remaining in bed on your back does not help your body. Standing, walking, squatting, swaying, and other movements may help move your labor along.

WHAT TO EXPECT

Unless you've already had one, a C-section can seem a little scary, particularly because the entire procedure is completely out of your control, yet it happens right in front of you. Understanding what to expect can make the process easier and more comfortable.

Preparation

Before your C-section, if it is not an emergency, you will talk with your health-care provider about the decision to have a C-section. This is the time to ask any last-minute questions or express any concerns. You will talk to the anesthesiologist, who will get a medical history from you and discuss your anesthesia options. If you do not already have one, an IV will be started in your hand so that medication can be administered. You will be taken into a surgical delivery room. Your abdomen will be washed and shaved. The anesthesiologist will administer your medication. A catheter will be inserted into your bladder. Sheets will be set up to block your view of the procedure. Your partner and/or coach will be allowed to join you.

....

Pregnancy Pointer

If you will be having, or think you may be having, a C-section, you may want to join C-Section Support, an online group for moms who have had or are about to have a C-section (online at http://groups.msn.com/CSectionSupport).

....

The Surgery

Your physician will make an incision into your abdomen. There are several types of incisions. The most common and most preferred is the low-segment transverse incision, or bikini cut. The physician cuts through your abdomen and then through your uterus. It only takes about three minutes from the time of incision to the time of delivery. You will feel nothing, other than some tugging. The physician will then reach in or push on your stomach to get the baby out. The baby will be suctioned (to clear the nose and mouth), and your incision will be closed. The skin incision is usually closed using surgical staples or with subcuticular sutures (sutures under the skin). The subcuticular sutures are more cosmetically appealing just after the surgery, and there is nothing to remove. However, staples are faster to place, and removal causes minimal discomfort. The wound looks the same with either method within several weeks after the surgery. Rarely, a drain may be placed temporarily inside the wound, usually attached to a small plastic bulb or circular cylinder for draining the wound.

Throughout the procedure, you will be surrounded by nurses and physicians who are there to care for you. If you feel uncomfortable in any way, let them know. After your baby is born, you will be able to see her, and your coach or partner will be able to hold her.

After your surgery, you will go to the recovery room, and your baby will go to the nursery for evaluation. Once your condition is stabilized, you'll be moved to a regular room, and your baby will join you.

Preventing Problems

The risk of uterine and abdominal wound infections is very high following a C-section, especially if labor occurred or membranes ruptured prior to the procedure. Preventive antibiotics are given as a single IV dose after the baby has been delivered to prevent problems.

Pregnant women are at higher risk for blood clots in general. When a blood clot forms in a large vein in the body, it is called deep vein thrombosis (DVT). If part of this blood clot breaks off and embolizes (moves) to the lung, it is a pulmonary embolism (PE). PE and DVT are called thromboembolic disease or complications. Women who have C-sections are at higher risk for these complications especially if they are older, obese, have varicose veins, or smoke. Women who have a C-section after labor or who have a uterine infection at the time of delivery are also at greater risk.

Thromboembolism after C-section is prevented using a small dose of blood thinner (Heparin) or sequential pneumatic compression stockings (stockings that gently squeeze your legs). Heparin must be given prior to the C-section and continued for a time period after the surgery. The sequential stockings are placed around the calves (they look and feel a lot like blood pressure cuffs) prior to the surgery and are connected to a machine that inflates and deflates the cuff. This pumps the veins in the lower extremities. There is some evidence that an epidural can help prevent deep vein thrombosis.

Another problem that a C-section can lead to is the need for a blood transfusion. For a routine C-section, the risk of needing a blood transfusion is relatively low. However, in certain circumstances such as placenta previa, especially in the presence of suspected placenta accreta (where the placenta invades the wall of the uterus, more common after a prior C-section), the need for a blood transfusion is relatively high.

....

Belly Basics

In most hospitals, a sample of blood is taken from the umbilical cord after delivery and sent for analysis of the pH level of the baby's blood. This shows the baby's oxygen levels at the time of delivery and can be used to determine if problems occurred prior to or during labor and whether the baby may need extra attention. Talk to your pediatrician about these test results.

....

Autologous blood transfusion, in which the pregnant woman donates her own blood in advance of the surgery, is an option. There was controversy at one time regarding pregnant women doing this, but it appears to be safe if performed to certain guidelines. Having a friend or relative donate (if they are compatible) is also possible; however, it is not always possible to know for sure if the individual who you have chosen to donate may in fact be a risky donor. Another possibility is called Cell Saver. This procedure collects blood from the patient's own pelvis or abdomen, recycles it, and transfuses the blood back to the patient. However, there is a significant risk of amniotic fluid spilling into the abdomen, mixing with the blood, and causing an embolism. Finally, the hormone erythropoietin (available as Eprex, NeoRcormon, or Aranesp) can be given by injection for several weeks prior to the surgery. This drug stimulates the bone marrow to make more blood and can raise the concentration of hemoglobin. Both erythropoietin and Cell Saver are usually acceptable to patients who are Jehovah's Witnesses or oppose blood transfusions.

VAGINAL BIRTH AFTER CESAREAN (VBAC)

Vaginal birth after cesarean (VBAC) has become a hotly contested topic. VBACs were once encouraged across the board. Recently, however, there have been concerns about VBAC due to highly publicized cases of uterine rupture and serious injury to both mother and baby. Because a VBAC requires an anesthesiologist to be at the ready continuously in case an emergency C-section is needed, there has been a dampening of the initial enthusiasm for the procedure, especially in level-one (low-risk) obstetrical hospitals.

The recent trend toward patient-choice C-sections also shows a declining enthusiasm on the part of many women for vaginal delivery in general, VBAC or otherwise. There has never been a randomized controlled clinical study trial comparing VBAC with repeat C-section, and it is unlikely that one will ever be done.

Belly Basics

VBACs are drastically declining because of studies indicating they are not as safe as was once believed. The VBAC rate is down 67 percent since 1996 and made up only 9.2 percent of all 2004 births.

In deciding if you'd like to try a VBAC, you need to discuss the reason for your first C-section with your health-care provider. If you had a C-section previously for failure to progress in labor and this current baby seems to be about the same size, it's unlikely you will be successful with a VBAC. But a prior C-section because of breech position does not make it likely a VBAC would be unsuccessful. The most serious risk associated with VBAC is rupture of the scar from the previous C-section.

A study in the *American Journal of Obstetrics and Gynecology* found that the older a woman is, the less likely it is she will be able to successfully have a vaginal birth after a previous C-section. Among all women, about 20 to 40 percent of VBACs are unsuccessful. Those most successful with VBAC shared the following characteristics:

- Had a low-segment transverse incision with their prior section
- Have a normal-sized baby who is not in breech
- Have a pelvis large enough for the baby to fit through
- Spontaneously go into labor (are not induced)
- Have not had a C-section in the last two years
- Have not had a C-section due to a large-for-gestational-age baby

A trial of labor to see if you can progress might be something to consider, but studies show that C-sections done after failed trials of labor have higher complications than C-sections performed without any attempt at labor (that is, a scheduled C-section). You have the right to change your mind at any time during a trial of VBAC, regardless of your reasons.

In deciding whether to do a VBAC, you need to weigh the risks. A repeat C-section carries the risk of infection, a longer recovery, difficulty holding the baby, as well as all the risks of surgery, such as blood clots. A VBAC carries the risk of uterine rupture and the risk of being unsuccessful, leading to a C-section after hours of labor, which may have a higher complication rate than if it had been performed electively.

If you are induced for your VBAC, you may be at a higher risk of complications. Several recent studies have shown that the use of prostaglandin analogues for cervical ripening is associated with a higher incidence of uterine rupture for VBACs. Although Pitocin alone did not appear to increase the risk of uterine rupture, many obstetricians will no longer induce a patient with a prior C-section who wants a VBAC. However, Pitocin augmentation during labor appears to be safe in skilled hands.

NOTES AND CHECKLISTS

Things Your Partner Will Need to Do and Bring for Labor

Labor can be a nerve-wracking experience, for you and your partner. It might be helpful to have a checklist on hand for your partner when labor starts to help them calm down and feel in control:

- ☐ Call your provider (when contractions are no more than 5 minutes apart, last at least a minute, and have been regular for an hour)
- ☐ Your overnight bag
- ☐ Cell phone, calling card, or plenty of quarters for pay-phone calls (if cell phones are not allowed to be used in the hospital)
- ☐ Phone number list
- ☐ Lock doors in house
- ☐ Instructions for where you should go once you arrive at the hospital
- ☐ Name and number of anyone attending delivery
- ☐ Name and number of person to contact at work (if you're not on maternity leave yet)
- ☐ Your partner's hospital bag
- ☐ Baby bag
- ☐ Infant car seat
- ☐ A copy of your birth plan
- ☐ Camera

PART 6

LIFE AFTER DELIVERY

Chapter 17

POSTPARTUM YOU

Once you're finally a new mom, you will mostly likely be floating on air, wondering at the beauty of your new baby. However, this is a time when you must also focus on yourself and your own recovery from the birth. It takes time to recover from the actual birth process, just as it takes time to adjust to caring for the new little person who has joined your family.

RECOVERY FROM VAGINAL BIRTH

Although birth is a natural process, it can sure take a lot out of a person. When recovering from vaginal birth, it is important to give yourself time and not to expect an overnight recovery. Remember that it took nine months to carry your pregnancy and that recovery is something you should view as an ongoing process.

If you deliver in a hospital, you will mostly likely have a two-day hospital stay. If you deliver at a birth center, you will most likely go home the same day. If you deliver at home, you will want to take time to rest and recover there. You will likely experience soreness and discomfort from the birth as well as fatigue. If you had an episiotomy or have tears, you will need to care for the stitches or tears as directed by your health-care provider, which will begin with ice packs

in the delivery room. You'll need to wash your hands before and aft...
bathroom and avoid touching the perineal area as much as possible. A cl...
pad is applied (front to back to avoid bacterial contamination of the perine...
Warm sitz baths offer considerable relief, as does lying on your side and sittin...
on a pillow or inflatable cushion. Often sprays or ointments are offered for pain
relief, and oral pain medication is also offered. If a third- (torn anal sphincter) or
fourth-degree (torn rectum) tear has occurred and was repaired, stool softeners
will be important. If you've had stitches, it may take a few months to fully recover
from them.

....

Pregnancy Pointer

If you're anxious to begin an exercise program after birth, it's important that you talk to
your physician. After a vaginal birth, you should wait four to six weeks. After a C-section you
may be advised to wait up to ten weeks, although stretching is acceptable immediately after
birth. The key to beginning an exercise program is to start gradually.

....

About a third of women who deliver vaginally develop hemorrhoids, and
many others experience constipation. Make sure you get enough fiber in your
diet and drink enough fluids in the days after the birth. Your health-care provider
may prescribe a stool softener. If you have difficultly urinating after birth, you
may need a catheter at first.

After giving birth, you will have heavy discharge, called lochia. This can
contain clots and will continue for weeks. You may feel what are known as
afterpains, as your uterus shrinks back to its normal size, which can feel stronger
when breastfeeding. This is normal. Your breasts will feel sore as your milk comes
in. Recovery from a vaginal birth is generally thought to take about a month, but
every woman's experience is different.

ΟM C-SECTION

section is similar in some ways to recovery from vaginal
y is recovering from carrying a baby; however, because
very is more complicated. A hospital stay for a C-section
days, and total recovery takes about six weeks.

l birth, you will have a heavy discharge for weeks after the
birth, afterpains, sore breasts, constipation, and possibly hemorrhoids, as well
as trouble urinating on your own. If you went through labor, your recovery may
be more difficult because you're recovering from the surgery and the hard work
of labor.

After a C-section, you will experience pain and discomfort around your
incision when you try to move around. It can be helpful to hold a pillow against
your abdomen when coughing, walking, or laughing to help reduce discomfort.
It is important to get out of bed and move after the surgery, either the same day
or the next day, to help prevent blood clots. The incision may burn and itch as it
starts to heal, and this can last for several weeks. It is essential that you follow
your doctor's instructions for caring for the incision, which will probably include
keeping the wound clean and dry. It is likely you will have numbness at the site of
the incision that in some cases can be permanent.

The hospital personnel will encourage you to do some breathing exercises to
help clear your lungs after surgery. Digestive functioning may take some time to
get moving again, and it's not uncommon to experience uncomfortable trapped
gas. Because it takes time for digestion to resume normally, you will be placed
on a liquid diet until you are able to pass gas. Getting up and moving around can
help increase digestive functioning.

You'll be advised to avoid stairs and heavy lifting until your incision heals. You
will probably be advised not to drive a car for about two weeks or until you are
able to make sudden movements.

Your physician will most likely prescribe pain-relief medication for you after
the surgery, which may at first be delivered intravenously (often by a pump you
can control) and then switched to pills. Speak up about your pain, and don't be
afraid to ask for more pain relief if you need it.

Belly Basics

BABY'S BODY: AN OPERATOR'S MANUAL

Your baby will actually lose weight as she starts out in life, but she should be back up to birth weight by her 2-week checkup. Thereafter she may put on a pound every 2 weeks, doubling her birth weight by her fourth month. Premature babies sometimes grow a little slower, but most eventually catch up.

Your baby's eyesight is a bit hazy, although she can see you fairly clearly when you hold her 7 to 10 inches away from your face. Studies show that she knows your voice well from listening to it in the womb, and she prefers to hear it to a stranger's voice.

Your newborn arrives with a variety of natural reflexes or involuntary ways of moving:

- **Palmar (grasping) reflex.** When you touch your baby's open hand, she'll make a fist around your finger.
- **Rooting reflex.** If you stroke her cheek, her head will turn toward your touch. This reflex helps the bleary-eyed newborn find her food source, and you can use it to guide her to the breast or bottle.
- **Sucking reflex.** Once at the breast or bottle, baby's sucking reflex takes over as she automatically sucks on anything put in her mouth.
- **Startle (Moro) reflex.** When baby is startled, he will thrust his arms and legs out, arch his back, then quickly pull arms and legs in again.

- **Babinski reflex.** Stroking baby's foot makes him spread his toes and flex his foot.
- **Stepping reflex.** Hold your baby up with your hands under his armpits so that his feet are touching a firm surface. He will lift his feet up and down like he is about to take baby steps.
- **Tonic neck reflex.** When placed on his back, baby turns his head to the right and makes fists with his hands.
- **Blinking.** The reflex of closing his eyes when they are exposed to bright light, air, or another stimulus is one involuntary reaction that baby will keep for the rest of his life.

FROM SOFT SPOT TO CURLED TOES

The bones of baby's skull are not yet fused together, and unless you have had a cesarean delivery, your baby's head may look a bit, well, pointy. This cone-headed appearance is the result of pressure in the birth canal and will round out within a few days after birth. There are four small areas on your baby's head where the skull bones have not yet joined; these are called *fontanels* (soft spots). Three of these fontanels fuse within the first 4 months of life, but the longest lasting and most visible of these—the diamond-shaped area on the top of the head called the *anterior fontanel*—can take up to 18 months to close. Many a curious sibling has reached out to jab this pulsating spot, much to his parent's horror. Don't get too concerned; your baby's brain is well protected by a tough membrane called the *dura mater*.

....

Belly Basics

Baby's soft spot is called a fontanel. She has a total of four, but only the anterior and posterior are easily located.

....

The eye color your baby has at birth may change later in infancy or childhood. This is due to the ongoing production of the hormone melanin.

Baby's Skin

Your newborn's soft-as-butter skin may have some imperfections at first. Post-term babies are more likely to have some peeling, while preterm babies can still be sporting a substantial amount of lanugo and vernix. Although the vernix is fairly well rubbed off by the time you bring baby home, you may continue to find it in his creases and crevices until his first real bath. The lanugo will rub off over the next few weeks.

Baby may also be wearing one or more birthmarks on his birthday suit, including:

- **Salmon patches or "stork bites."** Red marks on the eyelids, forehead, and at the very back of the nape of the neck usually fade and disappear over time.
- **Hemangiomas (strawberry birthmarks).** These red, slightly raised marks can increase in size but may shrink and be gone by age 5.
- **Café au lait spots.** Light-brown birthmarks. Very rarely, large numbers of these birthmarks can be a sign of medical conditions. Talk to your child's doctor if you have any concerns.
- **Mongolian spots.** Dark-blue to blue-green spots on the buttocks or lower back are most common in African American, Native American, and Asian newborns, and many fade over time.
- **Port wine stains.** These bright-red or purple marks are considered to be more permanent. Laser removal is an option in later life if they are located in a prominent spot.
- **Milia.** Little whiteheads called *milia* are common on newborns, especially around the nose, and may come and go during the first few days.
- **Petechiae.** These are red-to-purple pinpoints that you may see on your baby's face from the trauma of coming down the birth canal. These will disappear in a few days.

The Umbilical Cord

Baby's umbilical cord stump looks just like it sounds—a dark, dried-up protrusion. Since it is basically dead tissue, it is black in color. You'll be instructed to clean it regularly and keep it dry to prevent breakage and bleeding. Keep an eye out for signs of infection, such as pus or inflammation. Within 2 weeks or so the stump will fall off, and your baby's perfect little bellybutton will be revealed.

Belly Basics

Your baby, boy or girl, may have swollen breasts that actually leak milk. This milk, known in folk medicine as "witch's milk," is the product of your pregnancy hormones at work on your newborn. Avoid massaging the area because this can trigger an abscess. The breasts will return to normal size within a few days.

Genitals

Before your partner congratulates himself too heartily on his well-endowed son, you might want to break the news that this is probably just a passing phenomenon. Newborn boys and girls are often born with swollen genitals, again due to the effects of your pregnancy hormones working on them. Girls can even have a bit of mucus discharge, possibly blood-tinged, from their vaginas.

Fingernails and Toenails

Baby's tiny curled fingers and toes usually emerge in need of a manicure. Growing for several months in the womb, they are typically long and ragged. The thought of trimming such tiny appendages might fill you with dread, but it's not as hard as you think. Just make sure you have the right tools (infant-sized clippers) and try to trim while baby is sleeping (if you'd like to avoid wrestling with a moving target). If you still can't seem to cut the nails, bring your clippers with you to your 2-week pediatrician appointment and ask for pointers.

Sleeping Like a Baby

In the beginning it will seem like your little one is sleeping quite a bit. In fact, she's snoozing up to 18 hours a day. If she's your first, you might be crouched outside her door waiting to run in and get some quality playtime at the first rustle. (Second-time parents, on the other hand, count down the minutes to naptime.) Although her sleep patterns, which involve 4-hour stretches of snoozing, won't have a huge effect on your day schedule, they're going to hit you hard at night. She'll be waking up to be fed several times an evening for at least the first 3 months.

Remember to always place your baby on his back when laying him down for a nap or bedtime. Back sleeping has been shown to reduce the incidence of sudden infant death syndrome (SIDS). Make sure baby's crib is clear of stuffed animals, quilts, pillows, and other soft bedding when he heads to bed.

POSTPARTUM DEPRESSION

Feeling down is a common postpartum emotion that typically passes in a few weeks. For many women, however, these feelings go beyond the basic baby blues and signal a more serious depressive or endocrine disorder.

The Baby Blues

The majority of new mothers experience what is commonly known as the baby blues, a short-lived period of mild depression that appears in up to 85 percent of postpartum women. A severe shortage of sleep, disappointment with the birth experience, seesawing hormone levels, anxieties about baby's health and well-being, and shaky confidence in your own parenting skills all can lead to feelings of sadness or inadequacy. Fortunately, most cases of the blues resolve themselves between a few days to 2 weeks after birth, as balance returns to the new mother's life.

When It's More Than the Blues

More serious is postpartum depression (PPD), which occurs in about 10 to 15 percent of new mothers and can drag on for up to a year. If you're experiencing one or more of the following symptoms, talk to your doctor about PPD:

- Feelings of extreme sadness and inexplicable crying jags
- Lack of pleasure in things you would normally enjoy
- Trouble concentrating
- Excessive worrying about the baby or, conversely, a lack of interest in the baby
- Feelings of low self-esteem
- Decreased appetite

Fortunately, PPD can be effectively treated with counseling and/or antidepressant drugs, so ask your doctor for a referral to a mental health professional. Even if you're breastfeeding, you have medication options; there are several antidepressant drugs on the market that are thought to have minimal effect on nursing infants. A number of studies involving sertraline (Zoloft), for example, found that even though the drug passes into breast milk, the levels it reaches in the nursing infant are clinically insignificant, in some cases too low even to be detected in standard laboratory blood tests.

Belly Basics

Several studies have indicated that low postpartum hemoglobin levels (iron-deficiency anemia) increase the risk of postpartum depression. Ask your doctor about your blood hemoglobin levels, especially if you have a history of iron-deficiency anemia. Increasing dietary iron intake and taking daily iron supplements will improve hemoglobin levels and may alleviate depressive symptoms.

Safety cannot be guaranteed, however; studies on how antidepressants affect a breastfed child in the long term are not available. On the other hand, clinical research has demonstrated a measurable detrimental effect on children of depressed mothers when PPD goes untreated. Each woman must evaluate the risks of treatment versus the benefits when deciding whether drug therapy is right for her.

If you experience symptoms that worry you or are making your life difficult, it is essential that you tell someone about them. Talk to your partner as well as to your health-care practitioner. There is nothing to be embarrassed about, and none of it is your fault or due to any deficiency on your part. Seeing a therapist or taking antidepressants, or both, have proven to be very effective in treating postpartum depression. Women who already suffer from severe depression or manic-depressive illness are at extremely high risk for postpartum depression; it is important that such women keep in close contact with their mental health-care provider in the immediate weeks following delivery.

In addition to talking to your health-care provider, rest as much as you can. Get others to help you around the house and with the baby, and talk about your feelings to anyone who will listen. Keep busy with activities and people, and remember that you have just gone through a very significant life-changing event. You can't expect to bounce back immediately.

Belly Basics

Your health-care provider will let you know when you can begin to have sexual relations again, usually about four to six weeks after birth. Generally you'll be given the all-clear at your postpartum checkup. Remember to have patience with your body. It has done a lot of work and may not respond in the same old ways.

Postpartum Psychosis

An estimated one in every 1,000 women experiences a severe form of PPD known as postpartum psychosis (puerperal psychosis). Symptoms include hallucinations, delusions, fantasies of hurting oneself or others, insomnia, and turbulent mood swings. Postpartum psychosis is a medical emergency that needs immediate treatment and usually hospitalization. The good news is that with proper medical care, full recovery is expected.

Thyroid Problems

Thyroid problems are fairly common after childbirth, but the symptoms can be confused with other postpartum conditions. Milk supply difficulties, extreme fatigue, hair loss, depression, mood changes, problems losing weight or unusually rapid weight loss, heart palpitations, menstrual irregularities, and sleep disorders are all common signs of postpartum thyroid conditions.

Some women have temporary postpartum hyperthyroidism (an overactive thyroid), with the result of weight loss, diarrhea, racing heart, anxiety, and other symptoms of a revved-up metabolism. Your doctor may prescribe drugs to ease symptoms, although this condition often resolves itself quickly.

Other women can develop temporary postpartum hypothyroidism (an underactive thyroid), resulting in fatigue, weight gain, constipation, depression, and other symptoms of a slowed-down metabolism. Again, medication may be prescribed depending on the severity of symptoms, and frequently the thyroid returns to normal within 6 months to a year after the birth.

New mothers with a family or personal history of autoimmune or thyroid disease can benefit from routine thyroid testing in the first month postpartum. It can be hard to tell what's normal after having a baby, but if any of the aforementioned symptoms become debilitating, a thyroid test can quickly rule out or diagnose a thyroid problem.

Women who experience temporary postpartum thyroid problems are at a higher risk of developing thyroid disease later in life and should talk to their doctor about regular follow-up screening.

DISCOVERING YOURSELF AS A MOTHER

Becoming a mother is a life-altering experience. Your entire perspective shifts, and suddenly you have a baby who is your number-one priority. Discovering yourself as a mother is an amazing experience, but it can also be challenging.

Some women come into motherhood determined to conquer it like a career. If you've waited a long time to have a baby, it can be easy to feel you've got to make the most of it or that you must let your baby become your world. There are many types of mothers and endless appropriate ways to parent. Reading parenting books can help you get a feel for what style of parenting you are most comfortable with, and it can open your eyes to options you may not have considered or thought possible.

The most important thing you can do as a mother is listen to yourself and follow your instincts. You might believe you don't have parenting instincts, but you do have instincts about how you want to live your life, what kind of family you want to have, and your general approach to life. Listen to these instincts and let them guide you as you make parenting decisions. More than anything else, it is important that as you parent, you remain true to yourself. If it doesn't feel right to you, don't do it, even if all the books and your mother and your best friend tell you otherwise.

Belly Basics

The American Academy of Pediatrics recommends that mothers and babies sleep "in proximity to each other" to encourage breastfeeding. This stops short of endorsing co-sleeping or family beds. Some physicians believe family beds are dangerous and can lead to suffocation or increased risk of SIDS. Others believe that if done safely, it can enhance bonding and make breastfeeding easier.

All mothers make mistakes, and you will, too. You can't avoid it, and you shouldn't waste your time worrying about it. Mothering is a challenging undertaking that requires twenty-four-hour management. It is your flaws that will give your family its unique character. You can probably think of things your parents did that you swear you'll never do to your child. It's terrific that you already have some ideas about what you want to avoid, but you can be sure that you will make other mistakes and errors in judgment along the way. In the scheme of things, they won't matter because your baby will have a devoted and loving mother who has good intentions.

Your Relationship As Parents

Having a baby is a major change, and it can be a big change for your relationship with your partner as well. Learning to love each other as parents can be wonderfully rewarding, though, and working together to raise a child can bring you closer.

If this is your first child, you are undergoing a major change from being a couple to being a family. Previously, you and your partner decided things together and focused on each other. Now, suddenly, a new demanding person wants all of your time and energy. Instead of focusing on each other, you and your partner now are focusing together on your baby. After a while, you may miss the time and attention you used to be able to give each other. To keep your relationship as adults alive, plan time to spend alone together. You don't have to get a sitter and go out to a restaurant; just sitting and talking about adult things for half an hour while the baby sleeps can be enough.

Learning to parent together takes time and patience. It takes time for your parenting styles to emerge, and the most important thing to remember is that you are both learning as you go. You may not always agree about how to parent, and that's okay. You probably have parents who employed different parenting styles, and so you come to parenthood with a different set of expectations and experiences.

Chapter 18

BREASTFEEDING BASICS

Breastfeeding is one part instinct, one part practice, and a whole lot of persistence and patience. It's this last part that makes the difference between breast and bottle for many women, particularly in the first weeks of motherhood when even minor nursing difficulties can seem insurmountable. Stick with it, and take advantage of help and advice from other moms and from your health-care providers. The good news is that breastfeeding usually becomes easier and more fulfilling over time.

BREAST OR BOTTLE?

Deciding how you are going to feed your baby is a difficult task. Are you going to breastfeed or go the formula route? If you were comparing breast milk to formula strictly on a nutrient basis, few would disagree that the best choice is breast milk. But since the issue is also loaded with social, emotional, and personal considerations, things are seldom so black and white. In the end, breast or bottle is an individual choice.

Your Body and Breastfeeding

Some babies seem to be breastfeeding champs from the get-go, while others need a little coaching. You're both new at this, so have patience and remember that you'll get better with practice. If you're having a hospital stay after your birth, the nurses on the maternity ward can give you some pointers on technique and check baby's latching on. In some cases there will be a lactation specialist on staff to consult with.

....

Belly Basics

Sore or dry and cracked nipples are common phenomena as you get on the breastfeeding launch pad. Never fear: They will toughen up. In the meantime, try vitamin E oil for moisturizing, or pure lanolin ointment for easing abrasions and pain. You'll only need a tiny dollop of each, applied right after nursing. Just wipe the vitamin E oil off your nipples thoroughly before baby feeds again.

....

Start with a comfortable position for the two of you. Baby's whole body should face yours—not just her turned head. The cradle and cross-cradle holds are two common positions. The cradle holds your baby close across the front of your body, with her head in the crook of your arm and your hand supporting her bottom. The cross-cradle switches arms and puts your hand under her head. Lying down with baby facing you is a good choice for the utterly exhausted.

The football position (clutch hold) tucks baby under your arm, again facing your body and breast. If you've had a C-section, this can help by keeping the weight off your incision. It's also a favorite of moms with twins who are doing double nursing duty.

The seated Australian hold (in which the baby sits in your lap facing your breast) might be a good choice if you'd like to try to keep baby awake during and after his feeding. With all nursing positions, make sure your baby's head is well supported.

After you're settled into position, brace your breast with one hand cupped under your breast in the shape of a C. If you have small breasts, this may not be necessary after a time, but try the C-hold initially to make sure baby latches on correctly.

Encouraging baby to get a successful latch is the most important part of the process. Stroke her bottom lip with your nipple until she opens her mouth wide and yawn-like. This is called the *rooting reflex*. Insert your nipple into her mouth, and she should instinctively close (latch) onto it.

With all nursing positions, make sure your baby's head is well supported. After you're settled into position, brace your breast with one hand, cupped into the shape of a "C." Encouraging baby to get a successful latch is the most important part of the process. Stroke her bottom lip with your nipple until she opens her mouth wide and yawn-like. This is called the rooting reflex. Insert your nipple into her mouth and she should instinctively close, or latch, onto it. A proper latch:

- Encompasses the entire nipple and most, if not all, of the areola
- Positions her nose almost directly on your breast
- Can be verified by her visible and possibly audible swallowing
- Will not hurt (unless the nipple is in poor condition to begin with)

In the first few days following birth, your breasts will produce a clear to yellow sticky substance called colostrum. Colostrum contains antibodies that help strengthen the infant immune system. It also is important for getting baby's digestion off on the right track. The low-carbohydrate, high-protein concoction is easily digestible for these early days and helps to establish beneficial bacteria in your baby's gastrointestinal tract.

Colostrum comes out in small amounts compared to later breast milk. You'll know when your milk "comes in" because your breasts will become:

- Engorged with milk
- Very hard
- Sore to the touch

Nursing your baby will relieve some of the pressure quickly, although it's possible you may need a little additional help to ease soreness.

Simple but effective pain relief options include:

- Cold compresses between feedings
- Warm compresses
- Gentle breast massage
- Refrigerated cabbage leaves, draped over the breast, inside bra
- Warm showers

There's a lot to think about when it comes to choosing how your baby will be fed. Here is a list of the pros and cons of breastfeeding so you can make the right decision for you and your baby.

PRO: Breast milk is custom-made for your child's nutritional needs and provides essential antibodies.
CON: If you have a medical condition that requires drug treatment, it's possible your medication may pass into breast milk.

PRO: Breastfeeding is a low-maintenance feeding routine. Never needs mixing, warming, or other preparation.
CON: You will always need to be close at hand. Breastfeeding can be physically taxing.

PRO: Nursing gives you special one-on-one bonding time with baby.
CON: No one else can pitch in on the feeding duties.

PRO: Breastfeeding is a big cost cutter. Aside from the high cost of formula, you can save on bottles, bags, and other formula-feeding purchases.
CON: You may have to purchase or rent a breast pump and buy a personal kit to use with it, which can be costly.

PRO: Many women who breastfeed experience faster postpartum weight loss.
CON: Although you may be taking your figure back, your breasts belong to baby—leaks, sore nipples, and all.

PRO: Feeding isn't only mom, all day and all night.

CON: The special mother-child bond and skin-to-skin contact that breastfeeding brings may be harder to achieve.

PRO: You can give your baby a bottle just about anywhere, anytime without feeling self-conscious or raising eyebrows.

CON: Make sure you pack sterilized bottles and nipples, formula, bottled water for mixing, a can opener for opening formula concentrate, and more.

PRO: No worries about keeping up your milk supply when you return to work.

CON: You may miss out on a golden opportunity to spend special nursing time together at home once your work schedule starts.

PRO: You can assume control of your body again.

CON: After so many months as one, you're suddenly severing a close physical bond that nursing can prolong.

Supply and Demand System

When the process operates as designed, the more baby nurses, the more milk your breasts produce. A breast that baby has completely drained will produce milk at a faster rate than one that has only been partially emptied. Your milk production takes its cue from baby. So, if your child is premature or ill and isn't nursing, or is latching or sucking ineffectively, your milk supply will adjust downward. A breast pump can help keep the milk flowing until baby is ready to nurse full-time again.

Belly Basics

Newborns don't believe much in schedules. In some cases constant nursing in a fussy baby can indicate an insufficient milk supply. But as long as he's growing fine and is having six to eight wet diapers and about three dirty diapers daily, you can be assured he's getting plenty to eat.

....

Nursing ten to twelve times a day is normal for a newborn. That may seem like a lot, but just bear with it; as the weeks pass and he develops, he'll spend more time exploring and less time eating. In the meantime, his frequent snacks are helping to establish and grow your milk supply, which is great.

Practical Matters

Button-up blouses, shirts with zippers, and other easy-access clothing make nursing easier on a day-to-day basis. There are varieties of nursing bras available; make sure you try them on before purchase to ensure a good fit. You might opt for the comfort of a simple jogging or sports bra that slides up easily, especially if you like the added support of wearing a bra to bed.

Nursing pads for catching leaks before they soak through your shirt are also a must. These come in several different materials and configurations, including cloth, plastic, and disposable. Disposable has the advantage of high absorbency, while cloth can be washed and reused. Accidents do happen, even with pads, and carrying an extra shirt in your bag or car can save you a mortifying moment or two.

NUTRITION AND BREASTFEEDING

During pregnancy, the body naturally begins to prepare itself for breastfeeding. In the first few days after birth, a woman's body produces a fluid called colostrum. This is the first milk that the infant receives. Colostrum is a thick, yellowish substance that is produced just prior to the flow of breast milk. It contains antibodies and immunoglobulins, which help protect the newborn from bacteria and viruses and help to prevent the infant's immature gut from becoming infected. Colostrum is high in protein, zinc, and other minerals and contains less fat, carbohydrates, and calories than actual breast milk.

Between the third and sixth day after birth, colostrum begins to change to a "transitional" form of breast milk. During this time, the amounts of protein and immune factors in the milk gradually decrease while fat, lactose, and calories in the milk increase. By about the tenth day after birth, the mother begins to produce mature breast milk. One of the special qualities of breast milk is its ability to change to meet the needs of your growing baby throughout the course of breastfeeding.

Belly Basics

The size of breasts is not a factor in how much milk a mother produces. Instead it is the infant's feeding habits that control milk production. In other words, the more a woman breastfeeds her infant, the more milk her body will produce.

The Nutrition of Breast Milk

At this point, human breast milk provides the most optimal nutrition for infants. Breast milk seems to have the perfect balance of carbohydrates, fats, and proteins as well as vitamins and minerals that the infant needs. Breast milk contains just enough protein to keep from overloading the baby's immature kidneys. The protein in breast milk is mostly in the form of whey, which is what helps to make it easily digestible. The fat in breast milk is also easily absorbed by an infant's digestive system. Breast milk provides liberal amounts of vital essential fatty acids, saturated fats, triglycerides, and cholesterol. It contains long-chain polyunsaturated fatty acids that are essential for proper development of the central nervous system. Breast milk is relatively low in sodium and provides adequate amounts of minerals such as zinc, iron, and calcium, which reduce the demand for these nutrients from the mother.

Is My Baby Getting Enough Milk?

A worry for many breastfeeding moms is whether the newborn is getting enough to eat. With formulas, you are able to tell exactly how many ounces the baby has consumed, but with breastfeeding this is harder to identify. It may seem at first that the baby is hungry all the time, which makes some moms wonder if he has had enough. This is completely normal. Babies should be hungry quite often because breast milk is digested within a couple of hours after consumption. After the baby's first few days of life, he will want to nurse about eight to twelve times per day. The baby should be fed on demand, with no worry about schedules, until you have breastfeeding down pat and can begin to recognize your baby's own schedule. The baby's pediatrician will be able to tell if your baby is getting enough to eat by how much weight he gains at each visit.

There are other ways to tell if your baby is getting enough to eat. After the fifth day of birth, she should have at least six to eight wet diapers per day and three to four loose yellow stools per day. She is most likely getting enough if she is nursing at least ten to fifteen minutes on each breast. Your baby should show steady weight gain after the first week of age. Her urine should be pale yellow and not deep yellow or orange. You should find your baby wanting to eat at least every two to three hours or at least eight times per day for at least the first two to three weeks. In addition, she should have good skin color. If you become concerned about whether your baby is getting enough to eat, contact your pediatrician or lactation consultant. Babies who are not getting enough to eat can become easily dehydrated.

....

In general, most babies lose a little weight, 5 to 10 percent of their birth weight, in their first few days of life. They should start to gain at least 1 ounce per day by the fifth day after birth and be back to their birth weight by two weeks after birth.

....

Is Breast Milk Enough?

During the first six months of life, most babies who are breastfeeding will not require any additional water, juices, vitamins, iron, or formula. With sound breastfeeding practices, supplements are rarely needed because breast milk provides the infant with just about all the fluids and nutrients he needs for proper growth and development. By six months of age, it is generally recommended that babies be introduced to foods that contain iron in addition to breast milk.

While the water supply in most U.S. cities and towns contains plenty of fluoride, a mineral often found in tap water that is important for strong teeth and prevention of cavities, in certain rural areas the levels can be too low. Breast milk contains very low levels of fluoride. However, babies under six months of age should not be given fluoride supplements, even if levels in your water supply are low.

Vitamin D Controversy

Though breast milk is a complete source of nutrition for your baby, there is some controversy surrounding the need for supplementing with vitamin D. Vitamin D is found in only small amounts in breast milk and is necessary to absorb calcium into the bones and teeth. However, the vitamin D in breast milk is in a very absorbable form and therefore is generally adequate for most infants. Babies who may be at higher risk for vitamin D deficiency include those who have little exposure to sunlight. Moderate sunlight helps to produce vitamin D in the body, and mother and babies with darker skin may have a harder time getting enough sunlight to produce vitamin D.

Mothers deficient in vitamin D also create a risk of low levels in their babies. The amount of vitamin D in breast milk is directly related to the level of vitamin D in the mother's body. If you are taking a prenatal or vitamin/mineral supplement that contains vitamin D, drinking milk, and getting moderate exposure to sunlight, your breast milk should contain optimal levels of vitamin D. The American Academy of Pediatrics recently began recommending that all infants, including those who are exclusively breastfed, have a minimum intake of 200 international units (IU) of vitamin D per day beginning in the first two months of life.

Other Concerns

Babies sometimes react to certain foods that the mother eats because they may pass through to the breast milk. After eating spicy or gassy foods, the mother may notice the baby crying or fussing as well as nursing more often. However, these symptoms may also show up in babies with colic. You will know it is a reaction to food you have eaten if the symptoms last less than twenty-four hours. Symptoms caused by colic generally occur daily and often last for days or weeks at a time. If your baby seems to react to certain foods that you eat, eliminate those foods from your diet. There is no need to eliminate foods from your diet unless you have a specific reason to suspect a particular food is bothering your baby. If you have a family history of allergies, including asthma, you may want to avoid foods you are allergic or sensitive to while breastfeeding.

Belly Basics

The American Academy of Pediatrics suggests that breastfeeding mothers of susceptible infants (with a family history of allergies) are wise to eliminate peanuts and peanut-containing foods while breastfeeding.

Although the reaction is rare, some babies are allergic to cow's milk and foods that contain cow's milk in the mother's diet. Symptoms will usually appear a few minutes to a few hours after a breastfeeding session. They can include diarrhea, rash, fussiness, gas, runny nose, cough, or congestion. Talk to your pediatrician if your baby experiences any of these symptoms. Other foods you consume that may cause reactions in your newborn include chocolate, citrus fruits and juices, and common food allergens such as eggs, wheat, corn, fish, nuts, and soy.

NUTRITIONAL REQUIREMENTS FOR THE BREASTFEEDING MOM

As with pregnancy, it is vital that a mother eat a healthy, well-balanced diet to ensure that she gets all of the nutrients she needs for successful breastfeeding. The mother's diet needs to fulfill her own nutritional needs as well as additional needs, which increase during breastfeeding. At this time your body's first priority is milk production, and if you lack the right type of nourishment in your diet, your personal needs may not be met.

Belly Basics

Women who were obese prior to pregnancy or who gained excessive weight during pregnancy may not require the full 500 extra calories per day. Your doctor can help to calculate the amount of additional calories you may need during breastfeeding.

Calorie Needs

Your body's fuel supply for milk production comes from two main sources: extra calories, or energy, from foods you eat and energy stored as body fat during pregnancy. For your body to produce breast milk, it uses about 100 to 150 calories a day from fat that your body naturally stored during pregnancy. That is why breastfeeding moms often lose pregnancy weight more quickly. In addition, you also need to eat about 500 extra calories per day (or 500 calories more than your maintenance calorie level) during breastfeeding. In general, consuming 500 extra calories per day than before pregnancy will meet your energy needs for breast milk production.

Figuring on light to moderate activity, on average a woman needs about 2,700 calories per day. You need more calories if you are a teenager or more active. You can easily get these extra calories by eating nutritious foods from all of the food groups in the Food Guide Pyramid. The following number of servings from the Food Guide Pyramid would provide about 2,700 calories:

- 10 servings from the bread, cereal, rice, and pasta group (choose whole grains and whole-wheat products more often)
- 4 servings from the vegetable group
- 4 servings from the fruit group
- 3–4 servings of dairy (choose nonfat or low-fat dairy products); teens should shoot for 4 servings per day
- 2 servings (6–7 ounces) from the meat, poultry, fish, dry beans, eggs, and nut group (choose leaner meats more often as well as occasionally choose nonmeat selections such as legumes, nuts, or seeds)
- Use fats and sweets sparingly

Once breastfeeding is well established, a mother can reduce the number of excess calories modestly. This will increase the rate the body uses stored fat without an adverse impact on breast milk production. Be cautious not to cut calories drastically during breastfeeding, which can reduce daily milk production.

How to Fuel Your Body

While you are breastfeeding, it is still important to remember that you are still eating for two. You need to continue the healthy diet you followed during pregnancy through breastfeeding and beyond. Not only is it important to get extra calories, but those extra calories need to come from healthy foods. Eating a healthy, well-balanced diet will ensure you are getting the carbohydrates, protein, and healthy fats you need for breastfeeding. Focus on fueling your body with whole-grain starches, fresh fruits and vegetables, and lean protein foods that will provide plenty of protein, calcium, and iron. Simply adding empty calories to increase your caloric intake, such as with sugary or high-fat foods, is not going to be advantageous to you or your baby. Eating a variety of foods is important because this way, you can be sure to obtain different nutrients. Eating in moderation is the key, not too much of any one food or item.

Belly Basics

Rapid weight loss and cutting calories too low can pose a danger to your baby. Since milk production requires extra calorie expenditure, even increasing your caloric level by 500 calories will allow for a safe amount of weight loss. Losing weight gradually through a healthy, well-balanced diet and regular exercise is the safest route.

Harmful Substances

As with pregnancy, is it essential to think about all the substances you put into your body that can pass through to your breast milk and on to your baby. Many medications are safe to take during breastfeeding, but a few, including herbal products and/or supplements, can be dangerous to your infant. Always get approval from your doctor before taking any prescription or over-the-counter medications while breastfeeding. Alcohol should be avoided because it can pass through your breast milk to the baby. You would be wise to cut back on caffeine due to the fact that it can build up in a baby's system. A cup or two a day of coffee or cola is not likely to do harm, but too much can lead to problems. The guidelines for eating fish also pertain to women who are breastfeeding. Habits such as smoking and illegal drugs can cause a mother to produce less milk, and chemicals such as nicotine can pass through the breast milk.

Breast milk contains large amounts of lactose, or milk sugar. Lactose is utilized in the tissues of the brain and spinal cord and helps to provide the infant with energy. Breast milk contains only a small amount of iron, but the iron is in a form that is readily absorbed. Fifty percent of the iron in breast milk is absorbed, compared with only 4 to 10 percent of the iron in cow's milk or commercial infant formula.

BABY'S BODY AND BREASTFEEDING

Trying to impose a strict feeding schedule on your newborn will result in much heartache and little success. Unless you have multiples, there's really no good reason to start scheduling baby's meals at specific times. If you do have twins or more, you may want to wake them all when one gets up for a feeding in order to get them on a similar routine—but that still doesn't mean feeding by the clock. Only your baby can determine how much he needs to satisfy his tummy, and feeding on demand is the best way to accomplish this.

The health rewards for your nursing child's body and mind are tremendous. Breast milk improves immunity, is thought to offer protection against certain chronic diseases (for example, type 1 diabetes), is associated with a reduced risk of SIDS, and is easy on baby's digestive system. Clinical studies have also indicated that breastfeeding can enhance cognitive development in small-for-gestational-age (SGA) babies.

So, how long do you breastfeed? From a clinical standpoint, the American Academy of Pediatrics has recommended exclusive breastfeeding for at least 6 months and promotes breastfeeding for a year or longer, as long as both mother and child are still comfortable with the arrangement. The best answer is probably as long as both of you are still enjoying and benefiting from it.

BOTTLE BASICS

If you do choose to bottle-feed, there are literally hundreds of bottle types and nipple configurations on the market to choose from. Figuring out what works and what doesn't is largely trial and error, but there are some factors you can look for:

- **Low air flow.** Designs that minimize air or that can be de-aired prior to feeding can reduce baby's gas.
- **Convenience.** If saving time is a priority, features like presterilized disposable bag bottles are a big plus.
- **Easy to clean.** Pick a bottle with minimal parts, one that looks relatively easy to clean and sterilize.

- **Built for baby.** Make sure to start baby with a newborn-style nipple that has a smaller opening so that she doesn't face a formula tidal wave. If her sucking reflex is weak, however, you might have to upgrade to a larger opening.

Both breastfed and bottle-fed babies require regular burping during a meal. You'll quickly pick up your child's cues that a bubble needs bursting; she may arch her back and fuss at the breast or bottle. In the beginning, burping at least twice during a feeding session can help to ensure her comfort.

An infant's tiny stomach can only hold 2 to 4 teaspoons of fluid at birth. Spitting up is his signal that the tank is full. Swallowing air and engaging in too much activity with a full tummy can also cause spitting up. However, if baby's spit-up becomes excessive and forceful (projectile vomiting), or is accompanied by gagging or difficulty swallowing, call your pediatrician immediately. It could be a sign that your baby has a formula intolerance or a gastrointestinal problem.

LACTATION PROBLEMS

Learning to read baby's body language and hear vocal cues is an acquired art, one that takes time to acclimate to. It's easy to miss hunger signals or mistake them for other needs. For now, familiarize yourself with the warning signs of insufficient feeding. If your baby is having fewer than six wet and three dirty diapers a day, is excessively fussy at the breast, has a sunken fontanel (soft spot), acts lethargic, and is not at or above birth weight by 2 weeks postpartum (or steadily gaining thereafter), he is probably not getting enough milk and needs to see his pediatrician immediately. Fortunately, with some work and a little guidance, you should both be able to get back on track.

Why Your Body Isn't Cooperating

There are dozens of reasons why milk supply or nursing itself may not be making the cut, but most of them can be overcome with patience, special equipment, and/or professional training and guidance.

- **Medications:** Antihistamines, decongestants, contraceptives, and some other medications can have a detrimental effect on milk supply. Talk to your doctor before taking any medication while nursing.
- **Inverted nipples:** If you have inverted nipples, a good latch may be elusive. Breast shields designed to pull out the nipple can help.
- **Prior breast surgery:** Many women nurse successfully after breast surgery, but certain types of breast augmentation (enlargement) or breast reduction surgery do have the potential to hinder your milk supply, depending on how they are performed. Talk to your doctor if you've had breast surgery and are having lactation problems.
- **Hypotrophic breast disease:** Some women have structural problems with the breast tissue that decreases the number of milk-producing ducts. You may still be able to nurse, but baby might require supplemental feedings. Again, speak with your provider about your options.
- **Retained placental fragment:** Lactation problems can be a sign that a piece of your placenta was retained in delivery. Because this can also cause severe hemorrhage and infection, a suspected retained placenta should be assessed by your provider immediately.
- **Stress:** New motherhood and all its related stressors can inhibit milk supply, and tension can make letdown (milk ejection) difficult. If you're uptight about nursing problems, the cycle perpetuates itself. Try to look forward to nursing as a relaxing, *de*-stressing time.
- **Poor technique:** Letting baby empty one breast before moving on to the next will stimulate milk supply and allow her to reach the fatty and filling hindmilk at the end of her drink.
- **Poor nutrition and hydration:** Good eating habits and plenty of water are essential to your milk-production efforts.
- **Nipple confusion:** The mechanics of drinking from a bottle are very different from those of feeding from the breast. If a bottle is introduced before breastfeeding is well established, it's possible for your baby to

develop a preference for it.

Babies born prematurely, those with a poor sucking reflex, or those with a cleft lip or other health problem can have problems nursing initially. If your baby needs supplemental feeding in the hospital for any reason, you can request that it be administered with an eyedropper, syringe, feeding cup, or supplemental feeding system to avoid nipple confusion. You should also talk with your pediatrician and a lactation consultant about adaptive techniques and other options.

Lactation Consultants

A lactation consultant is a health-care provider who specializes in breastfeeding support and training. If you're having difficulties with nursing, a consultant can be a huge help in overcoming breastfeeding difficulties. Your OB/GYN or your child's pediatrician can provide a referral if needed. Some large pediatric practices retain lactation consultants on staff.

A board-certified lactation consultant will have the designation "IBCLC" (International Board Certified Lactation Consultant) or "IBCLC, RLC" (Registered Lactation Consultant). These mean she meets specific eligibility and experience requirements and has passed a board examination administered by the International Board of Lactation Consultant Examiners (IBLCE). Sometimes consultants are nurses who have earned board certification.

Many certified lactation consultants are also La Leche League leaders. Don't overlook the value of La Leche League support if you have no lactation consultant in your area. The organization can be a tremendous source of emotional support as well as practical advice and expertise.

Pump Primer

A breast pump can be useful in ramping up your milk production if you're having supply issues. It's also a great tool for moms heading back to work who want to keep nursing, as well as for mothers of babies who are temporarily unable to nurse for various health reasons.

A pump may be manual (hand powered), battery powered, or a plug-in unit.

The hand-powered pumps have the advantage of being inexpensive and portable but can take some getting used to and take longer to empty a breast. They use a piston-like action or a squeeze bulb to create the suction that removes the milk from your breast.

Hospital-grade electric units are probably the most efficient and allow you to pump both breasts at the same time, though they are bulky to transport and costly to purchase. Weekly or monthly rental units are frequently available through lactation consultants, hospital programs, or private businesses. For safety reasons, you will have to purchase a personal kit for use with the rental unit to obtain all the elements that come in contact with your breast milk, including tubing and bottles. The kit can be used for as long as you plan to pump and usually runs between $20 and $45 monthly for the basics.

....

Belly Basics

Beyond the immediate physical benefits of helping to speed your postpartum body back into shape, breastfeeding can have long-term benefits for maternal health. Studies have suggested that women who breastfeed have a lower risk of developing premenopausal breast cancer and ovarian cancer and postmenopausal osteoporosis and hip fractures.

....

Supplemental Feeding

If you're having breastfeeding problems, a supplemental nursing system (SNS) can help you provide baby with added nutrients of pumped breast milk or formula while still giving the benefits of suckling. A bottle or bag milk reservoir hangs around your neck, and two narrow silicone tubes channel milk flow from the reservoir to your nipple, where the open end of the tube is taped. As baby feeds on both the supplemental milk and breast milk you're providing, her suckling action further stimulates your milk production.

Women who are having problems producing enough milk for whatever reason may be able to supplement from a local breast milk bank if one is nearby. Milk donors are screened for health problems in a process similar to blood-donation screening. Again, a lactation consultant or pediatrician should have further information on what's available in your area.

Mastitis

Mastitis is an infection of the breast that can be caused by a plugged milk duct. If you develop mastitis, you can and should keep nursing. Your baby cannot get ill, and the breastfeeding process will actually help the mastitis resolve itself faster by easing the pain and draining the milk ducts.

Signs of mastitis include:

- Breast warm to the touch
- Red, tender streaks on the breast
- Pain and swelling
- Fever present

If you develop mastitis, stay on your nursing schedule and try to get sufficient rest to help your body heal. A warm water bottle, warm wet compress, or soak in a hot shower can help to ease the discomfort. If the mastitis doesn't start to clear up in a day or so or begins to worsen, you might need an antibiotic. Your health-care provider can advise you as to what medications will be safe for breastfeeding.

JUST FOR DADS

Although it may look easy, breastfeeding can be hard work, particularly the first time out. Your support is vital to this venture. Let your partner know you value this unique gift she's bestowing on your child. Be a voice of support when things get tough, and do what you can to create a warm and welcome environment for your nursing twosome. If the whole process has you bewildered, don't be embarrassed about asking questions.

Getting Comfortable with Breastfeeding

Be honest. Somewhere in the back of your mind (or perhaps unabashedly front and center), you were a little freaked out at the notion of your partner as food source. If you weren't, more power to you, but it's normal to need a little time to adjust. Learning more about how beneficial breastfeeding is for your new baby can help increase your comfort level.

When you're both up to sex again, try to respect your partner's feelings about touching on the feeding zone. Nipple soreness, leaking milk, and breast sensitivity might have her feeling better left alone. Or she could be willing while you are hesitant, given whose mouth was there last. Whatever the situation, it's important that you each get your current viewpoint out in the open so that no one's feelings are hurt. Your outlook may evolve over time, or you may both decide to focus on other sources of pleasure.

....

Belly Basics

One thing you'll quickly learn about infant timing is that you'll be interrupted in the heat of passion at least once. And when your partner returns from nursing baby, realize that switching gears from nurturing mommy to adventurous sex kitten can be a tall order to fill. Don't force an uncomfortable and awkward situation if the moment has passed for either of you. Remember that you won't have an infant forever; making adjustments to your sex life is just one of the many detours that parenting brings.

....

Getting In On the Act

You're probably grateful for your gender at those middle-of-the-night feedings, but during the day it might be nice to be able to feed baby once in a while.

Just because your partner is nursing doesn't cut you out of the feeding picture completely. At some point you will want to familiarize baby with a bottle of breast milk, in case mom's absence requires feeding her expressed (pumped) milk. To avoid any nipple confusion, breastfeeding should be well established first.

Once a bottle is introduced, you can do the honors for a regular feeding if your partner has other obligations or perhaps in order to allow her to get some much-needed sleep at night. Some babies are hesitant to take a bottle from mom when they know her nice warm breast is just an arm's reach away, so your fatherly presence is necessary for this task.

FORMULA

Formula is an excellent alternative to breast milk. It is not difficult to prepare and very portable if you use individual cans or powder. Formula allows anyone to feed the baby and can offer more freedom to a busy mom.

Formula does require a lot of washing of bottles and nipples and requires more work for a middle-of-the-night feeding. It's easier to overfeed a formula-fed baby since the tendency is to try to get the baby to finish the bottle rather than let the baby end the feeding when she is full.

Commercial formulas come in all types of varieties. There are ready-to-feed liquids, concentrated liquids that require diluting with water, and powders that require mixing with water. You should always follow closely the instructions on the label for preparing bottles. As well as varieties of formulas, there are many different types of bottles and nipples available to choose from. You may need to experiment with a few different brands before you find a combination that works best for you and your baby.

Bottles should be warmed just slightly before feeding. Never heat a bottle of formula in a microwave! The formula can heat unevenly and leave hot spots, which can burn a baby's mouth. A microwave can also heat the formula too much, making it too hot for an infant's mouth. The best way is to heat water in the microwave, take the water out, and then heat the bottle in the water. Always test the formula to make sure the temperature is not too hot. Always wash bottles and nipples thoroughly in hot water, and wash your hands before preparing them.

Belly Basics

Do not leave bottles out of the refrigerator for longer than one hour. If your baby doesn't finish a bottle, the contents should be discarded. If formula bottles are prepared in advance, they should be stored in the refrigerator for no longer than twenty-four hours.

How Often to Formula Feed

Experts agree that for the first few weeks, you shouldn't try to follow too rigid a feeding schedule. As the baby gets older, you may be able to work out a more established schedule. You should offer a bottle every two to three hours at first as you see signs of hunger. Until she reaches about 10 pounds, she will probably take approximately two to 3 ounces per feeding. From there, intake will gradually increase. Don't force her to eat if she does not seem hungry. You may see certain signs when the baby has enough such as, closing her mouth or turning away from the bottle, falling asleep, fussiness, and biting or playing with the bottle's nipple. One advantage to bottle-feeding is that you can know exactly how much your baby is eating. Your pediatrician can advise you on optimal amounts to feed your baby as she grows.

Chapter 19

LIFE AFTER BIRTH

Babies need round-the-clock care. Coupled with the physical recovery from childbirth, this can make a person very, very tired. It might be hard at first, but your body and schedule will adjust to your baby before you know it.

SLEEP DEPRIVATION

Coping with sleep deprivation can be challenging. Many parents are geared up for all-nighters when they bring a baby home, but often the first few weeks are not that difficult, since many babies do a lot of sleeping. Just when you think things are working out quite well, your newborn may surprise you with increased nighttime activity. Whether you're walking the floors when your baby first comes home or a few weeks later, it can be exhausting and frustrating.

....

Belly Basics

More and more women are seeking out help not only with the baby but for their own recovery after a birth. Postpartum doulas are trained assistants who come to your home and help with baby care and more by meeting your needs and those of your household, including light cleaning, cooking, and errands, as well as comfort measures for the recovering mom.

....

Try these tips to help you manage the difficult weeks and months when you feel like a walking zombie:

- **Sleep when the baby sleeps.** It's old advice, but it works. There are times when you must get things done; if possible, try to do them with the baby awake, so you can sleep when he does.

- **Get serious about sleep.** Pull the shades, wear a sleep mask, turn off the TV, get in bed, turn off the phone, and do everything you can to maximize your sleep.

- **Get help.** Everyone needs a break. Ask your partner, friends, family, or hired help to assist you. Even if you are breastfeeding, someone else can give the baby a bottle of expressed milk at night, or at the very least, change and soothe her.

- **Relax your standards.** Because you're going to need to get some sleep during the day, you're just not going to be able to do it all, all the time. Cut back on work, reduce your household cleaning requirements, or use paper plates to make things easier.

- **Avoid tired traps.** Sometimes when you're exhausted it's easy to overeat, park yourself in front of the TV instead of going to bed, or skip exercise. None of these things will make you feel better; in fact, they'll just make you feel worse. Drinking caffeine to stay awake will only make it more difficult to fall asleep when the opportunity presents itself.

If you're heading back to work, getting enough sleep at night can be crucial. Share the burden with your partner if at all possible. If necessary, schedule a fifteen-minute catnap for yourself to get through the day. Going to bed early in the evening will also help ensure you get enough sleep.

ADJUSTING TO YOUR NEW SCHEDULE

Many aspects of your life are different now that you are a parent. You probably feel that your priorities are altered since you have a little one to think about. But taking time to care for yourself is equally important.

Bonding with Baby

These early weeks and months are a precious time of mother and child getting to know each other and of your building confidence in mothering. Yet after your baby has cried for 20 minutes straight and you still haven't guessed what's wrong (is she hungry, dirty, tired, colicky, gassy?), you might start to wonder about your mothering abilities. Trust yourself. Although it takes time to learn baby's language, the patience and persistence you invest in decoding her signals will pay off. You'll crack the code eventually, and in the process you'll establish a bond of trust and communication that lasts a lifetime.

Setting Priorities

You aren't going to be able to do it all. If you try to keep up your preparenthood schedule in addition to your new motherhood duties, something or someone has to give. Usually it's your sanity. Let matters that just aren't that important, usually anything in the domesticity arena, lag a bit. As the motivational gurus like to say: work smarter, not harder. Buy the birthday cake at the bakery instead of baking it yourself. Use a delivery service to get your groceries. Pay the kid down the block to mow the lawn.

Don't Forget to Have Fun

Once you get past the fatigue, the uncertainties, and the occasional frustrations, being a new mom can be incredibly entertaining. You have a legitimate excuse to play, explore, rhyme, sing, and generally revisit your childhood. You have an adoring little person who hangs on your every word and movement and loves you unconditionally. And you get to witness all of his incredible firsts as your tiny miracle learns to smile, roll over, crawl, and eventually walk and talk. A year from now, this postpartum time will be a distant memory. Treasure it while it's here.

FINDING TIME FOR YOUR PARTNER

After time for yourself, time for your partner is often the next thing to get lost in the busy days of motherhood. Making time to connect with your partner and share things together is an important way to keep your relationship alive.

Once you become parents, it can be hard to find time for just the two of you. For many months, you may feel as if you're just trying to survive and get enough sleep. Once you've settled into your routine, finding time for the two of you can be complicated, involving babysitters, feeding schedules, naps, and considerations of what time you have to get up in the mornings.

Here are some ways you can find time for each other:

- Schedule time together at home when you'll simply talk, snuggle, or watch a DVD together. Planning at-home dates means much less pressure than trying to go out and doesn't involve a babysitter.
- Talk on the phone and use texting and IM. You don't have to be in the same room to communicate and feel close to each other.
- Support each other's interests. If you don't allow each other time to do the things that inspire and interest each of you, when you are together, you will have nothing to talk about other than the baby.
- Plan to have sex. It may be the last thing you're interested in, but if you do it, the ingrained reactions will kick in. You will rediscover how nice it can be, and it will help you feel closer to each other.
- Rely on relatives. It might feel like too much to book a sitter so you can go out to dinner. Not only is it complicated, but it can be expensive too if you're living on reduced income due to maternity leave. Grandparents, aunts, uncles, and other relatives adore having time with the baby, and the baby deserves to get to know them, so rely on them some of the time. It's a win-win situation for everyone involved.
- Connect while the baby is occupied. If she's happily drooling away in her bouncy seat, use this as a few minutes to talk about something important.

- Make chores work for you. Washing the dishes together is a great time to just kid around or talk about something that's been on your mind. Link your minds while your hands are occupied.

Belly Basics

A twenty-year study performed by the RAND Institute on Education and Training found that children of older mothers had higher test scores than children of younger mothers.

It is not uncommon for your partner to feel a bit left out in the early months of your baby's life. Particularly if you are breastfeeding, you are using a lot of your time and energy to care for your baby. Even if you aren't breastfeeding, becoming a mother is a very physical commitment. Many women feel too tired for sex, and some partners feel they are somehow left out of the very intimate mother-baby circle.

In addition to finding time for you and your partner to connect as a couple, it is also important to find ways for your partner and the baby to have time together. It can sometimes be tempting as a mom to feel like you're the only one who knows how to care for the baby; if you spend all day with the baby, it is likely you will be more skilled, at least initially. However, your partner deserves a chance to parent, too, and that means walking out of the room and letting him change the diaper, do the feeding, or soothe the baby, even if he doesn't do it quite the way you would. He needs time and space to learn his own parenting techniques, and he needs your support to do that.

FINDING TIME FOR YOUR OTHER CHILDREN

If this isn't your first child, you're already well versed in what to expect as a new mom, but you may find adjusting to being a mom of more than one to be a challenge. You have the same number of hours in the day, but you now must divide them among your children. You also have to learn how to deal with siblings. Even if you already have two or more children, adding another one changes the dynamic of the family.

Other Young Children

If you are raising other young children, the demands on your time are very physical. Chasing after a toddler while caring for an infant can be challenging. The hardest part about caring for young children is that they aren't able to understand that you can only do one thing at a time and are not able to be patient. Caring for two little ones means learning to do a lot of things with one hand. Wearing your baby in a sling can be a good solution a lot of the time. A double stroller is another good answer, since it allows you to become mobile. You also can multitask during feedings; read a book, do a puzzle, color, or do another quiet, stationary activity with your older child while you are feeding the baby.

....

Belly Basics

If you're finding it difficult to adjust to being a mother and find that sometimes it simply seems too difficult of a life change, you're not alone. A 2003 study conducted in Australia found that first-time mothers who were over age 35 reported that adjusting to motherhood was extremely challenging.

....

Young children are often jealous of the very close physical contact you share with the baby. They may want to try to nurse or push the baby out of the way. Using feeding time as cuddle time for all of you is an effective solution, and young children are so active it's unlikely they'll stay put through an entire feeding.

Older Children

If you have a family that includes children who are older and have now added an infant to the family, the logistics of mothering can be hard at times. For example, you need to nurse, but your older child needs to be driven to soccer practice. Or your baby needs to nap, but your child has friends over and they are keeping the baby awake. These and other scenarios can truly put a mother to the test.

Belly Basics

Half of U.S. presidents were firstborn children. Many newscasters and talk-show hosts are firstborns as well.

The best way to approach a family of diversely aged children is to help everyone understand that needs must be balanced. Nobody gets what he wants all the time, and compromise is necessary. Older children are often enamored with a baby for longer than younger children. Your older child may be more understanding about the seemingly unreasonable demands a baby makes on you and on the family, but it does help to explain to the older kids that the baby doesn't mean to be demanding and annoying.

Older children can be a definite blessing because they can help you in significant ways. For example, an eight-year-old could be trusted to stay in the family room and watch the baby for a few minutes while you go to the bathroom, can answer the phone while you're feeding the baby, or can hold the baby for a few minutes while you pay for groceries.

As you already know, your older children need you in a different way than younger children do. Older kids need your mental and emotional attention more than your physical hands-on attention. The key to offering this kind of attention is affirming their needs—you know that they need to talk to you, need help with homework, or need you to help fix their hair—and pinpointing when you will be able to do that. If you're walking a screaming baby, you cannot give your older children your undivided attention. Ask them to be patient with you and the baby, and let them know that as soon as you physically can, you will turn your attention to their needs. The good thing about older children is that a little bit of attention can go a long way, so be sure to offer quality attention when you are truly focusing.

Stepchildren

If your partner has children from a previous relationship, you may wonder how bringing your own baby into the mix will work out. Your new baby is the product of both families and is in a way a unifying factor—although your stepchildren definitely may not see the baby that way! Before the baby is born, reassure your stepchildren, just as you would children of your own, that the baby will not take away their role or importance in the family. Stress how much it means to you that the baby will belong to all of you and will be related to all of you.

....

Belly Basics

Fifty percent of U.S. families are stepfamilies, according to the Stepfamily Foundation, and in fact the U.S. Census predicted there will soon be more stepfamilies than traditional two-parent families.

....

Don't be surprised if your stepchildren, just like biological children, at first resent the baby or are slow to warm up to him. It takes time to build a relationship, and it takes time to build trust in a family's love. Encourage your stepchildren to help care for the baby. Stress how grateful you are for their help, and point out how much the baby enjoys their company.

If your stepchildren do not live with you, they may be angry or jealous that this new child gets to live with their father all the time, whereas they are only able to visit. Help them know that your home is their home just as much as it is the baby's home.

FINDING SUPPORT

Parenting can feel like a lonely occupation. You spend much of your time with a demanding, fickle, uncommunicative little person who, though the love of your life, can certainly put you through the wringer at times. This a time in your life when you need support. Just having someone else to talk to who knows what you are going through can make you feel immeasurably better.

Friends and Family

Friends and family can provide important support. Your own mother or mother-in-law can be a great support person for you. She's been through it all and has made it to the other side. Although a lot of things about childrearing have changed over the years, the basic skills have not.

Sisters, sisters-in-law, and other close relatives are another great source of support. Since they're closer to your age, they are more likely to understand about today's parenting challenges. Friends with children are important. Not only are they going through the same things, they are able to offer advice without the added baggage or expectations that sometimes comes with advice from family. Forging close relationships with friends or relatives with children close in age to yours can give you a sense of community and let you rely on each other for things such as babysitting, play dates, and shoulders to cry on.

Mothers' Groups

Reaching out and finding a local mothers' group is a great way to make new friends who are mothers and who may be experiencing a lot of what you are. Mothers' groups can be formally organized or casually drawn together. You can find listings of formal clubs in church newsletters, regional family magazines, on community bulletin boards, and through word of mouth. Some mothers' clubs form among those attending the same childbirth education class or prenatal exercise class.

Other groups come together in less organized ways. You might strike up a conversation with a mom at day care and eventually meet her and another friend of hers for coffee. Moms in your neighborhood or on your block might become friends.

While moms' groups can be a true lifeline, there can be some difficulties navigating them. If you're joining an established group, you may feel like an outsider until you get to know everyone. There may be people in the group you simply don't click with, or as your children grow, you might find that the kids don't get along very well. Ultimately you have to do what is right for you and your child in these kinds of situations.

Online Support

While having a friend who can hug you and baby-sit for you is a great thing, it is possible to make friends whom you don't know in person. You can now find any kind of specialized support group online that you could ever dream of. Some women join due-date clubs while they're pregnant and converse online with other women due in the same month they are. Many of these groups last for years, as the women support each other through the many stages their children go through.

....

Pregnancy Pointer

Babycenter.com has bulletin boards for pregnant moms over 35 and over 40 at *www .babycenter.com/boards/bcuspreggen* and *www.babycenter.com/boards/bcusparentage*. Clubmom.com has a work/life balance board for moms at *www.clubmom.com/jforum/ forums/show/49.page*.

....

Online groups can be a convenient way to make friends since you can read and send messages at any time of day. It's important to be careful and not offer personal information (such as addresses, phone numbers, and so on) online unless you really and truly know someone very well.

NOTES AND CHECKLISTS

What You'll Need When You Bring Baby Home

- ☐ Lots of bibs
- ☐ Cotton wool pads or balls
- ☐ Baby bath
- ☐ Bouncy chair
- ☐ Baby monitor
- ☐ Bath thermometer
- ☐ Baby wipes
- ☐ Nail scissors
- ☐ Baby bath towel with hood
- ☐ Room thermometer
- ☐ Changing mat
- ☐ Newborn diapers
- ☐ Hat
- ☐ Booties or socks
- ☐ Bottles, if not breastfeeding
- ☐ Baby sling
- ☐ Breast pump
- ☐ Crib with sheets

Notes

Use the remaining space to write down any notes about your pregnancy.

_____

_____

_____

_____

_____

FREQUENTLY ASKED QUESTIONS

Will the bottle of champagne I shared with my husband on the night we conceived our baby be harmful?

Put this night of celebration behind you and stop feeling guilty. Binge drinking or regular abuse of alcohol when you are pregnant can cause birth defects, but an isolated episode of too much champagne probably has not harmed your unborn baby.

Heavy drinking, including binges or daily use, is associated with congenital defects. Babies born with fetal alcohol syndrome (FAS) show retarded growth, have central nervous system problems, and characteristic facial features, including a small head, a thin upper lip, a short upturned nose, a flattened nasal bridge, and a general underdeveloped look of the face. Because of the critical nervous system involvement, many show tremulousness, can't suck, are hyperactive, have abnormal muscle tone, and are later diagnosed with attention deficit disorder as well as mental retardation.

Relying on alcohol out of habit or cravings can also end your pregnancy abruptly. Heavy to moderate drinkers seem to experience a higher incidence of miscarriage in the second trimester, as well as problems with the placenta. Other complications linked to alcohol use are congenital heart defects, brain abnormalities, spinal and limb defects, and urinary and genital problems.

What should I take for a headache?

Most doctors say that aspirin is fine for most of your pregnancy. You should avoid it in the last month. Tylenol, or an analgesic based on acetaminophen, is also recommended for headaches, but be sure to ask your doctor before taking any medication during pregnancy.

I have terrible allergies. Is there anything my doctor is going to be able to recommend?

For some women, pregnancy can feel like a bad head cold. The increased volume of blood to your mucus membranes can make the lining of your respiratory tract swell. You may even experience nosebleeds. Fortunately, there are safe medications available to ease the symptoms, so consult with your doctor. See about taking extra vitamin C. A humidifier can also be helpful. If you experience nosebleeds as a result of allergies, try packing the nostril with gauze and then pinching your nose between your thumb and forefinger. To shrink the blood vessels and reduce bleeding, try putting an ice pack on your nose.

If I develop an infection, are there any antibiotics safe for expectant moms?

Yes. Pharmaceutical companies are coming up with new antibiotics all the time, and a number of them are safe for pregnancy. Many doctors believe that natural and synthetic penicillins are the safest antibiotics to take during pregnancy, so if you are not allergic to these oldest weapons against infection, you are definitely in luck. If you do get sick, make sure that your obstetrician is aware of anything your family doctor or another specialist may be prescribing.

What are the dangers of X-rays to my unborn baby?

According to the American Academy of Family Physicians (AAFP), the maximum safe fetal radiation dose during pregnancy is 5 rad, or the equivalent of 50,000 dental X-rays or 250 mammograms. CT scans, fluoroscopic studies, and nuclear medicine tests involve slightly higher doses than conventional X-rays, but in general still fall well within the range of acceptable exposure. In each case, the benefits of imaging need to be weighed against the potential risk to the fetus, and if at all possible, tests involving radiation should be avoided in the first trimester of pregnancy.

Can ultrasounds give misleading information?

While it's possible that you may be having a baby boy even if his external sex organs aren't visible in the ultrasound and therefore you may incorrectly think you are having a girl, most technicians won't state your baby's gender unless they are absolutely certain. If the sonogram indicates a due date that seems wrong, you might ask, "Could I possibly have dated the start of my pregnancy incorrectly?" Experts say that an ultrasound done at sixteen weeks is more accurate in regards to gestational age than an ultrasound done later in your pregnancy. When dating the length of a pregnancy, the ultrasound technician can be accurate within a few days. Ultrasounds date your pregnancy from the point of conception, which is a few days different from the point of your last period. Later ultrasounds are more accurate when determining your baby's gender. A very clear image must be obtained for the ultrasound to determine whether you are expecting a boy or a girl, and this may be more difficult to see in the early stages.

Why do I feel so hot and sweaty?

Your metabolism works overtime during pregnancy. Your body is burning more calories, and as a result, you often feel warm. An increase in blood supply to the surface of your skin, as well as hormones, all have an effect on how hot you feel. Keep cool by dressing in natural fibers and layering clothes so that you can always cool off by removing a layer. Hop in the shower; pat on a little talcum powder afterwards. You may need to change antiperspirants if your normal brand isn't working. To avoid dehydration as your body is working hard to burn calories and produce more blood, drink plenty of water.

Why do I often feel scatterbrained?

Increased hormones can make your thinking a bit foggy—just as they can during your menstrual cycle. Manage the situation by reducing your stress load, making lists, and going easy on yourself.

What is toxoplasmosis, and should I worry about getting it?

Toxoplasmosis is rare, but it is a virus that can affect your baby in the womb. When cats are allowed to run freely outside they can end up with a parasite that settles in the intestines and is passed on through cat feces. Toxoplasmosis can cause brain damage and other medical problems in your unborn child. Cats also frequent gardens and sandboxes, so wear gloves and wash your hands thoroughly after being outside. Don't clean any litter boxes during your pregnancy (ask your partner or a friend to help you).

My doctor recommends lots of iron, but it makes me feel nauseated. What should I do?

Take iron-rich prenatal vitamin supplements between meals with plenty of water or along with a fruit juice rich in vitamin C, which enhances the absorption of iron. Avoid drinking milk, coffee, or tea with your iron supplements because these beverages inhibit iron absorption. Add liver, red meat, fish, poultry, enriched breads and cereals, green leafy vegetables, eggs, and dried fruits to your diet to increase dietary iron.

What kinds of food cravings are normal?

Many pregnant women crave sweet or salty foods. Cravings for nonfood items such as dirt, soap, ash, or coffee grounds are different. A phenomenon called pica, which has shown up in medical literature since the sixth century, results in strange cravings that can cause serious problems for a pregnant mother and her unborn baby. If you have a craving to eat clay, ashes, laundry starch, or other unusual substances, seek medical attention right away.

Does intercourse hurt the baby?

Unless you have a high-risk pregnancy, you are not going to harm your baby by having sex. Sex is quite safe in a normal pregnancy. Vaginal bleeding, a history of miscarriage or premature labor, or a diagnosis of placental problems are good reasons to restrict intercourse, however. During the last month before your due date, you also should proceed with caution. Ask your practitioner if you have any concerns.

Should I circumcise my baby?

The American Academy of Pediatrics takes the stance that there is currently no firm medical or hygienic ground for performing routine circumcision (removal of the foreskin that covers the head of the penis) in newborn boys. However, the AAP also cited the importance of weighing cultural and religious beliefs and considering the child's best interest when deciding whether or not to circumcise a newborn male. If circumcision is performed, analgesia can be used to relieve the pain.

How soon can I have sex after the baby's birth?

Many doctors recommend waiting four to six weeks before having intercourse. Very few couples are able to swing back into a sex life immediately after the birth of a baby. Keep in mind either way that you can get pregnant in the period following birth. You should get back into your contraceptive routine before the mood strikes. Your doctor can give you a prescription before you leave the hospital, if necessary.

I'm getting varicose veins in my legs. Is this common in pregnancy?

The hair-fine marks, also known as spider veins, usually appear on the lower legs and are caused when increased blood volume and pressure damage the valves that regulate blood flow up out of the blood vessels of the legs. The result is pooled blood in the vein and that telltale squiggly red or blue line.

Supportive stockings, putting your feet up, resting on your left side, and taking an occasional walk when you need to stand for long periods of time may relieve leg soreness associated with varicose veins.

I've had a miscarriage in the past. Is there a way to prevent it this time around?

Many miscarriages occur due to factors completely beyond anyone's control—a defective egg or sperm, or implantation outside of the endometrium. Other triggers, such as teratogen exposure, may be avoided with special precautions in pregnancy. Speak with your health-care provider about your concerns and any special instructions given your medical history (such as restrictions on your activity).

What if I don't get to the hospital in time?

Every woman has heard stories of impatient babies being born in the backseats of taxicabs, but these impromptu deliveries are not common. Most women have plenty of time to make it to the hospital safe and sound; the average labor period runs twelve to fourteen hours. If you're concerned, you can take some basic precautions. Work out a route to the hospital in advance with your partner, keep your gas tank full, and have cash on hand for a cab just in case your car chooses the moment you go into labor to conk out.

If I'm overdue, will my provider induce me if I request it?

Whether or not to induce depends on a number of factors. Is the cervix effaced or dilated? Are you fairly sure your due date was accurate to begin with? Have you had a previous C-section? Have you had other complicating factors during pregnancy (e.g., placenta previa, umbilical cord prolapse)? Generally, if you've hit the thirty-nine-week mark, you have no history of C-section or other medical contraindications, and your provider thinks induction is indicated, she will schedule one for you.

What is umbilical cord blood banking?

Blood from the umbilical cord contains stem cells, those blank-slate cells from which all organs and tissues are built. Cord blood collected immediately after birth is placed in a collection kit and flown to a facility where it is cryogenically frozen and "banked" for later use if needed. The theory behind cord blood banking is that if your child ever develops a disease or condition requiring stem-cell treatment, the blood can be thawed and used for her treatment. If it matches certain biological markers, cord blood can be used to treat other family members as well. However, banking is cost prohibitive for many and requires an annual storage fee for as long as you would like the cord blood frozen. In recent years, some facilities have also made placenta blood banking available. The AAP has stated that "private storage of cord blood as 'biological insurance' should be discouraged." Many experts recommend donating cord blood to a public cord blood bank instead.

I have splotches of discolored skin on my face and abdomen. Is this normal?

Yes. Pregnancy hormones can cause hyperpigmentation of your skin, which makes certain areas of your skin (most commonly around the forehead, nose, cheeks, abdomen, and areolas) to darken. These discolored spots are usually dark on light-skinned women and light on dark-skinned women. Don't worry, though—these discolored patches will fade and eventually go away after your baby is born.

Are there exercises I should avoid during pregnancy?

Yes. A few sports are considered inappropriate during any phase of pregnancy. Mostly these sports are dangerous for reasons related to balance and risk of physical blows. It is not recommended that pregnant women ride horses, scuba dive, downhill ski, play rugby, or engage in other contact sports.

How do I know if I'm doing Kegel exercises right?

If you are doing Kegels correctly, you will not be tightening other muscles like your buttocks or thighs. You will be isolating this internal muscle and not straining other ones in the process.

Will eating too much sugar during pregnancy lead to gestational diabetes?

No, eating too much sugar does not directly cause any type of diabetes. Diabetes is a disorder in which the body cannot properly utilize insulin or does not produce insulin, which regulates blood sugar levels. Gestational diabetes is the result of changing hormones within a woman's body.

Do folic acid supplements really make that much of a difference in preventing certain birth defects?

According to the United States Centers for Disease Control (CDC), when taken one month before conception and throughout the first trimester, folic acid supplements have been proven to reduce the risk of neural tube defects by 50–70 percent.

Can eating more than three times a day be part of a healthy diet?

Yes. For women who are pregnant or for anybody who enjoys a healthy lifestyle, eating several small meals during the day can fit nicely into a healthy eating pattern. It can help you to fit in those extra calories and food group servings without having to eat large meals all at once, which can be difficult for women who may be having a problem with nausea or morning sickness.

Is it okay to take a calcium supplement if I don't eat dairy foods?

If you can't get enough calcium from the foods you choose, a supplement can be a good idea. The rule of thumb should always be food before supplements, though. First, include calcium-containing foods in your diet as much as possible, and then supplement on top of that. Never let a supplement take the place of an entire food group or nutrient such as calcium.

Is it unhealthy to have an aversion to vegetables during my first trimester?

It is common for women to have food aversions even to healthy foods such as vegetables. Try drinking vegetable juice instead of eating whole vegetables. You can also eat more fruit, since many of them contain some of the same nutrients as vegetables. Keep taking your prenatal vitamins to ensure you are getting all of the nutrients that your body needs at this time. However, it's always best to get your nutrients from food before supplements. If you have a temporary aversion to a healthy food, make substitutions. If you're not sure what to substitute, be sure to speak to a dietitian.

How can I tell whether I am experiencing morning sickness or something more serious?

If you vomit more than three or four times a day, are hardly able to keep any food down, lose weight, feel very tired and dizzy, and urinate less than usual, you may have something more serious than run-of-the-mill morning sickness— specifically, you may be suffering from hyperemesis gravidarum (HG). Additional symptoms include increased heart rate, headaches, and pale, dry-looking skin. It is important to diagnose and treat HG as soon as possible, so contact your doctor if you feel any of these symptoms or feel that your morning sickness is more serious.

INDEX

Conception, 141, 361

Constipation, 129–30

Contractions. *See also* Labor

    Braxton-Hicks contractions, 207, 226, 228–29, 234, 241, 288

    exercise and, 106

    length of, 290–91

    real contractions, 241, 288

    reporting to doctor, 207

    stress test for, 36

    timing, 106, 241

Cord

    blood banking, 366

    care of, 320

    cutting, 257–58, 294, 366

Co-sleeping, 159–61

Couvade syndrome, 166

Cribs, 149–50, 154, 156, 159–61, 321

D

Dad-to-be

    breastfeeding views of, 346–47

    parenting with, 326

    sharing pregnancy with, 166

    time with, 352–53

Day care, 155–58, 261–62

Deep vein thrombosis (DVT), 186, 306–7

Delivery

    of baby, 293–95

    care following, 314–15

    checklist for, 311

    cost of, 161

    forceps delivery, 257, 282–85

    impromptu delivery, 366

    life after, 313–60

    natural childbirth, 247–48, 256

    pain-relief for, 256–57, 281–83

    photographs of, 253

    prepping for, 288–89

    vacuum extraction, 257, 282–85

    video of, 253

Dental care, 136–37

Diabetes, gestational, 24–26, 52, 55, 59, 367

Diagnostic tests

    blood work, 25–28

    common tests, 22–25

    screenings, 32–36

    swabs/smears, 28–29

    ultrasounds, 30–31

Diagnostic tests/screenings, 22–36

Diapers, 164, 239, 261–62

Dick-Read, Grantly, 248

Diet

    for breastfeeding, 332–33, 337–40

    caloric needs, 57, 70–71, 78–80, 337–38

    carbohydrates, 70–71

    eating disorders, 84–85

    eating frequency, 57, 58, 368

    fad diets, 83–84

    fats, 71–73

    fiber, 74–77

    fish concerns, 48–50

    improving, 56–85

    log for, 119–20

    minerals, 65–68

    myths about, 56–57

    protein, 69–70

    recording, 119–20

    skipping meals, 57

    soy concerns, 50

    vegetarian diet, 108–19

    vitamins, 62–65

    water, 59–61

    weight gain, 77, 80–84

Dieting, 83–84

Triple screen test (AFP-3), 32
Tylenol, 133, 362

U

Ultrasounds, 30–31, 304, 363
Umbilical cord
    blood banking, 366
    care of, 320
    cutting, 257–58, 294, 366
Urine culture, 25

V

Vacuum extraction, 257, 282–85
Vaginal birth, 285–88, 293–95, 314–15.
    See also Childbirth
Vaginal birth after cesarean (VBAC), 297,
    308–10
Varicella, 27, 177
Varicose veins, 365
Vegetarian Food Guide Pyramid, 111–12
Vegetarian/vegan diet
    aversion to, 368
    benefits of, 109–10
    fatty acids, 118
    Food Guide Pyramid for, 111–12
    meal-planning tips, 112–13
    minerals, 113–17
    pitfalls of, 110
    protein, 117–18
    safety concerns about, 108–11
    servings for, 111–12
    vitamins, 113–17
Vernix, 178, 319
Vibroacoustic stimulation (VAS), 36
Vitamins
    in breast milk, 335–36
    fat-soluble vitamins, 62–63
    during pregnancy, 62–65, 113–17

prenatal vitamins, 16, 38, 64, 110,
    115–17, 126, 136
    for vegans, 113–17
    water-soluble vitamins, 63

W

Warmth during pregnancy, 363
Water, drinking, 59–61
"Water breaking," 107, 241, 283, 284, 291.
    See also Membrane rupture
Weakness, 102–3
Weight gain, of baby, 334
Weight gain, of mom, 77, 80–84
Weight loss, of baby, 317, 335
Women, Infants, and Children (WIC)
    program, 162
Work/career
    announcing pregnancy, 192–93
    comfort at, 196–97
    discrimination and, 190
    doctor visits and, 197
    goals for, 193–96
    legal rights for, 189–91
    maternity leave from, 182, 193–94,
        196–200, 244, 259
    "mommy track" trap, 193–94
    occupational hazards, 191–92
    pregnancy and, 189–200
    stress and, 197–98
Worries, 187–88, 214–15

X

X-rays, 193, 362–63

Z

Zinc, 67, 116–17

ABOUT THE EXPERTS

General pregnancy advice and organizer information

Paula Ford-Martin, MA, is the author of *The Everything® Pregnancy Book* and *The Everything® Pregnancy Organizer*. She has published extensively on health and wellness topics for patients, providers, and caregivers, and has a website at *www.wordcrafts.com*. Paula is also an award-winning health television producer, and is currently the Director of Content and Programming for The Wellness Network, an in-hospital television network that includes The Newborn Channel. Paula has four children and resides in Old Saybrook, CT.

Advice on nutrition during pregnancy

Britt Brandon, CFNS, CPT, is an ISSA-certified Personal Trainer and Fitness Nutrition Specialist. She is also a competitive runner, clean-eating enthusiast, and author of *The Everything® Eating Clean Cookbook*, *The Everything® Eating Clean Cookbook for Vegetarians*, *The Everything Green Smoothies Book*, and *What Color Is Your Smoothie?* Britt runs the popular website *www.UltimateFitMom.com* and lives in Jensen Beach, FL with her husband, daughters Lilly and Lonni, and son JD.

Advice for women over 35

Brette McWhorter Sember is a mother of two, pregnancy expert, and author of *Your Plus-Size Pregnancy* and *Your Practical Pregnancy Planner*. Brette is a contributing writer to more than 150 parenting publications and a member of the American Society of Journalists and Authors and the Association for Health Care Journalists. Her website is *www.BretteSember.com*.

Advice for vegan women

Reed Mangels, PhD, RD, LD, FADA, is a nutrition advisor for the nonprofit educational Vegetarian Resource Group, as well as nutrition editor and a regular columnist for *Vegetarian Journal*. She is the coauthor of the American Dietetic Association's position paper on vegetarian diets as well as their new food guide for vegetarians. Dr. Mangels is an instructor in the nutrition department of the University of Massachusetts at Amherst.